SCANDALS OF CLASSIC HOLLYWOOD

Chugach Peaks Photography

ANNE HELEN PETERSEN received her PhD from the University of Texas, where she studied the history of the gossip industry. Her work on celebrity and Hollywood history has appeared on *The Hairpin* and *The Awl*, and in *The Believer, Slate, Virginia Quarterly Review, Lapham's Quarterly*, and numerous academic journals and collections. Find her blog, *Celebrity Gossip, Academic Style*, at anne helenpetersen.com.

Praise for *Scandals of Classic Hollywood*

"Engaging . . . Petersen is an author for our age."
—*The Boston Globe*

"Insightful." —*Time*

"Clear and convincing . . . Although Petersen's book benefits from intelligent analysis of archival research, she writes with the verve of an enthusiast." —*Los Angeles Times*

"Terrific and thoughtful and fascinating."
—NPR's *Pop Culture Happy Hour*

SCANDALS OF CLASSIC
HOLLYWOOD

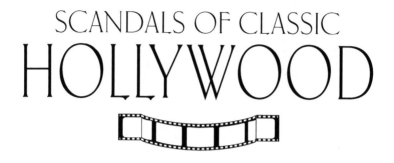

Sex, Deviance, and Drama from the Golden
Age of American Cinema

Anne Helen Petersen

A PLUME BOOK

PLUME
Published by the Penguin Group
Penguin Group (USA) LLC
375 Hudson Street
New York, New York 10014

USA | Canada | UK | Ireland | Australia | New Zealand | India | South Africa | China
penguin.com
A Penguin Random House Company

First published by Plume, a member of Penguin Group (USA) LLC, 2014

REGISTERED TRADEMARK—MARCA REGISTRADA

LIBRARY OF CONGRESS CATALOGING-IN-PUBLICATION DATA
Petersen, Anne Helen,
Scandals of classic Hollywood : sex, deviance, and drama from the golden age of American cinema /
Anne Helen Petersen.
pages cm
Includes bibliographical references.
ISBN 978-0-14-218067-9 (paperback)
1. Motion pictures—California—Los Angeles—Biography. 2. Motion picture industry—California—
Los Angeles—Anecdotes. 3. Scandals—California—Los Angees. I. Title.
PN1993.5.U65P48 2014
384'.80979494—dc23   2014001814

Set in Bembo Book MT Std.
Designed by Leonard Telesca

146122990

For my Granddad, who looked like Fred MacMurray, acted like Jimmy Stewart, and smoked like Humphrey Bogart

Contents

Contents

VOLUME FIVE: Broken by the System

VOLUME SIX: Three Angry Men

Introduction

On July 26, 2006, Mel Gibson—'80s hunk, '90s director, '00s oddball—was arrested for driving under the influence. He was visibly drunk and combative, and hurled misogynistic, anti-Semitic slurs at the arresting officers. Within hours, Gibson's disheveled mug shot had gone viral, as had the audiotape of his arrest, thanks to upstart website TMZ.com. The story made TMZ, but more important, it destroyed Gibson, whose personal and professional lives immediately fell apart. His marriage collapsed; work dried up. The man so powerful that he could make a film graphically detailing the death of Christ—a millionaire many, many times over—couldn't make a hit film in Hollywood. Today, Gibson is slowly reappearing in supporting roles, but save some remarkable, redemptive gesture, his career as a leading man is over.

Had this happened just seventy years ago, Gibson's fate would have been dramatically different. He would've been signed to a studio contract, complete with a morality clause to govern his behavior, and he'd have had studio-employed "fixers"—the hidden yet essential cogs in the star-making machine—to clean up after him in case of scandal. The fixers would erase all traces of the incident: the police would be paid off; the report would disappear. To the public at large, he'd continue to be a gallant husband, doting father, and responsible citizen—the very paragon of contemporary masculinity. Any whispers of chronic drunkenness would be silenced by well-placed mentions in the gossip columns concerning his commitment to his adoring children and devoted wife. Gibson's image would remain intact, his earning power for the studio secure. Because in the golden age of Hollywood, scandal was a roadblock, but rarely an endgame.

During this period, stars weren't born; they were *made*. Scouts would bring in "raw" star material, culled from the vaudeville circuit, the theater, or the soda fountain counter. The potential star would be given a name, a sanitized (and sometimes dramatized) backstory, a makeover, and a contract. After assigning him or her a few bit parts and gauging audience reception (usually through the amount and tone of fan mail), the studio would figure the performer's fate. An actor could be kept around to "pleasure" visiting execs, relegated to the stock character pool, or promoted to bona fide stardom, with first choice of roles and directors. Stardom was what happened when the raw star material and studio magic created an image that was not only beautiful but sublime; not only likable but charismatic. For an actor to become a star, he had to become more than the sum of his exquisite parts. His image had to demonstrate a particular way of life, a way of being in the world that resonated and inspired emulation—the boy next door all grown up, the rough cowboy with a heart of gold, the adventurer with a romantic streak.

This book tells the story of how these extraordinary stars were made, but also, as the title indicates, how they were unmade—or at least how the emergence of scandal compromised their carefully constructed public personas. The stars in this book were immaculate productions: the result of tremendous toil on the part of press agents, stylists, directors, and cooperative gossip columnists and fan magazine editors. But even the most perfect productions can crumble beneath the weight of their accumulated cultural meaning. Over the course of the next fourteen chapters, you'll see how that pressure served as a catalyst for all manner of misbehavior: drug use, gambling, and illicit sexual encounters in various shapes and styles. In other words, the bigger the star, the more meaningful she becomes to the public, the higher the chance for scandal to emerge.

Yet a star's actions, behavior, or lifestyle choices are never de facto scandalous; rather, they become scandalous when they violate the status quo in some way. A divorce in 1920 was potentially scandalous; today, it's par for the course. In 1950, homosexuality was unspeakable; today, it's doable, if difficult, with the help of a well-orchestrated coming-out narrative. Scandal is amplified when a star's actions violate not only the status quo but the underlying understanding of that star's image as well: when "Saint Ingrid" (Ingrid Bergman) ran off with an Italian director and gave birth to a child out of wedlock, the scandal was rooted not only in the infidelity but in how brazenly she violated her fans' understanding of her image and what it seemed to represent.

Scandal thus functions as a rupture—not only in a star's image, but in whatever cultural value that star represents. With carefully planned publicity, that rupture can be repaired. A star can repent; her actions can be reframed. See, for example, the dramatic reconfiguration of Brad Pitt's divorce from Jennifer Aniston, or Robert Downey Jr.'s phoenix-like rise from the ashes of addiction. The status quo is seemingly restored.

The scandals discussed in this book are more than just smut. They're history lessons, teaching us about what it meant to be a man, a woman, a child, a straight person, a fat person, a person of color, or a sex object during specific time periods in our past. But they're also love stories, tragedies, and comedies—lessons in the way stars come to embody a culture's hopes and aspirations and the harshness with which they are treated when they fail to meet expectations. Above all, these stories are page-turners: the very stuff of the very best of Hollywood films, complete with crackling narrative tension, breathless ascents, and dramatic downfalls. Many of these scandals end in tragedy, but others are raucous, screwball comedies, filled with wit, double entendres, and generalized rascalry. These stars lived *big*—and the narratives of their lives, their loves and losses, the way they rose and fell from fame, are just as impressive as their conspicuous spending habits.

This book will introduce you to new stories, broaden stories you know, and revise those you *thought* you knew. Chances are, you're familiar with many of the stars and scandals to come— Clark Gable, Humphrey Bogart, Judy Garland, James Dean. These stars endure for specific cultural reasons, co-opted by new generations, plastered on dorm room walls, and evoked in magazine photo shoots as signifiers of authenticity, rebellion, or class. But this book also includes the stories of much less familiar names: Jean Harlow, Wallace Reid, Clara Bow, Dorothy Dandridge, to name a few—stars who once enjoyed tremendous popularity but have, for various reasons, faded with time.

By familiarizing ourselves with the contours of stardom and scandal that shaped the past, we can see how they shape the present. Today, as before, there are certain types of stars for whom we will forgive all manner of trespass, and other types of stars who, once they step over the line, can never return. If our stars are reflections of our values and ourselves, then the way we elevate, denigrate, and dispose of them also functions as a sort of cultural mirror, however distorted, clumsy, and unbecoming. The aim of the book, then, is not simply to titillate, nor is it to propagate old, worn-out rumors. Rather, it will help rescue gossip, the study of stars, and scandal from the cultural wastebasket. With every chapter, you'll see how these stories are crucial to understanding our present and our past—history dressed in an evening gown and pearls, holding a flute of expensive champagne. But beware: Once you read one, it's difficult not to read them all. Your list of must-watch classic films will grow exponentially. You might develop a hankering for well-tailored double-breasted suits. Rest assured, it's all natural—once you become familiar with these stars, their complex narratives and their bewitching charisma prove impossible to resist. And you'll never think about stars, Hollywood, or the machinations that create them in the same way again.

TWILIGHT OF THE IDOLS

When the moving image first began to circulate in the late nineteenth century, it wasn't as if stars suddenly popped up along with it. Audiences were mostly just fascinated with the technological marvel they saw before them—the moving image *itself* was the star. Even as cinema developed in the early 1900s, huge, unwieldy cameras made it difficult to film anything other than a full-length shot. Because viewers couldn't see the actor's face up close, it was difficult to develop the feelings of admiration or affection that we associate with film stars. Gradually, close-ups became more prevalent, various actors became more recognizable, fans began to know the stars' names, and slowly but surely, audiences pieced together "types" associated with each star—the hero, the villain, the damsel in distress, the virtuous heroine.

It wasn't until the early 1910s, however, that stars as we understand them today came to be: an actor with a recognizable type on-screen—a "picture personality"—accompanied by information about her off-screen, made available through the proliferating fan magazines. A star was the combination of her on-screen and off-screen selves—selves that complemented and amplified each other. An actor who played a cowboy on-screen would stable a horse just outside of Hollywood; a sporting heroine would fit in a game of golf between taking care of her children and cooking dinner. Crucially, these off-screen images were always squeaky clean. Women were married or seeking marriage; men were eligible bachelors or devoted husbands. Throughout the 1910s, these narratives served a distinct purpose: to make Hollywood seem less scandalous.

Because the "film colony," as it was then called, was populated with young people, mostly poor immigrants, it was assumed that these actors, now flush with cash and lacking in so-called moral hygiene, would run wild. The logic of the time went something like this: if Hollywood was filled with immoral behavior, that selfsame behavior would seep onto the screen, thereby corrupting the impressionable youth so irresistibly drawn to the picture show. To sustain their business, then, and calm the anxiety propagated by reactionary moralists, the studios collaborated with the gossip press to make the stars' lives seem squeaky clean.

Working together, the studios, fan magazines, and gossip columnists painted a becoming, believable portrait of the players on the screen. By providing details from actors' domestic, ostensibly private existences, studios enabled fans to feel as if they had access to the true, authentic star. Knowledge about the star's living room, dress purchases, or other patterns of conspicuous consumption became de facto knowledge about how he or she "really was." In this way, Hollywood was able to convincingly suggest that the stars were without scandal. Until, that is, the stars started making decisions that no matter of fawning publicity could cover up. These cracks in the image of both the star and Hollywood as a whole provided a dim, shadowy peephole unto a new layer of the star: the scandalous, unspeakable, immoral core.

But as will become clear, this period of salacious scandal in the early twenties did not sink the industry; rather, it served as a catalyst for Hollywood to better manage its stars and their actions. The stars did not suddenly become less prone to scandalous behavior; the cover-up and management strategies simply got *better*. This pattern—the emergence of scandal; the subsequent emergence of techniques to manage it—has structured the dynamics of Hollywood for the past century. Sometimes scandal emerges due to a savvy new publication; other times, it's a rebellious star with a lack of oversight. The means of release and the methods of containment may change, but the pattern endures. As we trace that pattern, and how it adjusts with the cultural temperature, a vivid picture of the past American century begins to come to light.

CHAPTER ONE

Pickford and Fairbanks: American Royalty

With her immaculate curls, plaintive eyes, and porcelain skin, Mary Pickford bore a keen resemblance to a child's doll. And like a doll, she acted out the fantasies of others: her whimsical spirit and wholesomeness represented an American ideal under threat, proof positive that Victorian notions of girlhood and virtue could endure the onset of modernity. In this way, Mary Pickford became "a girl of all girls," an exemplar of femininity and desexualized youth. She began her film career in 1909 at the age of seventeen, but played roles much younger, usually as adolescent and prepubescent daughters. In 1909 alone, Pickford appeared in fifty films; by 1915, her salary equaled that of the president. In the years to come, she'd continue to play young girls—most notably in *Rebecca of Sunnybrook Farm* (1917), *The Poor Little Rich Girl* (1917), and *Pollyanna* (1920)—but she also worked, with mixed success, to sophisticate and texture her image. By the end of the 1910s, she was, without question, the biggest star in the world.

Audiences just *adored* her. A review in *The Bioscope* nails her appeal: only Pickford could be "ineffably sweet, joyously young, and sometimes, if one may put it so, almost unbearably heartbreaking in its tender pathos." She may have been "ineffably sweet," but she was also a savvy businesswoman, entrusted, from a very early age, with providing for her entire family. Her father, a drunk, had left the family when Pickford was three years old, and her mother concentrated on promoting young Mary's career. Throughout the 1910s, Pickford made a series of business decisions that afforded her more and more control over her image and salary; by 1916, her contract with Zukor Inc. gave her full authority over every production—along with five hundred dollars a week, an unheard-of salary. She was still playing little girl roles, but she had morphed into the first of many female actors bestowed with the title of "America's Sweetheart," neatly eliding her Canadian birth. Pickford may have been powerful, but any anxiety over that power was muted by how convincingly and consistently she radiated demureness and amiability.

Yet for all of her successes on-screen, her off-screen life was far from perfect. Pickford was entrapped in an abusive marriage to fellow silent actor Owen Moore, whom she had quietly wed in 1911 after meeting him on the studio lot. The marriage was kept secret due to Pickford's mother's disapproval of Moore, but IMP, their studio at the time, exploited the pairing, placing ads of the two together in a heart-shaped frame, paired with the catchphrases "She's an Imp!" and "He's an Imp!" Outwardly, Moore was "America's first juvenile," known for his boyish appearance on-screen. Off-screen, he was jealous of Pickford's success and embittered by his reliance on her connections for his new contract at IMP. Alcoholism, exacerbated by professional jealousy, led to bouts of physical and emotional abuse, but Pickford had to keep all traces of their unrest a secret lest it compromise her pristine image. By 1916, it was a deeply unhappy marriage, with Pickford and Moore living apart for long periods of time.

Enter Douglas Fairbanks: ascendant king of Hollywood,

swashbuckler, athlete, and all-American boy. Fairbanks was born in Denver, where his father was, at least between periods of drunkenness, a miner—a point that would be routinely exploited in the formation of Fairbanks's Old West image, with its undertones of wild, raucous adventure. He had been surrounded by stage aspirations from an early age, and profiles loved to emphasize how his father had read him Shakespeare before abandoning the family. Young Fairbanks also regularly performed onstage during high school, though he left before earning his diploma. Depending on the publication and authorial intent, Fairbanks would claim that he then spent time at Colorado School of Mines, Princeton, or Harvard Law before finding success on Broadway and marrying Anna Beth Sully, the daughter of a wealthy captain of industry.

Fairbanks's transition to film was part of a larger Hollywood migration of successful theater actors in the 1910s. He played the boy next door and the cowboy—the very embodiment of the American West, with its conflicting suggestions of wildness and honor. His hero was Teddy Roosevelt, and Fairbanks, at least publicly, aspired to all the connotations of rugged individualism that Roosevelt's name implied. His energy was seemingly endless, a frenetic liveliness that jumped off the screen. Much like Pickford, Fairbanks was universally beloved: as historian Scott Curtis describes, "This energetic, even indefatigable star became so popular because he projected an image of Americans as they wanted to see themselves, as they still want to see themselves: as youthful and athletic, optimistic and adventurous, decisive and democratic." He was the boy everyone loved to love, both on-screen and off.

Fairbanks's image was rooted in authenticity, but that sense of realness, the seeming lack of manipulation, was, of course, manipulation itself. The conflation of the "real" and "reel" Fairbanks was due to some exquisite, if slightly over-the-top, press management. On the set of the western *The Half-Breed* (1916), for example, Fairbanks supposedly spent most of his time away from the set, off romping in the woods, returning with bleeding hands and torn clothing. When the director asked, "What in the name of mischief have you been doing now?" Fairbanks replied, "Trappin'. . . . Bobcats, of course." The message: Fairbanks was a strapping explorer and would much rather spend time in the great outdoors than hobnobbing in the high society of Hollywood. Over the next decade, this apparent lack of pretense would serve Fairbanks well, as his statements and actions—especially those concerning his romantic life and the beloved Mary Pickford— were taken at face value and rarely questioned.

It's unclear when, or how, Fairbanks and Pickford first met or became intimate. The Movie Colony, as it was then called, was a small, cliquey place, and their paths would've certainly crossed. One overwrought tale has Fairbanks carrying her over a dangerous stream at a Hollywood party; others have them falling deeply in love at first sight. But such romantic meet-cutes were all mapped onto their relationship after the fact, long after they'd gone public with their love. The exact time line remains murky, but they had certainly become friends by 1916, and by 1917, Fairbanks was taking Pickford's business lead, leaving Triangle Film Corporation to set up his own production company, which would work exclusively with Pickford's distribution arm. Later that year, both joined mutual friend Charlie Chaplin in a nationwide tour to engender support for World War I war bonds, with an exhausting schedule that included dozens of stops and uncounted hours in intimate company. It must've turned hot and heavy in short order, but according to official reports, it was nothing if not a chaste friendship.

Over the course of their three war bond tours, the public became accustomed to seeing the pair together. Not romantically, but depicted in the same frame, smiling, joking, charismatically *together*—together for the good of the country, using their fame for a cause much greater than themselves. Even the April 1918 announcement of Fairbanks's imminent divorce, and subsequent rumors swirling around the "unnamed correspondent" (early twentieth-century speak for "person responsible for the breakup of the marriage"), widely believed to be Pickford, couldn't blunt the goodwill. With their winning, affable smiles, charismatic on-screen personas, and patriotic, selfless service to the country, it would've been nearly impossible to frame them as villains.

It didn't help that Moore came across rather poorly. "My wife," he told one reporter, "has always seemed to me to be little more than a child, with a child's winsomeness, appealingness, and trust in others." That childishness, according to Moore, accounted for her susceptibility to the likes of Fairbanks. Moore also claimed that Fairbanks had an odd personality that fascinated women—he was dangerous, with an "instinct for possession that has doubtless come to him from his Anglo-Saxon ancestors." Having effectively insulted an entire swath of the reading public, Moore eventually admitted that he, too, had succumbed to Fairbanks's charms—which was why he hadn't seen him stealing away his wife's affections. Once he did figure it out, he kept quiet (out of deference, so he claimed, to the Liberty Loan campaign), but when Fairbanks's divorce became public, he knew he had to speak. Still, Moore emphasized that it was Fairbanks who played the role of villain: "There is only one aggressor in the whole situation. The 'other woman' [Pickford] has been as much victimized as the rest, not wholly blameless, perhaps, but imposed upon."

Here, Moore—or Moore's press agent—performed a tremendous rhetorical feat. He underlined Pickford's "girl" image, an image that Americans adored, and then used the natural vulnerabilities of that image to explain any potential infidelity. Moore situated the blame firmly on Fairbanks—"there is only one aggressor"—while emphasizing his own propriety and patriotism. No matter what happened with Moore, Pickford could emerge with her integrity relatively unscathed.

Regardless of her seeming inculpability in the affair, the swirling rumors had become too much for Pickford. In April 1918, she announced her plans to go into total retirement. According to her sister, Pickford was on the verge of a nervous breakdown, "not only on account of the notoriety she has received in the papers in relation to a certain other star, but also because of her tireless work on the loan campaign." The message was clear: gossip was hurting Little Mary—the same Little Mary who had not invited the advances of Fairbanks, who had simply toiled, to the point of exhaustion, for the sake of her country.

Pickford did not, in fact, go into total retirement. After some time away from the spotlight, she resumed work. The rumors quieted, which isn't to say that the romance stopped, but Pickford and Fairbanks likely understood that their careers depended on the integrity of their images. The solution, then, was a marvel of carefully calculated publicity: they changed the conversation from one of gossip to one of business. Chaplin, Fairbanks, Pickford, and director D. W. Griffith founded United Artists (UA) in January 1919, with the goal of taking their careers into their own hands. Each would produce around five pictures a year with UA functioning as distributor. It was a loose artistic partnership designed to undercut the efforts of the studios, eager to tamp down the rising star salaries and demands. The move was ridiculed within the industry—according to one exec, "the inmates are taking over the asylum"—but it made headlines and further yoked Fairbanks and Pickford in the public eye.

By the time Pickford filed for divorce in March 1920, her

union with Fairbanks was a foregone conclusion. Still, she denied that she would remarry—Fairbanks or anyone else—claiming that she simply wanted freedom. Moore agreed not to contest the case, prompting rumors of a payoff, which Pickford was quick to counter. As for reports of attempts to avoid the press, her defense was irrefutable: "I regarded [the divorce] as a sacred matter, of no interest to anyone but myself. . . . I felt that, though my career and my work in films are the interest of the public, my personal affairs were not." Yet she demurred, "I now realize my mistake. I have learned now that I do not belong to myself. If I have done anything to offend the public I am so sorry. My life work is to make people happy, to fill their hearts with gladness through my appearance in picture stories." Here, Pickford simultaneously shamed readers for their curiosity *and* invited them to extend that curiosity—so long as it meant they still loved her, still wanted to let her make them happy. She was, in other words, preparing them to support her no matter what the future would bring.

As it turned out, the very near future brought a very romantic wedding, with Fairbanks and Pickford marrying in a "secret" wedding in Los Angeles. It was a gossip dream come true, and instead of being scandalous, the reports were jubilant: "Famous Film Romance is Crowned by Nuptials," exclaimed the *Los Angeles Times*, explaining that when Fairbanks was asked, "Are you happy?" he replied, "Oh gosh!" The pair were criticized for their choice of minister (a Baptist!), and Pickford's divorce from Moore was contested on a technicality, but the overarching public sentiment was one of companionate romance. The *Washington Post* framed the culmination as a "real life drama," telling the tale of how their love had been readily apparent for months, and "any one at all familiar with the strenuous methods of Doug was reasonably sure he would not accept 'no' as the final answer. Thus endeth the second reel in the life scenario of the most universally christened Pickfair, became the center of proper Hollywood society. Together, they marshaled the who's who of stars, deciding who was appropriate for dinner with visiting dignitaries and heads of state and who was too déclassé, improper, or otherwise unrepresentative of the Hollywood they wanted the world to see. Charlie Chaplin pontificated; Albert Einstein discoursed; they watched new movies in their private screening room; everyone went to bed early; and, of course, liquor was never served. It was an upright, West Coast version of the salon, only with more jumping in the pool and wrestling with Fairbanks, who purportedly insisted that all guests rise at dawn to accompany him on rides through nearby Coyote Canyon. *Photoplay* showed off their home whenever they remodeled, complete with customary tasteful menus, while Fairbanks framed the couple as ardent homebodies: "I've never been to any of the places in Hollywood and Los Angeles that the newspapers write about," he told *The Literary Digest*. "Why, Mary and I have only been to the Ambassador Hotel once since it was built. We spend practically all our evenings at home."

Judging from dozens of accounts, Fairbanks and Pickford did indeed live a quiet, almost suburban life. But the specifics of their lifestyle were almost certainly exaggerated—with the express purpose of making them seem high-class, gentile, wholly above scandal, and, most important, perfect companions. The scandal of their relationship never truly happened. And it wasn't because Pickford and Fairbanks were especially savvy, or even had any sort of phenomenal image management. These stars survived because they were just incredibly likable—and because fans so wanted them together, they would forgive all manner of rule bending in order for it to happen. The lesson, repeated dozens of times over the course of Hollywood history, was clear: a romance, properly played, can defuse even the biggest gossip bombs.

CHAPTER TWO

Fatty Arbuckle:
Fall Guy of the Film Industry

When Roscoe "Fatty" Arbuckle was arrested for the assault of a young starlet at a so-called gin jollification party, it was as if he had singularly confirmed the nation's very worst fears about Hollywood. These newly wealthy men and women didn't know how to control their money, their bodies, or their lives, spending, cavorting, and reveling in excess. And Arbuckle, with his two-hundred-plus-pound girth, was this type of excess embodied. Within a week's time, the highest-paid man in Hollywood, beloved for his physical comedy and chaste, boyish love stories, became the most hated man in America—a rapist, a drunk, and proof that the stars had, indeed, run wild.

Yet Arbuckle was none of these things. A drinker, yes; subject to revelry, of course—but he was acquitted of all charges against him. If a different star with a different image had found himself in Arbuckle's place, the situation may never have reached such a fever pitch. Yet as many historians and scholars have come to agree, Arbuckle was scapegoated. No matter his innocence—he was the right man to take the fall for the rest of Hollywood, to usher in reformatory measures that would reorganize Hollywood, wresting power from the stars and restoring it to the studios. It's not that his studio set him up. He just found himself in a position and charged with a crime that, given his image, was all too easy to believe he had committed.

For all of Arbuckle's raucous on-screen antics, his off-screen life was a page straight out of a Dickens novel. His childhood was not a happy one. He was one of nine children, and his slender father was harsh and unloving, in part, according to lore, because he didn't believe a child so large could be his own. His mother died when Arbuckle was twelve, and because his father refused to support him, Arbuckle was effectively on his own. Luckily, he developed his light comedic sense at an early age and cultivated his singing voice, which soon earned him notice and, eventually, a place on the vaudeville circuit. He attended Santa Clara College, where, in his words, "I matriculated in football, baseball and avoirdupois." He traveled the West with various troupes, learned to "fall without damage," and met and married fellow vaudevillian and rather petite Minta Durfee in 1908—a pairing that, like most things in Arbuckle's life, further emphasized his size. By 1909, he was in pictures—most notably Mack Sennett's famous *Keystone Cops* series. He refined his comedic act, partnering with Mabel Normand for an extended string of lovelorn comedies, such as *Mabel and Fatty's Wash Day* and *Mabel and Fatty's Married Life*.

The pictures were out-of-this-world popular. Arbuckle was so highly likable, and audiences loved him even more when he was paired with Normand, the straight woman to his comedic acrobatics. In *Mabel and Fatty's Married Life*; *Mabel, Fatty and the Law*; and *Wished on Mabel*, the pair fought, reconciled, fought some more, and routinely ended in a jumble of limbs, physical wreckage, and laughter. And when Arbuckle cross-dressed—most notably in *Miss Fatty's Seaside Lovers* and *Coney Island*—the result was transcendent in its simplicity.

But Arbuckle was more than just a comedian: he directed, conceived, and produced his own films, and helped kick-start the careers of Buster Keaton and several others. In 1914, Paramount offered him a sweetheart deal: a thousand dollars a day, 25 percent of the profits, *plus* complete artistic control. Over the next six years, the terms would only get more lucrative. By 1918, he had signed a three-million-dollar deal to make eighteen pictures over the next three years. He was championed as a master director, with an artistic touch that, according to one top producer, was "as full of poetry and sentiment as anything I ever saw." Arbuckle was the star-director-producer powerhouse long before the age of Clooney and Affleck, which is part of the reason the studios were so threatened by him. After all, if Arbuckle could rake in a salary of a million dollars a year, what would stars ask for next?

Despite Arbuckle's long-term marriage, the fan magazines wanted nothing of romance. Instead, it was all fat jokes, all the time. In fan magazine profiles, as in his own films, his size drove the narrative, structuring the piece and inflecting it with humor. Even his history was reshaped to emphasize and account for his fatness, continually playing up his alleged birth weight of 16 pounds. These jokes were never boldly malicious—they simply turned Arbuckle into someone defined, time and time again, by his size and appetite. A 1915 *Photoplay* article offered tongue-in-cheek advice from Arbuckle concerning how to perform "heavy-weight athletics":

> Arise before 9 a.m. Dress and lace your own shoes. This develops the abdominal muscles . . . if you feel that you have eaten too much, take a little exercise such as rolling a few cigarettes. If this exercise proves insufficient, join an athletic club where the bars open early. Transact what business is necessary to your affairs but do not overexert. By this time you will be

established. On Saturday, September 3, 1921, Arbuckle motored from Los Angeles to San Francisco, where he checked in to the St. Francis Hotel with plans to relax with friends. A day later, demi-starlet Virginia Rappe, best known for her appearance on the cover of sheet music, arrived at the hotel, along with two friends, Maude Delmont and Alfred Semnacher, Rappe's manager. On Monday, Arbuckle invited the trio to a party, reportedly at the request of one of his friends. When Rappe and her friends arrived, Arbuckle had yet to dress for the day and was still wearing his pajamas and robe. They lunched and began drinking; others joined the party; the phonograph was put to loud use. At this party, where gin and whiskey were in ample supply, the "alleged rough treatment," as it was first called in the press, took place.

At this point, testimonies diverge. According to Arbuckle and several others, "Everyone was feeling the effects of whiskey and gin." Rappe started making a scene and went into the bedroom of the hotel room. Lowell Sherman reported that her behavior was of no "great concern"—everyone simply thought she "had a bun on," or was drunk. Arbuckle had an afternoon appointment elsewhere in town, but in order to leave, he needed to change out of his pajamas. He entered the bedroom and locked the door, at which point he found "a woman writhing in the bathroom, writhing in pain" and "holding her stomach." He picked her up, placed her on the bed, and called for the other women at the party to assist. Two women, including Rappe's friend Delmont, came into the bedroom, where they found Rappe tearing off her clothes, "frothing at the mouth," and ripping her undergarments. Arbuckle left the room, returned to find that Delmont had put ice under Rappe's head (other reports place the ice on her stomach or, alternately, Rappe in the bath tub). Delmont told Arbuckle to get out of the room and leave Rappe be; Arbuckle then told Delmont to "shut up or I [will] throw you out the window." They carried her to another room, put her in bed, covered her up, and at last sent for a doctor.

That's one version of the story. The other version, propagated by Delmont, Semnacher, and party attendee Zev Prevost had the details somewhat different. Prevost testified that Arbuckle had been in the room for forty-five minutes with Rappe, at which point she knocked on the door and found Rappe "fully dressed, but her hair was hanging down, and she was moaning 'I am dying, I am dying, I know I'm going to die.'" They took off her clothes and attempted to place her in the bath to ease the pain; at some point, Rappe claimed, "I am dying, he hurt me." Semnacher alleged that Arbuckle had used "a foreign substance in an attack" and, the morning after, had told the other male guests at the party of "committing certain acts," presumably sexual, that injured Miss Rappe.

The day after the party, Arbuckle returned to Los Angeles. On Thursday, Rappe was moved to Wakefield Sanitarium, where she died the next day from peritonitis, caused by a ruptured bladder. That day, Delmont publicly accused Arbuckle. On Saturday, Arbuckle was in custody and the story was front-page news, with an arraignment planned for Tuesday, September 13. Over the course of the next six months, the pieces of what had or had not occurred in that room slowly became clear, only to be quickly muddled by allegations of witness tampering, blackmail, and contradictory testimony. It is uncertain exactly what happened in the room, and who undressed whom, at what point, and for what reason, and dozens of books have attempted to untangle the mess of the investigation. But here's what is certain: Rappe had suffered from chronic cystitis for several years. Whether or not Arbuckle did have sexual relations with her, it was her preexisting condition, not Arbuckle, that caused her death.

But in the weeks following Arbuckle's arrest, the truth mattered much less than what people wanted to believe of a man of Arbuckle's size, wealth, and vocation. It was a sensational story, with a seemingly endless stream of information, and the press pursued it with incredible stamina. In the days after the arraignment, the story was exploited as far as the bounds of mainstream journalism would allow, from "Arbuckle Born in Kansas Sod House" in the *Los Angeles Times* to "Weighed 16 Pounds at Birth" and "Remember Arbuckle as a Mischievous Lad" in the *New York Times*. It may have seemed like innocuous background reporting, but it was setting the stage for Arbuckle's public indictment. Even though his sister relayed his generous support of his family, and his childhood acquaintances recalled him as a "fat, overgrown lad, always seeking and getting into mischief but never given to cruelty or violence," the overarching emphasis was still on *excess*. He was a "heavy spender," paying one hundred thousand dollars for his home. He owned six cars, including the most elaborate vehicle in all of California, priced at twenty-five thousand dollars and specially designed for his size. What's more, he was negligent— the grave of his mother was unkempt, and his bulldog sat mournfully awaiting his return.

The papers framed the party as a "fatal wine orgy" and a "booze party," and within days, dozens of cities throughout the country had canceled or banned the showing of Arbuckle films. He proclaimed his innocence, appealing to "the Christian charity of the civilized world" until the court reached its verdict. But the sensationalism was just too much. As details of the party emerged, the "gin jollification" party morphed into the most nefarious circles of hell combined, indicative of an epidemic of parties filled with drugs, alcohol, and, worst of all, women dancing in the nude. Even men unconnected to the film industry were purportedly in attendance—a clear sign that Hollywood's immorality was spreading, and would continue to spread, if not contained. Rumors placed Arbuckle either crushing Rappe with his weight or, angry that he could not perform, raping her with a bottle. These rumors spread not necessarily because they were rooted in fact but because Arbuckle's image—or more specifically, Arbuckle's body—seemed capable of enacting them. That's the most insidious quality of gossip: it doesn't matter if it's true; it matters if it *seems plausible*. Arbuckle's image wasn't that of a rapist, but it was defined by excess and a certain asexuality, manifest in his films, in which he regularly cross-dressed, and he looked, to be blunt, like an overgrown baby. And when someone's sexuality reads as nonnormative, it's all the easier to believe him capable of anything, including rage at his own impotence and unspeakable sexual violence.

In this way, the baby-faced, bumbling, most beloved star in America became a drunkard, a rapist, and a murderer practically overnight. And who was to blame? Hollywood—and the fans who made it. Within days, condemnation began to flow. For Myra Nye, pontificating in the *Los Angeles Times*, the entire industry was at fault: "When a man may be raised from the position of corridor-cleaner in a bar-room to a pedestal of fame where he may make an income of 5000 a week simply because he is fat and can make faces, while the real talent of clearly youth passes unnoticed, the values of life are surely confused." The editorial's implicit message: poor people shouldn't get rich too fast, and they certainly shouldn't get rich for "making faces." In Los Angeles, dozens of religious leaders offered sermons on "Moral Degradation," "Hollywood and the Ten Commandments," and "Moralizations upon a Degenerate's Debauchery and Lust." "This sort of party is not American, it belongs to the ages of Nero, the depraved," declared one pastor. Producers must thus "clean out the libertines and harlots from their outfit before the public decides to clean the whole business." Senator Henry Myers claimed that Hollywood was replete with "debauchery, drunkenness, ribaldry," along with "dissipation and free love," and as a result, the movies were just as bad as the "open saloon" in their ability to corrupt the young.

Sin was a pathogen: the product of too much money and too little oversight, it seeped into the motion pictures, where it then infected all those who viewed them. Arbuckle's actions in a San Francisco hotel thus infected every man, woman, and especially child who had ever seen him on the screen. No matter that his actual films were some of the least offensive on the screen and that he had even made a pledge in 1917 only to create "clean" comedy, producing "nothing that will offend the proprieties, whether applied to children or grown-ups." The fact that they were innocuous—and thus framed as appropriate for children—made his off-screen offenses all the more grave.

But even the most arch of critics fell short of calling for a ban on motion pictures altogether. That would be too much: as appalled as audiences were at the allegations of Arbuckle's behavior, they still loved the movies. The solution, then, was censorship. Even before the events in September, censorship boards on the state and city levels were demanding cuts to various films—too much violence, too much suggestive sexuality, too much skin, too irreverent; the list went on. But each board asked for slightly different cuts, forcing the studio to provide unique prints of a film for dozens of different states and municipalities, a process that was both expensive and inefficient. It was also a slippery slope: if studios continued to heed the demands of individual censors, it might lead to a single, national censor. This scenario might sound feasible, but that censor would be government based—and therein lay the rub. More than anything, the studios wanted to keep the government out of their business, in no small part because their business models violated antitrust laws. To save their monopolies, then, they had to figure out a way to appease the calls for censorship, but to do so without actually appointing a government censor.

Thus the studios came together and created an organization—the Motion Picture Producers and Distributors of America (MPPDA)—and elected to censor *themselves*. They appointed devout Presbyterian and former postmaster general Will H. Hays as its head, luring him with a salary of $150,000 a year—approximately $1.9 million today. This appointment might seem an odd choice for the job, but recall that the postmaster general, at the time, wasn't just controlling the price of postage; he was responsible for rooting out obscenity sent through the mail—"stag" magazines, erotica, pornography, etc.—essentially acting as an arbiter of which media products could and could not reach a national audience. Just months before, a similarly appointed "czar" had successfully sanitized the sport of baseball following the Black Sox scandal, in which several members of the White Sox accepted bribes to "throw" the World Series; the idea was that Hays would do the same for the movie industry.

Hays's first act as head of the MPPDA, issued on April 18, 1922, was a blanket ban of all Arbuckle films. Arbuckle had still not been convicted, but the ban at least temporarily appeased groups clamoring for censorship. The ban resulted in the loss of ten thousand booking contracts at a cost of one million dollars, but it was a price the industry was willing to pay if it meant fending off the threat of national censorship and government oversight. With the full cooperation of the studios, Hays instituted mandatory "morality clauses" in star contracts, which effectively forced stars to hew to strict standards of moral behavior. If a star violated the clause, he or she would be released from the contract without question. In practice, these clauses meant little; outwardly, however, they signified a willingness on the part of both the studios and their stars to clean up Hollywood at large. Today,

Hays is best known for the "Don'ts and Be Carefuls" (don't, for example, use the Lord's name in vain or depict white slavery or miscegenation, and be careful about how you present the flag, rape, surgical operations, and "first night scenes"), which comprised the so-called Hays Code and governed the content of movies for decades to come. But these initial steps—and the ban of Arbuckle's films in particular—were crucial in avoiding government incursion and sustaining the status quo. Hays, in other words, set the ship aright, yet he did so at the behest of the industry and at the cost of Arbuckle's career.

Over the course of the next six months, Arbuckle stood trial three times, each time more complicated than the last. There was a hung jury, a retrial, and a final, resounding acquittal, issued by the jury with an accompanying statement:

> Acquittal is not enough for Roscoe Arbuckle. We feel that a great injustice has been done to him. We also feel that it was only our plain duty to give him this exoneration under the evidence for there was not the slightest proof adduced, to connect him in any way with the commission of a crime. . . . We wish him success and hope that the American people will take the judgment of fourteen men and women who have sat for thirty-one days listening to the evidence that Roscoe Arbuckle is entirely innocent and free from blame.

Hays even lifted the ban on his films in December 1922, as "Every man in the right way and in the proper time is entitled to his chance to make good. It is apparent that Arbuckle's conduct since his trouble merits that chance."

But it was too late. Hundreds of telegrams poured into the Hays office protesting the reinstatement. The National Education

Association publicly insisted Arbuckle's pictures remain out of circulation, lest they corrupt a new generation of young movie-goers, and the directors association refused to allow him back into their ranks. The official ban on Arbuckle's films may have been lifted, but his career was, for all intents and purposes, over. He had exhausted his finances on his three defenses and, stripped of his career, had no steady means of income. He spent the next ten years in relative poverty, directing sporadically under a pseud-onym. In 1932, with more than a decade between him and the scandal, he appeared in a series of two-reel comedies. Everyone loved them, and a comeback seemed just around the corner. He signed a contract with Warner Bros.; the press seemed ready to welcome him back. But on June 29, 1933, the very night he signed his contract, Arbuckle, all of forty-six years old, died in his sleep.

The fall of Fatty Arbuckle might seem like a simple tale: a man was in the wrong place at the wrong time and paid a tragic price. But Arbuckle's demise had much more to do with Ameri-can anxieties about class and gender than any actual wrongdoing. He became the figurehead for all that was dangerous about Hollywood—unbridled wealth, the unchecked vice—and no jury could acquit him of being an overweight, asexualized, overpaid man. It was easy for the public to forgive, or even ignore, the transgressions of Fairbanks and Pickford, the "King and Queen of Hollywood," by cloaking them in romance and destiny. But Ar-buckle's transgressions simply could not be reframed. Even if he did not rape or injure a young starlet, he was still Fatty. Not even the impressive rhetorical machinery of the fan magazines could refute that.

We don't call our stars "Fatty" anymore, and studios don't (of-ficially) ban them from Hollywood. But we do still allow stars to take on our personal anxieties, and shun them when they fail to embody them in ways that please us. We blind ourselves to corpo-

CHAPTER THREE

Wallace Reid: Hollywood's First Drug Addict

At 6'3" and 190 strapping pounds, Wallace Reid was a giant among men of the silent era. Between 1919 and 1921, he starred in five race car films, all variations on the same simple, appealing theme, from *The Roaring Road* (1919) to *Excuse My Dust* (1920). "I suppose I'm the original lucky individual," he told the *Washington Post*. "No matter how many accidents I am in, I always escape without serious damage, though I usually carry away some mark or another as a memento. Luckily, they've never been on my face." Lucky indeed, because Reid was classically handsome, with balanced features and earnest, sparkling eyes that added texture to his thrill-seeking persona.

A modern equivalent of Wallace Reid would be a hybrid of a *Jackass* cast member and a Judd Apatow man-child, a brawny boy next door. Yet this boy next door also had a long-term addiction to opiates and would eventually die from severe symptoms of withdrawal. There was no way to cover up Reid's death, so Will Hays, working with Reid's wife, changed the conversation entirely. It was a marvel of early publicity that helped establish the language of addiction and recovery that persists today. Reid could've been labeled a junkie—proof that despite

Hays's "cleanup," the filth of Hollywood persisted—but instead, he died a victim and a hero.

To understand how Hays spun the story, we have to understand Reid's image. Reid grew up in a theater family, but spent most of his time being athletic and handsome and successful—the all-American QB and homecoming king years before those things meant what they mean today. He starred in dozens of one-reel films before catching the eye of D. W. Griffith, who cast him as a blacksmith in *The Birth of a Nation* (1915). It was a small part, but he was shirtless—and the result was something akin to the way women responded to Brad Pitt in nothing but a pair of jeans in *Thelma & Louise*.

Over the next five years, Reid appeared in a slew of race car pictures, performing his own stunts and firmly establishing his masculinity . . . while also starring as a ladies' man in a string of exotic romances, most successfully opposite opera singer Geraldine Farrar. On-screen as the champion of the racetrack, he was equally at home as the plaything of the vampy Gloria Swanson. He was that rare Hollywood star who curried equal favor with both sexes: women wanted him; men wanted to be him. Yet Reid was keen to disassociate himself from the label of "matinee idol," lest it compromise his appeal to men. "May the Lord forbid that anyone ever think I'm a matinee idol," he told *Motion Picture*. "If I ever thought I'd have that label attached to me, I'd start to direct tomorrow. That's one reason why I like the race-track stuff—it gives me the chance to get mussed up and honest-to-goodness dirty!"

Unlike Douglas Fairbanks, whose image was also characterized by athleticism and strength, Reid's vigor was seemingly spontaneous. Fairbanks went to the gym; Reid was the type to play pickup football with some guys he met while walking home from work. Reid was also a bit of a dilettante; he was a jack-of-all-trades, even if he didn't do any of those trades all that well, except, perhaps, racing. But his "dabblings" marked him as a sort of new-money Renaissance man, equally invested in high-class hobbies (book collecting, painting, chemistry, music) and working-class diversions (racing and fixing cars). He was quick to make friends—a positive quality, save when it led him to hang with "the wrong sort of crowd." In this way, Reid's natural geniality was both the source of his charm and the catalyst for his downfall. He was reckless, but it wasn't his fault.

Even though Reid truly was a matinee idol, he was immune to the hordes of lovesick young girls, the proud husband to "Mrs. Wallace Reid," also known as Dorothy Davenport, with whom he led a quiet, domestic life with his young son and mother-in-law. Or at least that's what the fan magazines worked very hard to suggest: next to a photo spread of the pair dueting on violin and piano in their seemingly happy home, a quote from Mrs. Reid declares, "I have been married to my first and only husband for eight years, and I can say without fear of contradiction that Wally and I don't insult each other in public and have kept out of the Sunday supplements!" In "How to Hold Your Wife," supposedly penned by Reid himself, the star theorized that the best way to keep a woman content was to tell her you love her, tell her she's beautiful, and talk ceaselessly about your love; if you "take her to parties [and] arrange pleasures for her . . . she will be entirely happy." Today, Reid's advice sounds somewhat pedantic; in 1921, it made ladies swoon.

On October 21, 1922, at the height of his stardom, Reid was hospitalized for what the papers reported as a complete nervous breakdown. Rumors of drug use had been flying around the studio lot for months, further exacerbated when Reid pulled out of his latest film, *Nobody's Money*. The press explained that he had been under a physician's care, but his condition had reached a point at which his wife and a friend had taken him to the mountains to recover in private. The official line was that Reid was suffering from "klieg eyes," a common condition among actors, forced to work continually under the powerful lights necessary for the type of film stock in use during the time. Reid's press secretary claimed he was not, in fact, seriously ill—and certainly not in withdrawal.

Two months later, however, the jig was up. The reveal of Reid's addiction was carefully orchestrated. Instead of reporting that Reid was an addict, the press reported that he was *in recovery*. The title of the front page *Los Angeles Times* article was "Narcotics Given Up"—as opposed to "Reid Takes Narcotics" or "Reid a Total Junkie." His recovery was framed as "voluntary," forcing him to "play out the most heroic role of his life" in his "determined attempt to win out over drugs and whiskey." The Reid family acknowledged the rumors that he had been using for nearly two years; Reid's mother-in-law even referred to "wild liquor parties" that transformed the family home into something "more like a roadhouse." But those parties weren't Reid's fault. They were composed of so-called friends, "not even invited by [Reid]." These ruffians—completely unassociated with Reid, but whom he was just too nice to ever kick out—were the source of his addiction. Drugs and "uninvited guests" are thus clearly disassociated from well-intentioned, overly hospitable Reid. They were the contagion; he just wasn't smart enough to protect himself from infection.

The real story, then, wasn't of Reid's past. It was of his future, his recovery—a battle he could win because of his strength of will and character, so clearly evidenced on-screen. "My husband is a sick, sick boy," admitted Davenport. "I don't know if he will recover, but he has broken his habit and won his fight. He made this fight of his own free will and has won it by the strength of his own mind and will. I know that he will come back." And once he recovered, there'd be no more carousing, no more toxic friends— the Reids would move somewhere remote, with a tall fence and a "Not Welcome" sign on the door. In this way, an addiction that could've been figured as a weakness was refigured as a recovery predicated on strength, both moral and physical. Unlike Arbuckle, who spent months attempting to evidence his reform, Reid was already there, reforming before your eyes, fighting the righteous fight. Davenport and Hays thus invited readers to celebrate his reform rather than denigrate his sin—after all, only a hard-hearted moralist would condemn a man fighting for his life.

But suddenly, the problem spread beyond Reid and his addiction. In the days immediately after the public announcement, the papers were alive with speculation concerning "Hollywood dope parties." On page one, the *Washington Post* reported that Hays had been tipped off to a big-time producer who had supposedly "greased the skids" for Reid, starting him on the "poppy path." Even more damning, the man in question had supposedly collaborated with Hays in his efforts to clean up the industry. The article also alluded to the development of "vice rings," in which directors exploited young Hollywood hopefuls, setting them up, using them, and paying them off. These setups, according to the *Post*, were common knowledge in Hollywood—a simple investigation would bring them to light.

Testimony from Evelyn Nesbit Thaw, the young starlet at the center of the notorious Thaw-White scandal, in which Thaw's crazed lover killed her husband, painted a vivid picture of a "Hollywood dope hell." In Hollywood, according to Thaw, "a dope peddler and their victims are waiting there at every corner, in every home, at every party, for a chance to trap another victor." Thaw dramatically recalled a party where cocaine was served in a big sugar bowl—a temptation she resisted, but not for long.

Weeks later, she had a toothache; a friend gave her a compress soaked in cocaine to put on the tooth and a shot of morphine in the leg. One thing led to another, and her "fall" was complete. Like Reid, Thaw had been victimized; like Reid, it was an ailment that supposedly set her on her path to ruin. The clear culprit: Hollywood.

Thaw was likely just milking her final minutes of fame, but her very public account added fuel to what had quickly become a public relations disaster. If these allegations were true, then the entire "cleanup" effort could be exposed as a publicity stunt, illuminating the hypocrisy and greed still circulating just beneath the shiny Hollywood exterior. But Hays, working with Davenport, quickly neutralized this discourse. He demanded that Reid, "the poor boy," be "dealt with as a diseased person—not to be censured or shunned. Rather, let us all sanely and sympathetically try to help him, try to restore him to health." He likewise pledged full cooperation with all efforts to stop any lingering narcotics traffic in Hollywood. In this way, Hays was able to frame Reid as a victim while simultaneously highlighting the industry's amenability to an investigation, temporarily quelling anxiety concerning the persistence of the evil dope rings.

Because there was still the matter of the morphine. One could develop a morphine addiction after taking it for legitimate reasons—an injury, for example—but heroin was a criminal's drug, and one that was of particular concern as the so-called junkie population proliferated in New York City following the end of World War I. Various bits of information suggest that Reid was using both. Two years earlier, a young writer, Claude Tyner Waltman, was arrested on the studio lot for dealing heroin, and rumors suggested it was for Reid. New York was the headquarters of domestic heroin production, and it was also where Reid kept an apartment and hosted many late-night parties. When *Motion*

Picture interviewed him the morning after one such party, they alluded to its excesses, describing Reid as "weary" (read: hungover). Davenport also claimed that Reid had developed his addiction in New York and had periodically received packages of drugs from the city. Regardless of such suggestive reporting, Davenport and the press persisted in suggesting the addiction was one to *morphine*, never heroin or "dope." Davenport initially asserted that the rumors were untrue—that her husband *never* would've frequented a "dope party." Later, she somewhat unconvincingly averred, "I think he did go to one or two such affairs, but he found them distasteful and never went back again." His mother-in-law claimed he would return from a party, "sadly shake his head," and say, "Mother, I don't like it. That isn't the way to have pleasure. It's all so false."

In hindsight, these equivocations border on laughable, but at the time, they worked. Indeed, the denials were so effective that even today, the cited cause of death, on Wikipedia and elsewhere, is complications from withdrawal from morphine. Morphine was less salacious than heroin, but it was also a crucial piece of the complicated, highly malleable narrative woven by Davenport to explain Reid's addiction. In the weeks following the revelation, she traced the genesis of her husband's troubles to an illness on the set of *Forever* (1921), which he had filmed in New York over the summer of 1921. Because Reid was such a hardworking, selfless guy, he didn't want to slow down production, so he started taking morphine, acquired from a local physician. This explanation accomplished two crucial goals: first, Reid's relationship with opiates was initially sanctioned, was aboveboard, and was for his fans; second, the site of addiction was New York, not Hollywood. By shifting the locus of the drug culture to New York, Davenport (and presumably Hays, working with her) kept Hollywood "clean." But the *Forever* version of the story did not remain intact.

Davenport was soon suggesting that Reid's problem could actually be traced back to a train accident on the set of *The Valley of the Giants*, widely reported in the press in 1919. Several were injured on set and Reid was given morphine for a head injury. According to this explanation, he did not become addicted at that time, but the wreck was situated as but one of several accidents over the course of his film career, all of which he muscled through for the sake of his fans. He valiantly resisted the temptations of morphine until he became too weak to do so. It was a perfect cautionary tale, an object lesson in addiction. Reid's saga wasn't scandalous; it was a teachable moment.

But the story of the train wreck was a problem for the industry. It exculpated Reid, but it indicted the studios—they were the ones overworking the stars, putting them in danger, creating the very situations that could make a man as strong as Reid fall prey to addiction. Davenport thus changed her story *again*. The train wreck didn't happen while filming; rather, it was a "personal tragedy" and an "isolated case" that took place while Reid was traveling to the set. Reid attended to fellow passengers like a real hero, and then, "against the advice of physicians he went to work the next day and the picture was made on schedule. But from that hour Wallace Reid was never the same." So many explanations, so many contradictions—but the common narrative thread remained: Reid was a hardworking, self-effacing hero; the fault of his addiction was not his own.

These melodramatic explanations, along with repeated mention of Davenport as a "ministering angel," helped drown out rumors of a relapse. But no matter of publicity machinations could actually save Reid's life. On January 18, he succumbed to complications from withdrawal. His purported last words: "Tell them, Mamma, I have won my fight—that I have come back." Here, again, Reid's fight sounds like a page in a Hollywood script:

he wanted Hollywood to know that he had "come back"—he had "played hard," "worked hard," and "died game." He was, in other words, a conquering hero, gallant to the end. His equally heroic wife, also engaged in "the toughest fight a woman ever had," nearly collapsed following his death, but Reid's "indomitable will" had been passed along to her. Five days later, Hays announced that the Prohibition commissioner had performed an investigation, concluding that there was little foundation for the reports of narcotics rings in Hollywood.

With the diligent rhetorical labor of Davenport and Hays, the story of Reid's addiction had been transformed. No one was threatening to ban Reid's films—in fact, thousands were weeping, celebrating his struggle, and vowing to protect themselves against addiction, very much in the manner of the Hollywood melodramas of the time. But Hays also understood that any PR construction needs constant upkeep, especially as anxiety around Hollywood, drugs, sex, and general "den of iniquity" discourse remained, just below the surface. Another scandal and it could all reemerge, even more toxic and destructive than before.

Thus Hays, again collaborating with the very willing Davenport, sealed the well. The result: *Human Wreckage* (1923), a filmic "memorial" to Wallace Reid warning of the perils of addiction. Just weeks after Reid's death, Davenport announced her intention to make a motion picture to teach America a grand lesson, decrying "the insidious, poisonous serpent that has wormed its way into the bosom of our nation." Because Reid was pure "life," it was essential that she protect that life in others: "If I can drive the shyster doctors and the pandering peddlers from under cover, if I can bring into the intense light of the silver sheet these vile practices that have slunk about in the dark all these years—what better memorial can I erect to my husband?" It was all very, very serious, an early "Just Say No" Afterschool Special.

Human Wreckage hit theaters just six months after Reid's death, a potent, if extremely heavy-handed, means of securing Reid's legacy. Loosely based on Reid's story—or at least the public's understanding of it—the film starred both Davenport and Reid's own son. Trumpeted as "a great success" in *Photoplay*, *Human Wreckage* was reviewed as an impassioned cry for greater governmental responsibility in seeking out and destroying the "narcotic evil." It also helped accomplish the overarching goal of the industry protectorate: to show that the problem wasn't Reid, and it wasn't Hollywood; it was dope, those who peddled it, and the government's inability to destroy it.

Years later, the lasting impact of Davenport and Hays's ideological maneuvering remained. In 1925, *Photoplay* ran a nostalgic remembrance of "The Real Wally," effectively beatifying the star: Wally was a great dad; Wally loved his family so; Wally was just like a grown-up kid; Wally loved too much, gave too much, and thus lost everything. The profile prompted hundreds of teary-eyed fan responses, so many that *Photoplay* printed two full pages' worth. "There's no one equals Wallace Reid. There was a *man*," one fan wrote. "For us, Wally could do no wrong. No matter what might happen, our faith in him was and is steadfast." No mention of drugs or scandal; the means of his death had been omitted in favor of the triumphant narrative of his life as Hollywood hero.

Today, all of this seems rather standard—a bit saccharine, perhaps, but a natural means of mediating the scandal of addiction. But things that seem natural have only *become* so; they have histories and precedents that have been standard, in part through the endurance of Davenport in weaving a dramatic tale to explain her husband's addiction. Reid and the Hays office helped create a contradictory yet compelling tale of heroic recovery that was what the public desperately *wanted* to believe, even with its glaring holes and discrepancies.

These are the types of stories we tell ourselves—oftentimes prompted by the media—in order to make the world around us morally legible. There are heroes and villains, with very little gray area. In reality, Reid, Arbuckle, and Fairbanks and Pickford all resided in that gray area, as the vast majority of us do. But the combination of industrial logic and cultural mores made Fairbanks and Pickford the leads in a much lauded romance, and Reid triumphed even in death, while Arbuckle remained mired in villainy. And once cast in those roles, these stars are doomed or blessed, depending on one's perspective, to play them forever. Despite dozens of books and articles, popular and academic, Arbuckle casts a heavy shadow over early Hollywood history, exonerated under the law but not by popular history. His demise, and Hays's facilitation thereof, helped preserve the industry as it was; the revelation of Reid's "heroism" cemented it in a formation of top-down, highly regulated studio control that would endure for the next twenty years.

SILENT SEX SYMBOLS

Wallace Reid was Will Hays's test case: Could he spin a story? Could he protect Hollywood's reputation in the process? Clearly. But as the cases of Rudolph Valentino and Clara Bow show, it would be a much more formidable task when it came to the anxiety over the startling new representations of sex and desire that these stars seemed to embody. They weren't necessarily doing anything wrong—at least not in the same way that Arbuckle or Reid were. It was the little things of their lives—Valentino's "slave bracelets," Bow's resistance to Hollywood high culture—that made them unwieldy and, naturally, all the more alluring.

For some, Bow and Valentino embodied societal shifts that were both invigorating and intoxicating. For others, they incited tremendous concern over sea changes in gender norms, the place of the woman in the modern world, and the visibility of female desire. Their images, like any star images that seem to so precisely replicate the cultural temperature of a time, rose and fell with startling speed. Valentino's death, at the age of thirty-one, was a shock and a tragedy. But if he hadn't died, chances are high that his career would have fizzled in much the way Bow's did. Unless stars are able to modify their images along with the changing understandings of class and gender, their stardom is circumscribed, limited to the specific cultural moment from which they rose.

Stars are always symbols of something—of masculinity, of Americanism, of youth. But when their overarching symbolization is of sex, especially a new articulation of sex, their popularity becomes all the more mercurial. Bow's and Valentino's images were scandalous for the way they embodied sex and the way they incited desire. Valentino died before he could entirely fall out of favor and is thus immortalized, frozen as if at the height of his fervor, even when it's clear, to anyone who looks closely at history, that his image was already recycling itself and would soon exhaust its pertinence.

But Bow lived through her own decline. She refused or was unable to change the contours of her image to match what society wanted of her. She remained an outsider, neglecting whatever savvy advice she was given. Whether she stayed true to herself or was simply decimated by Hollywood, it's difficult to say. But it seems clear that the public was quick to reject what it had so recently loved, clinging to allegations that matched their desire to dispose of her. Bow was too much of the moment, a moment that, by 1930, America was eager to forget or, more precisely, to scapegoat for the economic disaster that echoed through the nation's new reality. These chapters chart the story of these silent sex symbols' rise and fall, inflected by turns with absurdity, tragedy, prejudice, and overwhelming success.

CHAPTER FOUR

Rudolph Valentino's Slave Bracelet

The craze for the Latin Lover, as Rudolph Valentino was dubbed, was one of the most significant events in cinematic history. For decades, no star would rise so suddenly, bewitch so many, enrage so many others, or disappear so tragically. But Valentino and the cloud of passionate devotion that surrounded him did not appear out of nowhere. His popularity was the product of a determined moment in American cultural history, characterized by the upheaval of gender relations following World War I. We commonly think of World War II as the war that sent women into the masculinized workforce, yet the same migration occurred during the Great War as well—one of several changes, including women's suffrage, that broke down the divide between traditionally public and private spaces: women, long thought to "belong" in the home, were walking unescorted on the streets, attending picture shows, shopping in department stores, and even living on their own. During this period, many women also became earners of their own incomes—incomes that they could, if these women were not yet married, spend exclusively on themselves, as the primary targets of the rapidly expanding postwar consumer economy. And the movies themselves were both a catalyst and a manifestation of these changes: women left the home to go see the movies; women read fan magazines with advertisements encouraging them to spend excess income; women watched and desired to copy the consumption modeled so tastefully by the "film idols" themselves.

Female moviegoers falling for a male star wasn't anything new. Women had fawned over Wallace Reid, Douglas Fairbanks, and dozens of other handsome young stars. But Valentino was not only the Latin Lover, but an immigrant during one of the most fervently anti-immigrant periods in American history. And not just any immigrant, but an Italian immigrant, the very group that incited the most anxiety and anger. But Valentino's Italianness was never disavowed or whitewashed. Instead, it was transferred into overarching otherness—he played sheiks, Arabs, Argentineans, Spaniards, with the resulting connotations of lustiness, swarthiness, and effeminacy.

And, let it be said, he was tremendously attractive. Valentino burned through the female population in much the same way that James Dean would thirty years later, or that Robert Pattinson did just recently. Part of Valentino's sexual power was rooted in his roles and the way he managed to embody both the menace and swoon of romance, and part of it was timing, some well-placed extratextual romance, and a very public war with his studio. Today, the dominant understanding of Valentino is that women loved him and men despised what he represented. In reality, Valentino had no small number of male fans, and many women disliked his particular brand of melodramatic romance. Yet when he died, his image was already morphing into the realm of myth, already erasing the titillating and intermittently hilarious details that accompanied his fame.

Narratives of Valentino's early life vary wildly—even the spelling of his name changed from year to year. But several themes remain constant: Born Rodolfo Alfonzo Raffaello Pierre Filibert Guglielmi di Valentina d'Antonguolla, commonly shortened to Rodolfo Guglielmi, he was a classic Italian mama's boy and youngest son who picked up some choice dance moves along the way. After some ne'er-do-welling in Paris, Valentino immigrated to the States in 1913 at the age of eighteen, where, unable to speak a word of English, he found employment as a "taxi dancer," which meant setting up regular residence at Maxim's Restaurant-Cabaret, dressing to the nines, and entertaining women of a certain income level and desire. He would dance with them, doing their bidding in an ambiguous play on the role of kept man, and make himself agreeable, taking on whatever persona the women desired.

It wasn't a very honorable vocation, but it paid the bills. Valentino, however, was ashamed of his dependence on women and eventually worked his way up to the more respectable ballroom circuit, purportedly amassing a new following of wealthy older ladies eager to buy him cars and pay for his dinners. After a stint with a touring company, he dabbled in the theater, finding his way to San Francisco and, upon the urging of a friend, moving to Los Angeles, where he found himself cast in a string of filmic bit parts. But the young Italian had the wrong look: at that time, dark-skinned actors were commonly relegated to parts as "heavies," aka bad guys. Leading men looked like Fairbanks and Reid—all-American boys with heaving chests and blue eyes, not slicked-back hair and olive complexions.

The "lounge lizard" bit parts he landed were displeasing. He played a "cabaret parasite" in *Eyes of Youth* (1919), opposite Clara Kimball Young, with the sole narrative purpose of luring the heroine to a club, seducing her, and then allowing her husband to discover them together. In *Stolen Moments* (1920), he's a skeezy Brazilian author who, naturally, spends a lot of time seducing young fans of his work. It's not surprising that Valentino was bored and frustrated with this type of role. But as critic Alexander Walker points out, even in these early films, there's a certain sophistication to Valentino's performances—the sort of poise that accompanies years of choreography, with "the professional dancer's manner of carrying his clothes, not being oppressed by them." The charisma was there; the parts just hadn't caught up to it.

Stolen Moments would be Valentino's last villainous role, because shortly thereafter, he got his break. According to lore, he had read the book *The Four Horsemen of the Apocalypse* while shooting another role, then agitated the producer for a role in the film. He was to play a supporting part, but director Rex Ingram, seeing some hint of the potential gravitas, expanded the supporting role to that of a star. In comparison to his costars, Valentino was making pennies—he even had to supply his own wardrobe—but he stole every scene. There was Valentino, dancing the tango, seducing, being a hero, and, most important, dying at film's end, thereby rendering his character, with its curious mix of romance and heroism, immortal. *The Four Horsemen* became the highest-grossing film of 1921, and Valentino became a phenomenon.

From the beginning, the press worked to construct Valentino as simultaneously pan-ethnic and Italian. A December 1921 article in *Motion Picture Classic*, subtly titled "Hitting the Hookah with Rudie," staged an encounter in an exotic restaurant "canopied in mauve silks," where they drank absinthe. The author underlines that although Valentino was born a Catholic, he "seems a pagan skeptical of creeds . . . things mystical fascinate him." He had the musculature of a Roman gladiator, but lest you associate him too heavily with Italianness, rest assured that "there is none of the volubility that we have come to expect as an Italian characteristic through commerce with push-cart financiers." And although the author admits that he's very dark skinned, with hair that appears almost lacquered, Valentino "is not florid or gesticulant." He may have been Italian, but he wasn't bad Italian.

This Gordian knot of exoticism was also on full display in *The Sheik* (1921), released at just the right moment to ratchet Valentino fever into frenzy. Valentino plays an Arab chieftain who abducts and threatens to rape an English gentlewoman, Lady Diana Mayo. The film is replete with sultry looks and unexpected switches between anger and desire, intercut with exchanges along the lines of "Why have you brought me here?"/"Are you not woman enough to know?" By film's end, we learn that the dusky sheik is, in fact, a Scottish earl, found in the desert when he was a baby. In this way, *The Sheik* gets the thrill of miscegenation without the ramifications or censorship troubles. What's more, the rape never actually takes place; the sheik just threatens the heroine, makes her wear ladylike clothes, and tells her to submit to his will. It's the thought of sexual menace, not the actual action, that truly titillates; the glower and firm embrace that frighten in their intensity. It's the knife-edge of rapture—the same feeling that has eroticized vampire stories for centuries.

The one-two punch of *The Four Horsemen* and *The Sheik* rocketed Valentino into public consciousness. And as with any cultural phenomenon, you knew it was powerful by the existence of imitators and parodies. In the months following the release of *The Sheik*, comedians were mocking his slick-haired look; Will Rogers played a buffoonish Rufus while Stan Laurel took on the role of Rhubarb Vaselino in *Mud and Sand*. And the vitriol began to flow: in "A Song of Hate," published in *Photoplay*, Dick Dorgan exclaims:

> I hate Valentino! All men hate Valentino. I hate his oriental optics; I hate his classic nose; I hate his roman face; I hate his smile; I hate his glistening teeth; I hate

his patent leather hair; I hate his Svengali glare; I hate him because he dances too well; I hate him because he's the great lover of the screen; I hate him because he's an embezzler of hearts; I hate him because he's too apt in the art of osculation; I hate him because he's leading man for Gloria Swanson; I hate him because he's too good looking. . . . The women are all dizzy over him. The men have formed a secret order (of which I am running for president and chief executioner as you may notice) to loathe, hate and despise him for obvious reasons. What! Me jealous?—Oh, no—I just Hate Him.

It's a magnificent piece of backlash, but it also illuminates why Valentino incited anxiety: he was beautiful and he was distracting women. And with that distraction, the unspoken fear that he was making women unsatisfied with what they *did* have—presumably men like Dorgan, who lacked Valentino's skills of romancing and inducing swoons.

Valentino wasn't helping his case with the male population. Following the release of *Beyond the Rocks* (1922), he offered *Photoplay* his thoughts on "Women and Love," theorizing that "We cannot know woman because she does not know herself. She is the unsolvable mystery, perhaps because there is no solution." But Valentino's message was mixed: he declared that he didn't like a woman who "knew too much" but also thought "a love affair with a stupid woman is like a cold cup of coffee." He was also a sexual conservative, or, at the very least, expected his female companions to toe that line, warning that if a woman offered her lips on the second or third meeting, he wouldn't care to accept them.

It was a fascinating reflection of Valentino's own love life, which had quickly become the subject of much speculation. In

June 1921, his first wife, Jean Acker, filed for divorce. After a drawn-out battle in the courts, it became clear that the couple had wed on a whim, spent very little time together, and fought constantly. Acker wanted to make a man out of Valentino and thought his dependence on her distinctly unmanly; Valentino countered that all her correspondence may have seemed full of sweetness and light, but it was, in truth, infused with bitterness. It was unclear as to whether the marriage had even been consummated—which, along with whispers of Acker's lesbianism, would fuel rumors of Valentino's own homosexuality. And according to Acker, Valentino had both knocked her down *and* used her perfume. While Acker's allegations were never substantiated, they meshed perfectly with Valentino's volatile, feminized, and impassioned picture personality. An interlocutory decree was eventually granted, with divorce contingent upon a yearlong waiting period.

In the meantime, Valentino busied himself with buying a luxurious new mansion (Falcon Lair, which *Motion Picture Classic* deemed "the most sensational and exotic piece of property in the movie colony") and going on the hunt for his soul mate. It did not take long—while filming *Camille* in the spring of 1922, he was swept away by art director Natacha Rambova, née Winifred Hudnut, the daughter of a New York perfume magnate. In May, the exotic pair eloped in Mexicali, spending a night of wedded bliss (with requisite publicity) before the DA threatened charges of bigamy and white slavery. Valentino, it turned out, had conveniently forgotten the terms of his divorce decree. Lest he be embarrassingly charged with bigamy, he and Rambova parted ways, promising to stay apart until the year was over.

Both were quick to exploit the separation, highlighting the inherent drama of the situation. A September fan magazine spread features pictures of their future home, which Valentino, dressed in a bright orange Chinese lounging suit, could not bring himself to enjoy alone. In *Photoplay,* Rambova established herself as the better of every reader of the magazine *and* exculpated herself from any role in the supposed bigamy: "She is very subtle, Natacha Rambova. She is white satin embroidered in gold, she is absinthe in a crystal glass, she is a copy of Swinburne bound in scarlet. She is beauty drugged with sophistication." In short: she was everything you weren't—and thus so very easy to despise. But she also had intimate knowledge of Valentino, whom she described as an emotional little boy, sensitive to the wounding words of others. Valentino's public may not have loved Rambova, but her words only ratified what fans wanted to hear: that he needed care, that he was sincere, that he was overflowing with emotion— enough to fulfill the needs of his entire fan base.

Such unabashed sympathy for Valentino came in handy—and not just to soothe the potential scandal surrounding his near-bigamy. At the same time of the bigamy scandal, he was warring with his studio, Famous Players–Lasky, over pay and artistic control. He had been unhappy for months: even after the runaway success of *The Sheik,* he was earning a mere twelve hundred dollars a week, a paltry sum when middling stars like Thomas Meighan were earning five thousand. But Valentino wanted more than money: he wanted artistic control over his next project, *Blood and Sand.* Famous Players offered to up his salary to seven thousand dollars a week, but also understood that "artistic control" was really code for "skyrocketing budget," and stood firm. In protest, Valentino pulled a classic movie-star move, charging up huge bills for Spanish and Moorish artifacts for use on set. Finally, in September 1922, he refused to accept further payment from Famous Players—no matter that he was already in the studio's debt for payoffs related to his divorce from Acker.

The case went to the courts, but Famous Players engaged its

option to extend Valentino's contract, thereby ensuring that if he wouldn't work for Famous Players, he wouldn't work for anyone. It was the beginning of what would become a nearly two-year absence from the screen, but Valentino was primed for a fight. He published a very plaintive "Open Letter to the American Public" in *Photoplay* and, with permission from the court, embarked on a massive dance tour with Rambova, performing in eighty-eight cities across the United States and Canada. The pair worked constantly: many appearances were single-night stands, and while on tour, they promoted their sponsor (Mineralava face cream) and judged beauty pageants.

Meanwhile, Valentino collaborated with *Photoplay* to craft a detailed and maudlin three-part story of his life, published at the height of the dispute. He wrote for *The Bookman*, a reputable literary magazine, prompting *Motion Picture* magazine to call him "a thinker who has the courage of his own convictions"—the exact sort of support Valentino was doubtless seeking. If all the Renaissance man activity weren't enough, Valentino also wrote and promoted his book of poetry, *Day Dreams*, purportedly inspired by "psychic communication." This type of artistic effort might have induced eye rolling, but it was a brilliant business move. When Valentino finally reached a deal with Famous Players, along with Ritz Carlton Pictures, on Christmas Day, 1923, he had been off the screen for nearly two years, yet had managed to keep himself constantly in the public eye. He maintained the fitness of his star image, despite the best attempts of the studio to wear him down, besmirch him in the press, and replace him, most blatantly with the likes of similarly swarthy Ramon Novarro.

And thus the studio capitulated at last: Valentino would make seventy-five hundred dollars a week and have full artistic control over his next project, the historical drama *Monsieur Beaucaire* (1924). His return to the screen was eagerly anticipated, but like most long-awaited comebacks, it fell short—in part because Valentino spent the film in over-the-top period clothing (think white wigs and silk pantaloons) that provided ample opportunity for public ridicule. If one looked closely, the film was actually satirizing the excess that attended the court of Louis XIV, but the satire was lost on most and the film underperformed.

Valentino's performance and wardrobe did little to quell the rumors of his effeteness: a spread in *Motion Picture*, for example, highlighted the contents of Valentino's dressing room, which held "all the beauty secrets of the boudoir of a fastidious debutante," overflowing with cosmetics and beauty accessories. He was roundly ridiculed for his platinum "slave bracelet"—a gift from Rambova that suggested his status as a kept man. As a writer for the *Chicago Tribune* exclaimed, "What in the name of all that's masculine is a slave bracelet?" What's more, his follow-up films to *Monsieur Beaucaire*—*A Sainted Devil* (1924) and *Cobra* (1925)—failed to make an impression. At this point, independent producer Joseph Schenck made him a sweetheart deal: $520,000 a year and 40 percent of the profits from his films . . . but only if he returned to his classic Valentino image. Stricken with lingering debt from his divorce and extended absence from the screen, Valentino begrudgingly accepted the offer.

The buildup to the release of his first film with Schenck, *The Eagle* (1925), coincided with the slow, very public demise of his marriage to Rambocha and the reactivation of Valentino's image as a domineering romantic. In late August 1925, he made a public statement that he and Mrs. Valentino had agreed to a "marital vacation." As *The Eagle* hit theaters, Valentino began championing the bachelor life, claiming he was much better off single, in part because he just loved to "appreciate beauty. I realize now that this is my nature." As he boarded a train to New York, where, he insisted, he would *not* see his tiresome wife, he added that he was just now realizing all the fun he had been missing while married.

Amid rumors of new dalliances, production began on *The Son of the Sheik* (1926), the 1920s version of the derivative blockbuster sequel. Valentino was to be paid more than one hundred thousand dollars, but the gossip was that he was all washed up. *Motion Picture Classic* wondered, "Has the Great Lover Become Just a Celebrity?" while *Motion Picture* declared that Valentino was old news: "Sheiks are dead as the proverbial doornail." Unoriginal as it was, *The Son of the Sheik* was a hit. The dubious publicity was perhaps a little unfair—but then Valentino made things much, much worse. On July 18, 1926, an anonymous writer for the *Chicago Tribune* visited a new public ballroom on the west side of Chicago, where he found a powder dispenser in the men's restroom, with instructions to put a personal powder puff beneath the dispenser and pull the lever. Powder in a men's restroom! Judging from the writer's reaction, it was tantamount to putting a little boy in a dress and, by extension, the downfall of American civilization. As he declared, "Why didn't someone quietly drown Rudolph Guglielmo, alias Valentino, years ago?" Valentino, however, was livid—and demanded retribution. Since American law forbade the "duello," he would settle for a meeting in the boxing ring or on the wrestling mat, "in typically American fashion, for I am an American citizen." In answer to the naysayers who would write the challenge off as a publicity stunt, Valentino would hold the duel *in private*, demonstrating to the writer that "the wrist under a slave bracelet may snap a real fist into your sagging jaw."

The press was not kind. *Los Angeles Times* columnist Harry Carr needled Valentino's bombast, backhandedly conceding that "his flourish has probably impressed all the Polish servant girls and stock-yard sausage stuffers; and Rudy is a hero once more." In the next day's column, he offered Valentino some unsolicited advice:

If he would "stop riding in automobiles with silver snakes crawl-
ing around the hoods; and take off his gold bracelets; and stop
kissing the hands of visiting ladies; and generally stop trying to
show himself off as a 'Latin lover' for the benefit of the overawed
telephone girls," he could save his career. As it was, he was making
himself purely, embarrassingly ridiculous. Over the next week,
Valentino practiced at a local gym and met with famed journalist
H. L. Mencken for advice on how to proceed. Mencken advised
him to drop the ordeal, but the melodramatic damage was done.
Valentino's attempt to re-masculinize himself—to defend himself
against claims that he had feminized the nation—had rendered
him absurd.

But before Valentino could become too much of a punch line,
he collapsed at his hotel in New York and was taken to the hospital, where he was diagnosed with appendicitis and gastric ulcers,
requiring immediate surgery. By August 20, 1926, the press was
reporting that Valentino was in recovery—he even chuckled at a
telegram from a fan that declared, "I need you. Live." But on
August 21, he developed a case of severe pleurisy in his lung, fell
into a coma, and passed away two days later, at the age of thirty-
one.

The national grief was embodied by actress and rumored lover
Pola Negri, who was reported to be lying prostrate in seclusion,
unable to speak. In the aftermath of Valentino's death, eulogizers
proclaimed his rise to stardom as "the beginning of a new regime
and the overthrow of an old one among the youth of the country." Even Carr, who had so mercilessly ridiculed Valentino just
months before, admitted that the star had broken the "barrier of
bitter prejudice" against Latins. According to Carr, "When I was
a little boy it would have been almost unthinkable to represent an
Italian in a popular melodrama as anything but the arch villain."
Valentino, though, "made the Latin the lover of the world."

Tales of women committing suicide in the streets have long accompanied the Valentino narrative, though these claims have been exaggerated. A young starlet, Peggy Scott, who had, according to very flimsy rumor, had an intimate rendezvous with Valentino in Biarritz, Spain, committed suicide in the week after his death, but the connection between her death and Valentino's was a tenuous one, exploited by the press. At the suicide inquest a month later, the connection between the two was effectively disproven—it seemed that Scott had, very likely, simply imagined herself an intimate of Valentino's—but the sensationalism of the timing remained. In September, a nineteen-year-old girl, reportedly an ardent movie fan, turned on the gas in her apartment and died with a picture of Valentino clutched inside her handkerchief; the next month, a twenty-year-old mother of two, claiming she wanted to be reunited with Valentino, drank iodine and attempted, unsuccessfully, to fire two shots at herself.

But three incidents does not make an adequate case for causation: months before Valentino's death, critics were decrying a "suicide wave" among students, traced, according to one prominent clergyman, to the large-scale abandonment of religion in favor of "physical pleasures."

Valentino did not inspire a wave of suicides, but he did make female emotionality visible: thousands of women attended his public funeral, and the stories of prostration and physical grief were easily co-opted into a story of "mass suicide," simply because that narrative seemed to match the emotional fervor that accompanied Valentino fandom. And it was this response—what Valentino *did* to women, making them publicly and privately unruly—that made columnists and the male public at large so uncomfortable.

Valentino was more than just a film idol. He inspired a particular type of devotion, a manifestation of female sexual desire, that exacerbated existing tensions about the changing role of women in American society. It's evident in the way writers spoke of his fans, the way they constantly framed them as working class, lacking in intelligence. Female desire can be powerful—which is exactly why masculine forces have sought to isolate, belittle, and ridicule it, whether in the twenties, in the sixties surrounding Beatlemania, or today with the so-called Twihards. Valentino was more than just the Sheik, more than a lounge lizard and a Latin Lover. He was a live conduit of female desire—and that, even more than his slave bracelets and his threats of dueling, was what made his body, his longing stare, his skill at the tango, and his brooding visage so very scandalous.

CHAPTER FIVE

Clara Bow:
The "It" Girl

Clara Bow was also a conduit of desire, only hers was framed in slightly different terms. Bow was the "flapper par excellence": she bounced, she danced, she fidgeted and *moved*. Bliss was written all over her body—she seemed constantly alight and alive. With her flaming red hair and wide, playfully mischievous eyes, Mary Pickford she was not. Like Valentino, Bow represented a sea change. She looked physically different from the stars that had come before—there was a certain lushness to her, a vibrancy and indelibly modern look. By 1927, she was arguably the biggest star in the world, the woman most resplendent with what screenwriter Elinor Glyn called "It"—a polite way of saying "sex appeal."

The flapper looms large in American conceptualization of the Roaring Twenties, Charleston-ing from one overflowing glass of champagne to the next. In truth, the flapper, which F. Scott Fitzgerald described as "lovely, expensive, and about nineteen," was merely the most vivid and controversial variation of the New Woman, a name that began to appear during this time frame. This title was the overarching designation used to describe the growing freedom for women and the reaction against conservative Victorian ideals of femininity. Not all New Women were flappers, yet the figure of the flapper—and Bow, as its most visible exponent—became the locus of both positive and negative critical energies, at once a sign of American vitality and a harbinger of the apocalypse.

In the press and on-screen, Bow was constructed as eminently changeable, able to alter her face, demeanor, and personality at a moment's notice. She could be sexy yet demure, playful yet scowling, a tomboy with no concern for the games of romance and a flirt who plays the game flawlessly. Bow's mutability mirrored the complicated, contradictory expectations of the New Woman, who had to be liberated yet passive, aggressive yet still desirous of man, "new" when alluring, "old" when necessary. These tangled ideological contradictions were what made it so difficult for Bow the person to function under the weight of Bow the image.

From the beginning, Bow was framed as a chameleon. Growing up in Brooklyn, she came from an impoverished family, and her mother was intermittently ill. Bow thus spent most of her time in the streets, playing with boys and ignoring girls, who would make fun of her ragtag outfits, most of which she put together from the leftovers of her mother's closet. As she told Adela Rogers St. Johns, she was a classic tomboy who "didn't give a darn about clothes or looks. I only wanted to play with the boys." But Bow wanted a way out. In 1921, after seeing an advertisement for a beauty contest in a fan magazine, she went to have her photo taken. According to a widely circulated anecdote, Bow attempted to put on a sweet, demure look for the camera. But the cameraman was a local guy, who recognized her from her time running around town, and he told her, "Kid, you're not angel. You just look saucy and you'll win." Bow pulled out her saucy look for the second set of photos, but her father would have none of it, insisting that she submit the sweet photos. As the story goes, Bow switched in the sassier photo at the last moment, ultimately winning the contest.

Whether or not the details of the story are true, its wide circulation helped frame Bow as capable of switching her personality with a single look. With time, she earned a contract with Preferred Pictures. On loan to First National Pictures, she played an over-the-top flapper in *Black Oxen* (1923)—but as *Photoplay* noted in the caption to a full-page photo of Bow, "It doesn't seem possible that this little school girl, with the wide-open innocent eyes, can be Clara Bow, the exasperating flapper in *Black Oxen*. There is a wistfulness, an ingenuousness about Clara in this picture that is not the flapper type." Here, Bow's performance as an "exasperating flapper" is framed as just that—a performance. Her real self, captured by a publicity photo, was the opposite of exasperating—all innocent eyes and schoolgirl earnestness.

Over the next two years, Bow appeared in a staggering number of pictures, almost always in some variation of the flapper type. She appeared as a college girl in her last film for Preferred, *The Plastic Age* (1925), which became a huge hit and ushered in her transition to Paramount, where she played even more flapper roles, mostly famously as Kittens in *Dancing Mothers* (1926). She became engaged to her *Plastic Age* costar Gilbert Roland, but as would be the case with all of Bow's engagements, it didn't last long. She moved on to Victor Fleming, who directed her in *Mantrap* (1926) and who, years later, would compare Bow to an exquisite violin: "Touch her and she'll respond with genius." Throughout this period, Bow was becoming a fan magazine darling: she was a product of a fan magazine contest, her life story was just maudlin enough, and she provided excellent copy, with her red, tangled hair bursting from the full-color renderings.

Part of the attraction of Bow's image was its apparent lack of manipulation. Despite clear evidence that her stardom had been the product of a fan magazine, she was described as a star seemingly without pretense. What you saw, what you heard, what you felt—it was all real, untarnished by publicity and mediation. *Photoplay* heralded her "artlessness" and "lack of self-consciousness," while columnist Alma Whitaker warned that whatever she did, Bow should *not* try to become a lady. "There's nothing highbrow about Clara," she explained. "She radiates sex appeal," but it was tempered with "an impish sense of humor." She was the original "cool girl"—unpretentious, charismatic, the life of the party.

Bow's artlessness made her a phenomenon, but it also excluded her from Hollywood high society. In the early twenties, the Arbuckle scandal, with its tales of "gin jollification," painted a picture of a sinful, wanton Hollywood. With the help of Pickford, Fairbanks, and other seemingly upright stars, Will Hays was able to transform Hollywood's image into one of genteel and clean living—a sort of high society in the Hollywood hills. Valentino was never wholly accepted into this society, but he was still a "model immigrant," engaging with the high arts and avoiding low-class diversions. His consumption patterns may have been over the top, but they were still always in relatively good taste. Bow, by contrast, refused to hew to the unspoken rules of Hollywood behavior.

This noncompliance was part of what the columnists meant when they referenced her refusal to become a "lady": she went around town in clothes inappropriate for high society, such as a "white flannel sport outfit—no sleeves, very short" with "kid sandals, no hose, and a jaunty little blazer cap." She loved going to football games, especially the local USC ones, to which she purportedly always wore red satin slippers. Most of all, she did not concern herself with good taste. She fumed at *Photoplay*, "What are the dignified people like? The people who are held up as ex-

amples . . . ? They are snobs. Frightful snobs." But Bow also understood exactly why she had become a Hollywood curiosity. She
was, in her words, "a big freak"—but that was simply "because
I'm myself." Whatever hurt she may have felt at her exclusion
from high Hollywood society made for tremendous publicity,
further underlining her genuineness and resistance to putting on
airs. Not even Hollywood could take the Brooklyn out of the
girl.

For all the praise heaped on Bow's *lack* of acting, it was crucial
to maintain a distinction between her on-screen, wanton lifestyle
and her off-screen lifestyle. By the mid-twenties, the Hays office
was wary of potential boycotts against flapper films, with their
depictions of a hedonistic lifestyle replete with dancing on table-
tops, flirting with boys, and consuming alcohol. Bow, then, was a
"flapper who flaps for screen purposes only." Or, as she told the
Los Angeles Times, "I'm not a flapper, really"—she avoided the
cabaret and the movies, and spent her time at home or driving
through the night, the wind in her hair. The disavowal of an off-
screen flapper lifestyle not only assuaged anxiety over behaviors
that might seep off the screen into real life but also made "flapperism" into a performance. If even the so-called super-flapper didn't
inhabit the flapper lifestyle off-screen, then flapper behaviors
weren't some new way of being—they could be put on and taken
off like a new coat.

Playful sex appeal, femininity without pretense, flapperism as
play—these constructs were the very foundation of Bow's image
and, not coincidentally, the hallmarks of her character in *It,* the
smash hit of 1927 and Bow's career-defining role. The concept of
the "It" girl is generally attributed to Elinor Glyn, a British writer
whose narratives became a mainstay of Hollywood in the 1920s.
Glyn was always cagey about the exact definition of It, inspiring
dozens of articles debating its precise meaning and potential con-

notations. The It factor lives in the girl who doesn't know she's beautiful, who's utterly without self-consciousness or pretense—all of which sounds a tremendous amount like Clara Bow. Bow goes unnamed in the article, but once cast in *It*, she became *It* and *It* became her. Even in her own description of It, she fulfills the definition: "As far as I know I think it must be my vivacity, my fearlessness and perhaps that I'm just a regular girl or a tom-girl, one that doesn't think of men much; maybe it's my indifference to them. I don't particularly care about men." As for Bow's engagements? No matter—indeed, her negligence of them only further testified to her indifference toward men. She attracted men because she cared so little; she was beautiful because she didn't care for beauty. She was It because she doesn't even care what It was.

The movie *It* is like a ninety-minute attempt to define It, with the added bonus of a department store backdrop. Bow plays a shopgirl, eager for love and, perhaps more important, the capital to buy the dresses and other goods she desires. Over the course of the film, she handily seduces Cyrus Waltham Jr., the owner of the department store in which she works, exploiting the affections of his best friend and getting Waltham to dump his inconvenient fiancée. She's a blatant social climber, but somehow, she also comes off as totally blameless—a girl who just wants to have fun, go to Coney Island with a boy, and fall in love. Any potential deviousness is obviated by the sheer joy of Bow's performance. *It* is also a classic romance narrative, in which a seemingly independent, free-thinking girl uses that independence to get a man—and, ultimately, become *dependent*. This was the same fundamental contradiction at the heart of the plight of the New Woman: independence was only a means to an end, a way for a single girl to become a wedded woman. Cultivate yourself, get a job, provide for yourself, but only as long as it takes to get a man who will then provide all those things for you.

Bow was supposed to live out that contradiction—prove, through her very existence, that it could be reconciled. The problem, then, was that she was having all the fun, getting all the boys, but refusing to marry and settle down. Her independence was, ironically, too unruly for the press and the public. Once the revelations of Bow's private life, and the flapperesque excess it contained, came to light, the artifice of the "flapper who doesn't flap" would begin to crumble. Yet in 1927, she was still the hottest thing in Hollywood: she rode the wave of *It* through several successful films, including a turn in the World War I drama *Wings*, the first film to win the Academy Award for Best Picture, and a dalliance with newcomer Gary Cooper.

Over the course of the next two years, however, Bow's actions began to take on a whiff of the absurd. Much like Valentino, she seemed to be becoming a caricature of herself. She became engaged to New York club owner Harry Richman—the latest in a long string of attachments and engagements for the girl who supposedly cared nothing for men—and the gossip columnists ridiculed it. One play-by-play of a rendezvous: "Harry gets up in the middle of the night (9 a.m.) to meet Clara when she hits New York. They hug seventy-five times for seventy-five sleepy reporters and cameramen."

But the story gets worse: In June 1930, Bow made a trip to Dallas to visit one Dr. Pearson, who had administered to her in Los Angeles and with whom, if rumors were to be believed, she had fallen rapturously in love. Bow claimed she just happened to be in Dallas visiting friends, but the damage was done. Pearson's wife, it was revealed, was six months pregnant, and Bow had tried to buy her silence and cooperation with a $30,000 payment. At this point, it appeared that Bow was stringing along three men—Richman, Pearson, and a new entry to the field, actor Rex Bell. The head of Paramount ordered her home; Richman, still her supposed fiancé, told reporters that he had no knowledge of Bow going to Dallas to romance another man, but if it were so, then maybe she ought to return her engagement ring. Rumors began circulating that Will Hays himself would force Bow home, but the star was unfazed: she didn't fear Hays, and she had plans to quit Hollywood entirely when her contract was up.

In the end, Bow emerged from the ordeal without punishment—or fiancé—but her stardom had taken a turn. First, there was the weight gain. In the spring, the gossip press began to note an expansion of her figure. One columnist ridiculed her multiplying chins; a reviewer called her "plump" in her role in *The Saturday Night Kid*. When fans wrote in protest, the reviewer shot back that if he were talking about anyone other than Bow, he would've just up and called her *fat*.

Then there was the gambling. In September 1930, Bow stopped payment on $13,900 worth of checks issued in a Tahoe casino to pay off her debts after gambling all night. She had ignored longtime friend and personal secretary Daisey DeVoe's insistence that the fifty-cent chips each represented one hundred dollars, thus believing she had lost fourteen hundred dollars, not fourteen thousand. Clearly, Bow was employing some faulty math, but her flippant reply was, "Let them sue!" But the studio was less amused: Henry Herzbrun, attorney for Paramount, intimated that if she went any further, she'd be putting her new contract—and her career—in serious danger. Between the weight gain and the gambling, it was easy to frame Bow as an unruly woman, with appetites quickly spiraling out of control.

At some point in October, Bow and DeVoe quarreled and DeVoe moved out. Bow had met DeVoe on the set of *It*, where DeVoe was working as a hairdresser; the two hit it off immediately and became inseparable, and after several months, Bow asked DeVoe to become her personal secretary. From that point forward, the pair traveled together, with DeVoe attending to Bow's notoriously messy financial affairs and complicated daily toilette. The women were so close, and DeVoe was so protective of Bow, that she regularly incited the ire of Bow's meddling family members and various suitors. The friendship soured, however, when Bow, acting on the advice of new companion Rex Bell, alerted the police that DeVoe had been skimming money from her accounts. On November 15, 1930, the case went before a grand jury, and on November 26, DeVoe was indicted on thirty-seven counts of grand theft committed by withdrawing small sums from Bow's accounts.

When Bow went after DeVoe, she failed to anticipate what the trial would make public—namely, the specifics of her finances. More than fifteen hundred canceled checks were entered into evidence, revealing expenditures of $350,000 over two years, including no small amount of whiskey, presents to male admirers, and clothing. DeVoe claimed that she was merely purchasing what Bow desired, and would regularly go to purchase clothing for Bow, fitting it to her own figure, as the two wore the same size. But as Bow testified, "things got worse on my trip last year to New York. . . . One of my maids called attention to the fact that Daisy's clothes cost more than mine, and that her wardrobe was much classier." Then she found out about the money, and "it was all over."

But DeVoe had taken more than money and clothing. She had also absconded with personal correspondence, including a set of telegraphs Bow had received from various suitors. These telegraphs were introduced into the record and, naturally, reproduced on the front page of the *Los Angeles Times*. From Dr. Earl Pearson: "Nighttime and lonesomeness may not be for long. Wire me darling. Earl." From Harry Richman: "Old homestead don't seem same since our Nell left and steam room won't steam any more. I love you, I love you, I love you, Harry." From Rex Bell: "Dearest sweetheart, darling baby, I do miss you, and this is only the beginning."

Bow was livid. She lashed out at DeVoe from the witness stand, taunting her. In a description dominating the front page of the *Los Angeles Times*, Bow seemed to behave like a small child losing her temper—she bit her lip, stomped her feet, and collapsed, weeping on the witness stand. She was especially enraged by DeVoe's testimony that one of her jobs had been to attend to the dyeing of Bow's hair—"Look at the roots," Bow said. "Why that hair was red when I was born, been red ever since and is red now and always will be." Her final stinger: "And don't forget this either—Daisy's hair is bleached."

DeVoe fired back, reporting that Bow played poker six nights a week and regularly arranged for liquor deliveries to her home—sometimes more than $275 worth. She bought jewelry for men—a three-hundred-dollar ring, a two-thousand-dollar watch. "There were so many it's hard to remember them all," DeVoe averred, while Rex Bell, sitting in the audience, reportedly looked down at the giant diamond ring on his own finger, with the unique and telling inscription of 'It.' The most tantalizing allegation, however, was that as Bow's companion, DeVoe had been entrusted with letting the men in Bow's life know when she was through with them. She had been in charge of Bow's dirty laundry, and now she was airing it out for the public to see.

The judge realized that DeVoe was simply using the witness stand as a means to smear Bow and banned "mudslinging" in the courtroom. But the damage was done: first by the tabloid press, propagating rumor, and second by the mainstream press, recounting what was seemingly true. There was nothing illegal about Bow purchasing whiskey, gambling, or gifting suitors with jewelry. Receiving amatory telegraphs from three men over the course of two years was by no means against the law. But the trial and its reportage revealed a culture of indiscriminate excess. Together, Bow's emotions, spending habits, and romances were all *too much*. The flapper "performance" had gone too far, become part of her real life, and, now that it had been revealed, demanded scrutiny.

Riverside, California, censors had already banned the most recent Bow film due to "notoriety,"and her new film, *No Limit*, which premiered the day after one of her courtroom breakdowns, sunk at the box office—perhaps because the film asked audiences to conceive of Bow as "virtuous heroine," an image wholly at odds with the discourse swirling around her and her "spending orgies." Paramount withdrew Bow from *City Streets*, publicly replacing her with a more stable actress.

But things were about to get much, much worse for Bow. Starting in late March, a pulpy tabloid, the *Coast Reporter*, began a massive smear campaign against her. The allegations were juicy, salacious, and totally preposterous: Bow slept with dogs; Bow liked sex in public; Bow had venereal diseases; Bow had had a threesome with two Mexican prostitutes while a "Mexican croupier" watched; Bow slept with her chauffer; Bow slept with her cousin; Bow slept with everyone and everything. It was a clear case of libel, but as *Coast Reporter* editor Frederic Girnau would later testify, the information came from an affidavit signed by DeVoe herself. DeVoe would deny this claim and file suit against Girnau for claiming as much, but as Bow's lawyer told the court, DeVoe had approached him in November demanding $125,000 for "what she wanted" (presumably, dropping the case); otherwise she'd "turn her information over to the newspapers." However, *where* the information came from mattered far less than the material itself, which, for all its outlandishness, was still circulating and impugning Bow's character.

Girnau was skilled at exploiting interest in the salacious, but he was not a savvy man. He approached Rex Bell and attempted to coerce him into buying the *Coast Reporter* for a sum of ten thousand dollars. Bell refused; Girnau raised the price to twenty-five thousand dollars. It was a blatant case of extortion: buy the newspaper or it will continue to libel Bow in its pages. Girnau was subsequently arrested on charges of sending obscene materials through the mail, having mailed copies of the *Reporter* to Will Hays himself.

Girnau was clearly in the wrong, but the damage to Bow's image was done. On May 7, she had a nervous breakdown, and doctors ordered her into confinement. On June 9, Paramount and Bow came to a mutual agreement to sever her contract. The exhausted Bow was pleased, but the saga had taken its toll on her public image—as *Photoplay* columnist Cal York reported, "It really doesn't look as though Clara Bow is ever going to get sense enough to keep out of trouble." Patience with Bow's antics—and her endless excuses—had run thin. She wasn't a sympathetic victim anymore; she was just pitiful.

On June 15, 1931, DeVoe's appeal of her conviction was denied. On August 1, Girnau was sentenced to eight years in prison, with the court officially decrying his publication as "unfit to be fed as garbage to swine." Bow reported that she had offers for independent productions, but opted instead to retreat to a simple life with Rex Bell on his Nevada ranch. As any student of contemporary scandal knows, however, interest in the subject of scandal only grows after the storm seemingly passes. What is she doing? How is she coping? Will she return? Bow was reticent, but she was willing to invite reporters to her Nevada homestead. Without a major studio contract, she had no studio publicist forcing her to submit to interviews. Rather, it seems that Bow, perhaps on the advice of Bell, who had become her de facto adviser, understood that without a contract and out of the public eye, she might never return.

And so the new, "rough" Clara emerged. These days, "Rex carries Clara pick-a-back. She is sixteen pounds over studio-weight, but Rex can handle her like a child." The rest of her body was seemingly going to seed: her hair was "blonde and straight and wild" and constantly in her face; her arms were patchy and sunburnt, but her back was a deep tan, which Bow demonstrated by whipping off her sweatshirt. She spent her days "shooting at tin cans, rabbits, buzzards, and fence posts." The implicit suggestion: Bow had gone feral.

But the simplicity of Bow's new life also seemed to suit her. It was, at long last, a chance to be herself: "No people, so I don't have to act. When I feel rotten, I don't have to fake a smile and act as though I feel good. I don't have to be on dress parade. I can do as I please, look as I please." This was a return to the natural, unpretentious Bow, the Bow before the excess. It would also seem the sole means through which Bow could recuperate her image and even regain It—by jettisoning the lifestyle that had made her performative and unnatural, the very worst manifestation of flapperism.

But as *Photoplay* columnist Leonard Hall pointed out, Bow's real problem was her unpopularity on the screen. "Bad publicity can be forgiven and forgotten," he wrote. "A little alleged misunderstanding on a gambling debt can be chuckled off as good clean girlish fun. A sweetheart every six months is just a maidenly prank. But failure to draw [audiences] is the Eighth Deadly Sin." It wasn't just the excess: Bow was out of fashion. The flapper was a symbol of the Roaring Twenties, but those twenties had crashed with the stock market. And while Hollywood didn't suddenly start excising glamour from its film, the stars of the early thirties tempered their extravagance: Joan Crawford, "hey hey girl" extraordinaire, had settled down with Douglas Fairbanks Jr. She was a clotheshorse, but she was a *reasonable*, married one.

Bow's comeback film, *Call Her Savage* (1932), was the first of a two-picture deal with Fox. Meant to invoke and lampoon the worst of the rumors circulated about her, it would also remind audiences of the classic Bow image and the new, remodeled one. The studio was careful to keep her away from anything that might signify as abject or excessive, "surround[ing] Clara with everything that spells good taste." *Photoplay*, ever eager to trumpet a comeback, exclaimed, "Who would have expected the rather plump and picture-weary star to emerge from her desert ranch, looking like this?" In the accompanying photo, Bow does indeed look rehabilitated, but also just a bit unhinged and on edge, despite the caption's claim of "A different girl now with a different and happy viewpoint."

Call Her Savage was a moderate success. The second planned film, *Hoop-La* (1933), did fine. But then her contract was over, and with no additional offers forthcoming, Bow retreated again to ranch life with now-husband Rex Bell. She officially retired from films in 1933, but her eyes were open. As she told a reporter, "My life in Hollywood contained plenty of uproar. I'm sorry for a lot of it but not awfully sorry. I never did anything to hurt anyone else. I made a place for myself on screen and you can't do that by being Mrs. Alcott's idea of a *Little Woman*." At twenty-seven years old, she had made more than fifty films. For a period in the midtwenties, she had been the biggest star in the world. Five years later, her career was over.

In many ways, Bow was right: her stardom was rooted in her difference, her startling deviance from the blandly palatable femininity of Victorian texts. Bow, and what her image represented, ruptured the ideological fabric. She tore down the conventions of how sexuality and femininity could and should mix, how women should act around men, how they should wield their bodies in public, and, most flagrant of all, how they should react to others' opinions of them. Of course, Bow's transgressiveness was always, in some way, compromised—her character's aim was always to get a man—yet she was unapologetic for the pleasure she took in being herself, reveling in the freedom of her body, and speaking her mind. She may not fit our contemporary definition of a feminist, but she trampled all sorts of expectations of what a successful, powerful, joyful woman might look like—and for that, she'll always be *It*.

THE BLONDE MENACE

By the early thirties in Hollywood, you could get away with a lot on-screen. After Will Hays's crackdown on on- and off-screen immorality in the early twenties, the studios began a gradual process of boundary testing. Sure, there were rules for what they could and couldn't show or suggest on-screen—but enforcement of those rules was nearly nonexistent. Thus emerged a motley genre of films, today known as Pre-Code Cinema, that weren't so much *before* the code as *flaunting* it. Gangster films, "kept-woman" films, films depicting insurrection and drug use and "white slavery," also known as prostitution—they were the hottest thing in theaters. At the forefront of this assault on American morals: Jean Harlow and Mae West.

Other female stars played hussies and harlots, but no one did it with more verve, or fewer apologies, than Harlow and West. Both served as an affront to traditional notions of female respectability: Harlow's platinum hair was unnatural, even an abomination, and she had a terrifying way of giving men the once-over that made them seem like little more than her next meal. She was a classic vamp with the face of an angel, and the confusion between how she looked and what she did was part of what made her so effortlessly beguiling. As for West, she was a bulldozer in a skintight gown, equal parts wit and sexual appetite. With her "dangerous curves," West reset beauty standards, forcing men and women to forget the flapper silhouette with the power of her well-sequined, voluptuous hips.

Harlow and West were either the most glamorous, beguiling thing to hit the screen in a decade—or a blonde menace, out to sully impressionable minds and turn them toward sin. Or they were both: female stars whose images exploited Depression-era appetites for the sumptuous and the suggestive. But as protests against the so-called immorality of the screen began to gain traction, Harlow, West, and their studios had no choice but to soften and desexualize their images—a shift that Harlow, who had always proved herself amenable to MGM's manipulations, survived, but West, at least in the short term, did not. The combustive sexual energy manifest in the performances of Jean Harlow and Mae West, and its brief tenure on-screen, forms a persuasive argument for the very real, very robust sexual appetites of audiences . . . and how the female star so often becomes the locus of the terror and confusion that ensues.

CHAPTER SIX

Jean Harlow:
The Platinum Panic

Jean Harlow was unlike anything Hollywood had ever seen. On-screen, she was brazenly sexual and uninhibited in her passions, taking tangible pleasure in plowing through a series of men. According to rumor, she seldom wore underwear and loathed the feel of a bra, preferring the sensation of satin against skin. With the perfectly arched, penciled-in brows fashionable during the period, she could look conniving or childlike, wholly guilty or perfectly innocent. In publicity shots, she almost always appeared in long, draping white gowns, which, paired with her hair and diamond jewelry, made her seem like something rare and incandescent. But that wasn't what made her novel; indeed, her sexuality combined the playfulness of Clara Bow and the predatory sexuality of cinematic vamps of the silent screen. What was new—and what made her a star—was her platinum blonde hair, which would serve as her trademark for the rest of her career and signify a sleek, brassy personality that seduced men before they knew what was happening. She was, as my grandfather would say, a total dame.

Harlow was the original "blonde bombshell," with a reputation, as one fan magazine put it, as "TNT and sex dynamite."

On-screen, her characters took what they wanted and did as they pleased. Unlike Mae West, who used wit and innuendo to manipulate men into her bedroom, Harlow's characters could be whiny and passive-aggressive, tricking men into believing they loved her when what they really loved was sex. Harlow and her studio claimed that her near-white hair was natural, but it, like her sexually voracious screen persona, was fake—a performance. But as time would tell, neither were actually all that far from the truth: her natural color was in fact a light, unremarkable blonde, and her personal life was riddled with men, destruction, and tragedy. By the time she died of uremic poisoning at the age of twenty-six, she had starred in more than twenty films, married and divorced three men, and weathered more scandal than stars three times her age. It should be no surprise that Marilyn Monroe cited her as her muse: both came alive before the camera, and both struggled to endure the ramifications of that sexual vivacity off the screen.

Harlow grew up in Kansas City, Missouri, the child of bourgeois parents and even more bourgeois grandparents. When she eventually made it in Hollywood, her patrician background would be exploited as a means of differentiating her from other, déclassé, stars: they were poor immigrants made good; Harlow was sophisticated *by birth*. She may never have been poor, but her life was not always classy. She was the child of an arranged marriage, and when her mother became frustrated with her disinterested father, the pair divorced in 1922, when Harlow was eleven years old. Her mother had dreams of stardom—a point that would become clear in her eventual micromanagement of her daughter's career—and moved to Hollywood.

But Mother Harlow was too old to break into pictures, and after some choice words from Grandpa Harlow, she and her daughter, whom she referred to exclusively as Baby, returned home. Jean spent most of her time in boarding school and at summer camp, where, at the age of fifteen, she developed a severe case of scarlet fever, followed by a serious kidney infection. The resulting damage to her kidneys led to high blood pressure, hypertension, and undiagnosed nephritis, which would plague her for the rest of her life—and eventually cause her death. But young Baby was too busy falling in love to worry about the aftereffects of a kidney disease. After her time at summer camp, her mother enrolled her in a Chicago boarding school; as a freshman, she was introduced to twenty-year-old Chuck McGrew, who must've seemed very cool and, as the son of a patent medicine king, very rich. The two eloped on September 21, 1927, when Harlow was all of sixteen years old. When her husband turned twenty-one just months later, his trust fund made them flush with cash; naturally, Harlow dropped out of school and the pair moved to Hollywood.

In Hollywood, Harlow and her husband did a lot of drinking and little of anything else, save, perhaps, fighting. According to lore, she was driving a starlet friend to the Fox lot when an exec goaded her into giving acting a try, signing her under her mother's maiden name, "Jean Harlow." She failed to make much of an impression at Fox, but in December 1928, at the urging of her mother, Harlow signed a deal with Hal Roach Studios for twelve dollars a day. At this point, the details get a bit hazy, in part because they were erased and rewritten so often when Harlow became a star two years later, but within the next year, her grandfather supposedly disinherited her, visited her in Hollywood, decided it wasn't so bad after all, and agreed to keep her in the will, but cut off her allowance. In narratives of Harlow's life, her grandfather's "disinheritance" would be repeatedly recycled as a means of invoking her high-class background and "good breeding"—and her commitment to stardom, even if it meant living without a safety net. She appeared in several bit parts, including some with Laurel and Hardy, got out of her contract with Roach, and on June 11, 1929, officially separated from her husband, whom she would later label in court documents as "profane and abusive."

Thus began the second act of Harlow's Hollywood life. She endured a few bit parts, some demoralizing extra work, and then, while she was working as an extra on the film short *Weak but Willing*, a scout for millionaire-turned-filmmaker Howard Hughes spotted her on the set and arranged to have her do a screen test. And it wasn't for just any role—it was for the lead in *Hell's Angels*, an over-the-top aviation film, years and millions in the making, that would make or break the reputation of Hughes. If you've seen Martin Scorsese's *The Aviator*, you know at least part of the story: Hughes had originally shot *Angels* as a silent film, but when the technology for sound became available, he became convinced that the film had to be reshot. But there was a problem: the film's heroine was played by Norwegian actress Greta Nissen, and her accent was, to put it bluntly, way too Scandinavian (and not in the sexy Greta Garbo sort of way), especially since the woman in the film was supposed to be British. So Hughes began scouring for a replacement, testing hundreds of starlets over six months until Harlow appeared before him.

Whatever she did, it caught Hughes's attention—or maybe he just saw the marketing potential in her blonde hair. Hughes was a megalomaniac and a perfectionist, but he was also a savvy businessman and understood the power of a well-placed nickname. Bow had ridden "the It Girl" to superstardom, and he wanted something similarly catchy for his new star. And so: "Platinum Blonde" was born. Hughes signed her to a five-year, $100-a-week contract, and began reshoots.

In *Angels*, Harlow handily seduces *and* betrays two brothers—a vixen role that would set the tone for her image for the rest of her career. But she was more than just the Platinum Blonde: according to press reports, she was a brand-new discovery, the hottest thing in Hollywood, and she certainly hadn't been toiling, undiscovered, for years. Rather, she was a Kansas City society girl, "given the advantages of birth and education that have not usually been evidenced in aspiring young leading ladies," who'd "actually read some books." It wasn't necessarily untrue, but it also wasn't strictly true. Her upper-class roots and Kansas City backstory, however, helped differentiate her from other stars, transforming her explicit sexuality into something less wanton and cheap.

To ballyhoo the movie, Hughes set up a contest challenging any hairstylist in America to replicate Harlow's particularly vivid shade of blonde, with a reward of ten thousand dollars. Thus began "platinum fever," with young women across the country using untrustworthy combinations of bleach, peroxide, and other noxious chemicals to try and bleach their hair. Tales of ruined hair, shaved heads, and crying teens abounded. It sounds like bad publicity, but it was genius: Harlow became the only girl in America with the perfect platinum shade, wholly singular and special. The exact shade evaded description—not silver, exactly, but "about the color of pale salt water taffy"; it was "startling, almost bizarre, but on the whole quite beautiful." Just as Bow's flaming red hair came to represent her wild, wanton sexuality, Harlow's suggested a sexuality that was ice cold, aloof. The press claimed that only one woman in a thousand had hair and coloring to endure the process; the wages of trying to emulate her hair and, implicitly, what she represented, would be "regret, and even disastrous results." It's no wonder she became known as the "Blonde Panic."

Harlow's performance in *Angels* was, to put it mildly, unimpressive. Print ads for the film promised she was bound to become "the greatest star of them all," but critics agreed that while she had the body for stardom, she lacked the acting ability. No matter: her hair, her role, and her appearance in one of the most highly anticipated releases of the year made her a hot commodity, and Hughes knew it. After sending her on tour for nationwide premieres of *Angels*, he began loaning her out to other studios at a tremendous profit. He'd get thousands for her services, yet still paid Harlow her contracted one hundred dollars a week. She worked for MGM, Universal, and Warner Bros., where she made a brief but memorable appearance as James Cagney's gun moll in *The Public Enemy* (1931).

But Harlow's star wattage was dimming. According to her most reliable biographer, David Stenn, she depended heavily on her new boyfriend, New Jersey mobster Longy Zwillman. Zwillman was well known as the "Al Capone of Jersey," with an income of around forty million dollars a year from bootlegging and other illicit, *Boardwalk Empire*–style dealings. But he loved Harlow, buying her all manner of garish presents (a charm bracelet; a red Cadillac), moving her and her mother into a nicer house, and, most notably, leaning on Columbia head Harry Cohn (read: paying him five hundred thousand dollars in cash) to make a two-picture deal for Harlow's talents. Since Zwillman knew that Hughes wouldn't up Harlow's salary, he upped it himself—to a startling one thousand dollars a week. These details are based on word-of-mouth testimony and certainly weren't public knowledge at the time, but for those looking back at Harlow's life, they seem credible—if only because she had just so perfectly embodied the role of the gun moll.

The first result of these supposed dealings was *Platinum Blonde* (1931), an obvious exploitation of Harlow's hair color. But Loretta Young clearly out-acted Harlow, and her second film with Columbia, *Three Wise Girls* (1932), was forgettable. What was noteworthy, however, was how much gossip Harlow was inspiring. In April, a catty *Motion Picture* columnist quipped that Harlow, in attendance at a cocktail hour, "was dressed in her own idea of an afternoon gown. What there was of it was black velvet. . . . Either black velvet or white organdie. Anyway, Jean was inside it (or mostly inside it) and it was swell." Every time she appeared in public, another rumor started—usually some variation on her "vamping" of husbands and associations with a large, ever-rotating cast of men. In September, *The Saturday Evening Post* emphasized how her dark eyebrows and violet eyes prompted "invidious" comments from female audience members, in part because "she is slim and has no particular notion of being otherwise, yet she holds no truck with such repellent things as diets. She eats lettuce, but does not live on it." She appeared on Hollywood Boulevard in nothing but her pajamas, and the rumors of her preference for panty-less-ness had begun to circulate. She was, in other words, the type of girl that other girls love to hate, treading the sharp division between jealousy and attraction.

It was a dangerous place to be. If she alienated enough women—specifically, the female columnists who gossiped about her and were largely responsible for the maintenance of her image—they might turn on her altogether. Some ideological maintenance was necessary, something to suggest that she was not, in fact, the vamping girl around town, off to steal your husband and make you feel bad about yourself. The must surefire tactic: emphasize her on-screen persona as pure performance. *Photoplay* led the way, publishing a feature article that promised to "Unmask Jean Harlow." The premise: Harlow's image is a construct, mostly of Hughes's making. Her backstory is false; the idea that she's a newcomer is false. She's just like any other starlet who has to struggle to assert her "real" personality against the weight of her on-screen one. The piece begins by partially indicting Harlow, describing a typical Hollywood party scene: "She removed her come-hither hat because her startling white hair was even more come-hitherish," and within seconds, she had attracted all of the men in the room. But "she was acting—just as she was acting in 'Hell's Angels.' She'd show them." And so the women gathered, gossiping, in part because their husbands were among those flocking to Harlow's side. "You can guess what they said," the article suggests. "You know women." Here, the author both fulfills the readers' worst thoughts about Harlow—and then, deftly, with utmost subtlety, shames them for it.

With that shame established, the article offers an alternate understanding of Harlow: Her vampishness is not *on purpose*. Rather, she attracts men *subconsciously* with her beauty and allure. You can't blame her for being beautiful! But, the article asserts, Harlow's been so hurt by the constant rumors that she's become a total homebody. She never leaves the house without her mother and father; she's always home by midnight; she refuses Hollywood invitations. After describing a night out on the town with two friends from home, a night when, she vowed, she had nothing to drink, the columns, hungry for scandal, had her falling down drunk. "I hate Hollywood," Harlow admitted. "I suppose it sounds like biting the hand that feeds you. . . . I just can't be myself—they won't let me." A feature on her autumn style emphasized how modestly she dressed in real life—still chic, but not so "daring." Once again, the reader is led to believe that Harlow is not only not the vixen you've seen on-screen, but that you should pity her for believing the gossip you've read about her.

It's unclear how effectively her image was softened, but in the beginning of 1932, Harlow was on the brink of stardom. After her two-picture contract with Columbia was over, MGM producer Paul Bern cast her in *The Beast of the City* (1932), playing yet another variation on the sexy gun moll. He likewise arranged for Harlow to go on tour, where audiences clamored for her. Bern

used her popularity to lobby MGM head Louis B. Mayer for a
long-term contract, but Mayer had a very specific idea of the type
of star that should be associated with MGM: namely, classy and,
above all, glamorous. Harlow may have seemed glamorous, and
the details of her childhood may have suggested a modicum of
class, but her image was nevertheless that of a harlot. A tacky,
gaudy, totally sexy harlot. Mayer wanted none of it.

Bern turned to Irving Thalberg, head of MGM production,
appealing to his sense of profit. And so, after much dithering,
MGM bought out Harlow's contract with Hughes, signing her,
on April 20, 1932, to a seven-year deal. The first order of business: actually change her image. Or, at the very least, soften and
domesticate it in a way that the fan magazines had not yet been
able to. The most visible means of doing so, of course, was to
change her hair color, easily achieved by starring her in *Red-
Headed Woman* (1932). The film was originally intended for fellow
MGM star Joan Crawford, and Harlow's takeover of the role was
but one of dozens of events that incited Crawford's infamous
wrath. (Whether or not Crawford ever actually feuded with Harlow or any of her other well-known adversaries matters little; it
behooved MGM to promote the idea of "star feuds," if only because it encouraged fans to take sides and, as a result, develop even
more intense fandoms.) While *Red-Headed Woman* was filming,
Harlow attended the premiere of MGM all-star vehicle *Grand
Hotel* (1932) on the arm of rumored boyfriend Paul Bern, with her
hair a very deep shade of red. You can imagine that Crawford, one
of the stars of *Hotel*, would've been furious when the press attention turned to Harlow's new shade.

As much as MGM wanted to class up Harlow's image, it also
understood that the films in which she starred—characterized by
fiercely manipulative sexuality and generalized titillation—were
big box office. *Red-Headed Woman* was thus sold with the inflam-

matory taglines "Take all men as you find them . . . but TAKE them" and "All men go too far . . . but most girls are a poor judge of distance." The film was a triumph and earned Harlow the first truly positive notices of her career; the reviewer for the *Los Angeles Times* even admitted that she had "transformed into something closely resembling an actress." And then she did something that, at least for a time, silenced those who refused to believe that the "real" Harlow just wanted to settle down, cook, and hang out in housedresses. She got married—and not to a handsome young star, but to a man of unremarkable looks and twice her age. That man, Paul Bern, just happened to have been responsible for her newfound success.

While rumors of the pair's romance had been in the air since the *Grand Hotel* premiere, the June 1932 marriage nevertheless came as a surprise. There was no real engagement, no lavish wedding—just a trip to the courthouse and a tremendous amount of explanation for the press. It was excellent publicity for *Red-Headed Woman*, which was still fresh in theaters, and a perfect opportunity to activate a new domestic discourse, emphasizing the ways in which Harlow's red hair had changed her. Before, her platinum hair had made her seem standoffish, with a "frozen glamour" that seemed to embody her entire personality. But during the filming of *Red-Headed Woman*, she would come on the set, all "aloof, mysterious, her sex appeal in an ice-box," put on her wig, and emerge "a bright, snappy little hoyden." It was the red hair that brought her love: as a blonde, she lacked steady boyfriends; as a redhead, she nabbed the long-single Bern.

No matter that the narrative of *Red-Headed Woman* suggested that Harlow preyed upon well-to-do men, dangled her sex appeal in front of them, and abandoned them when a more lucrative catch came along—that wasn't what was happening here! Because Bern, at least according to the fan magazines, was the ultimate catch. In order to explain why the gorgeous Harlow would marry a somewhat homely guy twice her age, they had to paint him as the paragon of kindness and charity, interested in Harlow for *her*, not her body, and most certainly not the real-life analog to the easily duped male lead of *Red-Headed Woman*. *Motion Picture* reported that Bern was well known as "the Good Samaritan of Hollywood," with a history of taking care of ill, fading, or otherwise damaged stars. He was so beloved, in fact, that *Photoplay* promised that if Harlow didn't make Bern happy, there were "hordes of women" who would be "willing to wring her shapely neck."

From the outside, the marriage seemed healthy. But on September 6, 1932, Bern was discovered in their home with a fatal bullet wound to his head—an event that sparked a year's worth of headlines and brought the future of Harlow's career into question. It was scandal—but was it *her* scandal? As would become clear, the public was able to differentiate between the actions of a husband and those of the star herself, and Harlow emerged from the mess of her husband's mysterious suicide with an earning power just as strong, if not stronger, than before. But Bern's suicide would cast a shadow across the remainder of Harlow's career: from that day forward, she would be Jean Harlow, tragic star.

The details of Bern's suicide are thoroughly tangled, the result of carefully calculated studio publicity, diverging court testimonies, and posthumous speculation. The approximate facts: Bern died of a bullet wound, almost certainly self-inflected, and he was discovered naked by a member of the housekeeping staff on the morning of September 6. Nearby, a cryptic suicide note, presumably directed at Harlow: "Unfortunately this is the only way to make good the frightful wrong I have done you and to wipe out my abject humiliation," with an even more cryptic postscript: "You understand last night was only a comedy." The note, released to the papers, set the tone for the bizarre coverage that was to follow.

Harlow had been staying with her parents and was alerted to Bern's death the evening of the sixth, at which point she reportedly attempted to fling herself off a balcony in despair. The story is somewhat unsubstantiated, but it suggested two crucial points: 1) Harlow loved Bern, and even more important, 2) she didn't murder him. Because no matter how little evidence there was to suggest that Harlow had participated, it was nevertheless the first and most natural rumor to start circulating. As police attempted to ascertain a motive for the death, they discovered evidence of a so-called second Mrs. Bern—a woman named Dorothy Millette, who was Bern's "common-law wife." At some point in the mid-1920s, she took up residence at the famed Algonquin Hotel, in New York, and Bern had been supporting her ever since. Bern's brother, Henry, was making his way to Hollywood to offer testimony that Harlow had, in fact, known of the existence of the previous Mrs. Bern, whose mental breakdown had apparently precipitated their separation. Regardless of when and how much Harlow knew about Millette, none of it boded well for the star's reputation.

At this point, the MGM fixers stepped in. Or, rather, they started to flex their muscles—they'd already been the first ones on the scene, the first to discover Bern's note, and the first to exploit it as a means of cementing the death as a suicide. But now the narrative seemed to be spiraling out of control. They needed a counter-narrative, and they needed it quick. First, they fetched Henry Bern from the train station just as he arrived. When he emerged from the MGM offices several hours later, he refused to offer his promised statement concerning Harlow's knowledge of the first Mrs. Bern. Several days later, inspectors discovered a pair of shoes and a coat near the railing of a steamship headed from San Francisco to Sacramento—items believed to have belonged to Dorothy Millette. The natural speculation was that Millette had killed herself, either in response to Bern's suicide or over her own guilt for his murder.

With attention effectively drawn away from Harlow's involvement, the fixers began phase two of their publicity campaign. On September 13, just a week after Bern's suicide, Harlow was back to work filming *Red Dust*. The next day, Bern's doctor, whose telegrams had all been directed through the MGM office, reported that Bern had been suffering from "acute melancholia" and had been an "unusually sensitive man" with "fits of depression." But there was much more: acting on pressure from MGM, the coroner's report relayed that Bern had "underdeveloped" sexual organs. *Time* extrapolated on the findings, explaining that Bern's so-called handicap would have "prevented a happy marriage." The implicit, however unspeakable, suggestion: Bern was a hermaphrodite and impotent; on the night of his suicide he had stripped naked, examined himself in the mirror, and shot himself in despair.

This sensational suggestion wasn't the press running away with the story—it was the work of the studio, throwing its executive under the figurative bus in order to save the reputation of its star and its brand. With Bern framed as both a bigamist *and* a hermaphrodite, he was "guilty" of scandal; Harlow, by contrast, was just looking for companionship and care—how was she to know that her husband wouldn't be able to consummate the marriage? Even when the coroner clarified that Bern was merely "undersized," not "underdeveloped," meaning he certainly could have had sex, the rumor endured. In "The Jean Harlow Story Hollywood Suppressed," published just months after Harlow's death, trusted fan magazine author Adela Rogers St. Johns forcefully reactivated the story, recalling how the impotent Bern had "denied [Harlow] her wifehood and motherhood and he knew it and she did not. It was no fair bargain." St. Johns's proof: she was close friends with Barbara La Marr, another star whom Bern had attempted to marry, only he'd been more honest with La Marr, asking for a "mental and spiritual marriage."

As letters between Millette and Bern soon revealed, Millette had planned to come to San Francisco, most likely made an unexpected visit to Los Angeles, perhaps threatened to go public with their past, and Bern had acted to protect his wife. The inquest endured for months—Harlow's testimony was sealed; a housekeeper provided additional testimony as to the presence of an unknown woman's bathing suit that showed up at the house the night before the suicide, along with a woman's scream from inside the home.

It was a mess—but somehow, it didn't seem to be Harlow's mess. In the weeks after the suicide, she offered one wholly banal interview, declaring her lack of fear and her commitment to the idea that "the best any of us can do in life is to try to build a strong foundation on which to stand." It reeked of publicity pabulum, but it set the foundation for the next act of Harlow's career, characterized by resilience and a renewed commitment to de-vamping her existing image.

Harlow's future was nevertheless framed as contingent on her fans: in the *Los Angeles Times*, Edwin Schallert repeatedly emphasized that *Red Dust*, released six weeks after Bern's suicide, would make or break Harlow's career. If people went to see it, then she had emerged unscathed; if they didn't, her career was doomed. But even before the film was in wide release, Schallert was declaring her victory: the film was a success, in part because Harlow's connection to the scandal was, to his mind, somewhat dubious. The film grossed $1.2 million—nearly triple its $408,000 budget—and was viewed as a testament not only to Harlow's resilience, but to an overarching cultural shift in expectations of stars: as Schallert proclaimed, "the saccharine age of idols, when people believed that players must be like the roles they did in pictures, has passed."

As several star scandals in the forties and fifties would prove, such a statement was overblown. There were still specific understandings of what stars could and could not do, and those understandings were still very much rooted in the stars' on- and off-screen personas. Harlow survived the scandal because MGM, in collaboration with Schallert and others like him, had so thoroughly disassociated her from Bern and the motivation for his death. The public didn't love her *in spite of* scandal—they loved her because they could still believe she wasn't scandalous.

To further distract from the scandal, there were hot love scenes with Clark Gable (neatly accomplished with *Red Dust*) and whispers of another romance (only after an appropriate mourning time) with the "Jewish Adonis," otherwise known as prizefighter Max Baer. The only problem: Baer was married. When gossip columnist Louella Parsons interviewed his disenchanted wife, her words were damning: "Max may be in love with her. I suppose he is. He loves glamour." If the relationship persisted, Baer's wife could file for divorce and very publicly name Harlow as "correspondent." Bern's suicide hadn't ruined her image, but this affair—still just over six months after Bern's death—very well could.

The best way to stop the rumors? Get Harlow to marry someone else—someone wholly without scandal—as soon as possible. The unknowing target was her longtime cameraman Harold "Hal" Rosson, who, much like Bern, was twice her age, "normal" looking, and one of the men operating behind the scenes to ensure Harlow's success. MGM planted a few gossip bits—*Motion Picture*, for example, reported that Rosson had purchased an expensive engagement ring, which Harlow roundly denied—so the pairing wouldn't seem entirely out of nowhere when, on September 18,

1933, just over a year after Bern's suicide, Harlow and Rosson eloped.

But even MGM's publicity machine couldn't take away the weirdness. Rosson maintained that he had loved Harlow for months, but could only tell her weeks before, when they actually spent some one-on-one time on the golf course. A proposal came in early September, and a week later, a studio-chartered plane whisked them to Yuma, Arizona, where they were wed at 4:30 A.M. with their pilot as the sole witness. Louella Parsons called the press reception afterward, with a still-stunned Rosson telling reporters, "It can't be true. . . . I can't believe she belongs to me," one of the strangest she'd ever covered. A lengthy feature in *Motion Picture* attempted to explain "Jean's 'Surprise' Marriage" by emphasizing that Rosson's age was part of his attraction: he was old enough to advise her, yet "young enough to be the most wonderful play-fellow and companion I've ever known."

Rosson was also presented as the reason for Harlow's success—*he* was the one who, since her arrival at MGM, had meticulously lit her, figuring out a perfect formula that would bring out her hair and sex appeal while also emphasizing her humanity and humor. Forget Bern: Rosson, the humble cameraman, was responsible for turning her from a simple sex object into a true star. As for elopement, Harlow did it out of deference—it would've been in poor taste to have a big, public wedding. She was, in her words, "truly and humbly in love."

Or maybe not. A week after the wedding, Rosson was off to Mexico to shoot a new MGM film while Harlow stayed put to promote *Bombshell*. Their planned honeymoon to Hawaii was canceled when Harlow was hospitalized for appendicitis, and by March, *Photoplay* was reporting that she was battling a "sea of rumors"—some concerning a potential pregnancy, but mostly centered on the imminent demise of her marriage. It was no tremendous surprise, then, when Harlow announced their formal separation on May 8, 1934, just eight months into their marriage. It's difficult to know whether the public believed her exhortations of love or saw the marriage as the sham it was. Either way, MGM's publicity department had done its job: when the wife of the "Jewish Adonis" at last filed for divorce, she did not name Harlow as the catalyst.

MGM's real worry, however, wasn't idle chatter about a potentially sham marriage. It was the Legion of Decency, which had singled out Harlow as one of Hollywood's most objectionable stars. Founded in 1933 by the Archbishop of Cincinnati, the Legion of Decency pledged to root out "vile and unwholesome moving pictures" by hitting the studios where it hurt most: the pocketbook. According to the Legion, Will Hays and the rest of the MPPDA had fallen short on their commitment to censorship: Throughout the early thirties, films featuring wanton women, generalized insurrection, and explicit violence on the part of valorized gangsters dominated the box office. The more these types of films succeeded, the more imitators they inspired. It was a sinful spiral straight to hell, and the Legion was committed to stopping it, even if it meant boycotting cinema altogether.

While many female stars had played "notorious" women, Harlow, along with Mae West, had done so most flagrantly, "enjoying sex without shame or embarrassment." And so the Legion issued an ultimatum: make Harlow a virtuous woman or they'd boycott every film in which she appeared. The threat of a Catholic boycott may not seem like much today, but in 1934 it was a serious threat that could sink a movie and, potentially, a star's career. MGM decided to play along, changing the name of Harlow's next project, *One Hundred Per Cent Pure*, to *Never Been Kissed*. Was it MGM's idea of an ironic joke? Maybe, but it still didn't satisfy the newly empowered censorship board, which, starting in 1934 and under the watchful eye of Hays's "deputy" Joseph Breen, was actually enforcing drastic cuts in dozens of Hollywood films. *Never Been Kissed* thus transformed into very sensible *The Girl from Missouri*, and the script became a moral Frankenstein, "vacillating," according to one reviewer, "between the necessity to 'justify' its chief protagonist and to let her be herself." The same could've been said for dozens of films that emerged during this period, as the studios attempted to balance the newly enforced rules of the Hays board with the appetites of their audiences.

The Girl from Missouri was only the first step in a renewed effort to remodel Harlow's image. Over the next two years, her screen persona would shift dramatically: pre-1934, plots had pivoted on Harlow's ability to seduce men; post-1934, in films such as *Wife vs. Secretary*, it was all about the protection of her virtue. Howard Strickling, head of MGM publicity, wrote an editorial in the *Washington Post* trumpeting her dramatic about-face: "Jean has grown, mentally and spiritually"—now she's "more tranquil than she's ever been" and "more poised and more satisfied," clearly code for "she's not plowing through a series of men." Her hair was a new, mousy brown shade—dubbed "brownette"—that disassociated her from the blonde bombshell connotations of her past. She was hanging out with William Powell, one of the most respected men in Hollywood, and an engagement seemed forthcoming, but for now, they were just taking it slow, enjoying each other's company—no matter the rumors that MGM had written a clause into her contract forbidding her to marry.

By 1937, Harlow was ascendant. The doyennes of the studio were all in decline, as Norma Shearer's executive husband, Irving Thalberg, had died of a heart attack, and Garbo and Crawford had both been somewhat dubiously dubbed "box office poison." But Harlow's repeated pairings with Gable, Powell, and Spencer Tracy were reliable moneymakers, and *Libeled Lady*, released in 1936, not only won an Academy Award nomination for Best Picture but proved her to be an effective comedienne. But over the course of the spring, Harlow's health gradually began to decline. She was drinking heavily—one report had her downing glasses of gin, yelling, "Here goes another baked potato!" She and Powell were supposedly on and off again, which only further fueled the drinking. Or so the retrospective story goes—at the time, the press said nothing. When *Life* put her on the May 3, 1937, cover, it used a picture that was two years old—that's how bloated, whether from drink or other causes, she had become.

In late May, Harlow complained of feeling ill while on the set of *Saratoga*, her latest project with Clark Gable. She was exhausted and nauseated, but insisted on working until she nearly collapsed on set. Over the next few days, she was misdiagnosed with the flu and bedridden; according to oft-cited legend, when Gable came to visit her, her breath smelled strongly of urine; "it was like kissing a dead person, a rotting person." Harlow's kidneys were shutting down. She slipped into a coma on the morning of June 7, 1937, and never awoke. The official cause of death: uremic poisoning, the symptoms of which she had likely been suffering for months.

Harlow's posthumous image was the same as her living image, only amplified. Obituaries and remembrances emphasized the "real" Jean Harlow, who always preferred slacks and sportswear to the slinky gowns for which she was, at least for the first half of her career, best known. A *Washington Post* headline promised that Harlow "Was Totally Unlike Roles She Played in Films"—an avid conversationalist, an aspiring novelist, and above all, not a tramp. She had inspired intense devotion from the men who loved her, and Powell had been at her side when she died. In his grief, he arranged for Harlow's burial in a tomb inscribed with "Baby," where he planned to eventually be entombed as well. It was all very romantic and melodramatic, taking on the same tragic narrative characteristics that attend the tales of all stars who die young. No matter how assiduously publicity departments try to disassociate these stars from their on-screen characters, audiences still think of them as players in a high stakes game of life and death, sex and betrayal, bliss and despondency. It's only natural that the understandings of their deaths should match the same emotional pitch.

In the months and years to come, two dominant explanations for Harlow's demise began to circulate. First, her mother, a devout Christian Scientist, had refused to allow her to undergo treatment—a claim that multiple accounts of sustained treatment clearly refute. Second, and most persuasively, the fumes from her hair dye—peroxide, ammonia, Clorox, and Lux flakes—had contributed to her kidney damage. That which made her a star, in other words, had also killed her. Other than a recent study indicating that chlorine gas inhalation apparently causes kidney damage in rats, there's no tangible evidence that Harlow's hair dye contributed to her death. Scarlet fever and kidney infection as a teen, sure, exacerbated by her drinking, but the hair dye narrative is nevertheless the one that sticks in popular memory.

The reasoning is simple. We love to think of stardom as both pleasure and pain; its participants reap its riches but must also pay for their transgressions. Harlow's platinum blonde hair was the source of her fame and her downfall—the signifier of her sexuality and, ultimately, the sin for which she was made to pay. It's a much more symmetrical explanation—indeed, the type of explanation of which the Legion of Decency would approve—and far less ambiguous than a preexisting condition and alcoholism.

Over the course of Harlow's career, her image became the playground on which all manner of desires, insecurities, and anxieties collided. She was, most likely, a victim of circumstance, subject to the manipulations of powerful studio heads who expected their young, seemingly naive starlet to do and act as they pleased. She was a victim, but she was also resilient, vivacious, and infectiously charismatic. Today, her hair seems otherworldly and garish; in the 1930s, she was a firecracker, impossible to ignore. Harlow's reception in life, and the heavy mythology of her death, emphasize just how pliable star images are to our whims, hopes, and fears.

CHAPTER SEVEN

Mae West:
When She's Bad, She's Better

If Jean Harlow was an ice queen, beguiling men with her aloof coolness, then Mae West was an incinerator, with enough heat to consume a man whole. With a supple, curvaceous figure and a comedic style she termed "down low," West was a wholly singular star creation. She spoke with a nasal, all-knowing tone, her words brimming with innuendo—she couldn't even say "good morning" without it taking on a devious double meaning. When she entered a room or a conversation, she always did it with her hands casually on her hips, an intoxicating nonchalance to her utter dominance of all, especially men, who crossed her path.

West's body, with its so-called dangerous curves, along with the turn-of-the-century fashions she clothed it in, inspired an entire trend against "reducing" (read: dieting). But from the beginning, she was marked as an outsider: she wrote all her own material and talked frankly about the process of authorship, and she opted out of the Hollywood nightlife, choosing instead to spend her nights at the prizefights. She never had a high-profile romance, nor did she endure any specific scandal, save the revelation of a long-forgotten teen marriage. After a meteoric rise to rival that of Valentino, her films were so successful that they were credited with "saving" Paramount from its Depression-era slump. Her body was different, her attitude was different, her humor was different—but they were what American audiences craved, at least for a brief period of time.

But West, along with Harlow, Barbara Stanwyck, and other stars featured in the cycle of "kept woman" films in the early thirties, was also a "blonde menace" whose on-screen actions were thought to threaten the moral fabric of the nation at large. Contrary to popular history, Mae West was not, in fact, personally responsible for the industry-wide crackdown on the depiction of sex, violence, and other illicit activities. But her films appeared at the crest of the wave of objectionable films and provided a rallying cry for those clamoring for renewed censorship efforts. Suddenly, West's body and humor—the site of so much pleasure—became something to be contained. And so a thoroughly unruly woman became docile and, at least ostensibly, pliant, with the censors muting, if not altogether silencing, the humor that had characterized her oeuvre. Over the second half of the thirties, her films made less and less money, and West receded in the rearview mirror of Hollywood history, a reminder of the ribald revelry that once snuck past the straitlaced, self-serious Hays office.

West was born in 1893 in Bushwick, New York, and while her working-class roots were often invoked in stories of how "Mae came to be Mae," the year of her birth was not. This elision was part of a publicity decision, on the part of West and her longtime manager, to omit her real age, which, when she arrived in Hollywood, was thirty-eight years old—ancient by industry standards. Her father was a semi-well-known featherweight fighter, a point that West and others used to explain her voracious fandom for boxing and, by extension, boxers themselves. Her mother was German, but West and others sometimes framed her as French, so as to explain West's nonchalance toward sex. As West recalled, even as a kid, she was thoroughly boy-crazy: "I thought *I* was supposed to do the kissing." In this way, her sexual forwardness was figured as "natural"—something she was born with, had even inherited, and that, as such, was neither perverted nor indecent. Put differently, West had *always* been West—a theme that would guide the formation of her Hollywood star image.

And if West had always been West, it was no surprise that her comedic talent emerged at a young age. At age five, she was already known around the neighborhood for her impersonations of various male entertainers, which she'd perform at church socials. According to oft-repeated lore, Hal Clarendon, who ran a prominent stock company, signed her to perform with his troupe; one gig led to another, and by age thirteen, West had made her way to Broadway, with a weekly salary of $150. When she recalled her past, she mentioned two stories from this period: first, that she spent a significant amount of time admiring the figure of the *Venus de Milo*, which she came to associate with womanliness. She claimed that to achieve the "fine figure" and "real bosom" depicted in the statue, she would apply coconut oil to areas she "wished to attain prominence." Second, she insisted that during her teens, it was *she*, and not various other dancers, who came up with the so-called shimmy dance. "I suddenly discovered that I was dancing just like everyone else—with my feet," West recalled. "Why not use my hips, my shoulders, and my torso and—everything?"

With these anecdotes, West staked claim on two additional cornerstones of her image: the voluptuousness of her body and the things, completely of her own imagining, that she could do with that body. She aligned her form, so unpopular when she burst onto the scene in the early thirties, with *classic* beauty; at the same time, she underlined that what she did with her body came, yet again, naturally. What's more, sex was her unique invention—she was the patent holder, in other words, on the particular brand of West sexuality.

Testimony from others on Broadway at the time suggests that even at a young age, West was West: according to one former costar, in 1915 she had already adopted the characteristics that made her name in Hollywood: "the same curves, bustles, curly blonde hair, floppy picture hat and all." West may have *seemed* very à la mode in 1933 and 1934, but it wasn't due to any publicity promotion; she was emphatically *not* the product of any press agent. In the words of one fan magazine headline, "Anecdotes of the Great Mae of Bygone Days Prove She Has Always Been Herself." West had always been West; the tastes of the consuming public were only now becoming sophisticated enough to hunger for what she had to offer.

After several prominent appearances in Broadway revues, West began to develop her own material for the stage, penning a play, frankly titled *Sex*, in which she would play the starring role. Despite the lurid title, the play was actually a rather philosophical meditation on sex and its place in history and culture. But West was already a burgeoning businesswoman: she knew that the publicity generated from the title, no matter how negative, would attract the audience numbers she needed to establish herself and her name. The newspapers refused to run the print ads for the play, but no matter: when she protested, claiming censorship, they wrote pieces covering the conflict, thereby sensationalizing the title and bringing in far more customers than any amount of paid advertising could. When West was arrested and jailed on indecency charges, the coverage reached a fever pitch, which she then exploited fully: upon her release, she sold her story for a thousand dollars, then turned around and used it to endow the Mae West Memorial Library at the prison. As she would repeatedly brag to Hollywood reporters, the stint in jail was a public relations dream, bringing in an estimated one million dollars in free publicity.

West leveraged her newfound notoriety to publicize her second project, *The Drag*, which, with its depictions of "female impersonation," was deemed too obscene to even make it out of rehearsals. Future projects—*The Wicked Age, The Pleasure Man*—benefited from the same type of publicity; when *Pleasure Man* was raided in 1928, West and her fifty-seven costars were all brought to very public trial. She wrote a book, *Babe Gordon*, and held a renaming contest for its adaptation to the stage. The fitting winner: *The Constant Sinner*, which told the lurid tale of a philandering woman who makes her way through a prizefighter, a black drug dealer, and the heir to a department store fortune. It was with this background, and no small amount of success behind her name, that West came to Hollywood.

Hollywood had first tried to nab West in 1930, when Universal began investigating the possibility of adapting her smash Broadway play, *Diamond Lil*, into a screen property. The question, however, was whether it could get past the increasingly strict state and local censorship boards. According to the advice of the MPPDA, no way: an internal memo, directed to industry heads within Hollywood, deemed it ill advisable given the "vulgar dramatic situations" and "highly censorable dialogue." When Universal floated the idea of employing West as a studio writer, the MPPDA discouraged that as well. And when the MPPDA formally discouraged something, there was essentially a tacit agreement among the studio heads that they would heed its advice.

In 1932, however, the somewhat desperate Paramount took a different approach. First, it signed West to a contract, casting her in a supporting role in *Night After Night*. Then it began behind-closed-doors plans to revisit the *Diamond Lil* script, but rumors soon began circulating within the industry, with Warner Bros. president Jack Warner particularly up in arms. The somewhat devious solution: Paramount could make the film, but *only* if they changed the title, didn't set it in a whorehouse, and eliminated some of the more salacious details, including dialogue that suggested that a man could be "had." And so *She Done Him Wrong* was "born"—with most, but critically, not *all* of the MPPDA advisements in effect.

In late October 1932, just as the *Diamond Lil* controversy was brewing, *Night After Night* hit theaters. West was billed fourth, but in her turn as a bawdy saloonkeeper, she stole the show. In her most famous line from the film, a hatcheck girl exclaims, "Goodness, what lovely diamonds!" to which West responds, "Goodness has nothing to do with it." West had rewritten the line herself—a point that publicity for the film was keen, from the start, to underline. The hoopla over her appearance in *Night After Night* took Paramount execs off guard: they knew that the *Diamond Lil* property was hot, but they didn't exactly realize that West was the reason for it.

It was the perfect buildup to *She Done Him Wrong*, which hit theaters like a tsunami in late January 1933. *Photoplay* ran an anticipatory piece, on newsstands in December, cautioning readers, "Look Out! Here's Mae West!" The article established the tenets of West's star image for the uninitiated: she was "blonde, buxom and rowdy," and spent her screen time "slithering across the scene in a spangled, sausage-skin gown." But lest you think her a vamp, she "specialized" in "naughty ladies with big souls and golden hearts." The hooker, as the cliché goes, with the heart of gold. The author also offered West's basic info: she was young ("it wasn't long ago that she turned thirty like a handspring"), lighter than she photographed ("she jiggles the beam at under a hundred and twenty), and a true looker ("believe me, you look three times as Mae West passes by"). This "firsthand" testimony from a male author painted West as a sex symbol par excellence, implicitly suggesting that readers should go, see for themselves, and be persuaded.

And persuaded they were. As a film, *She Done Him Wrong* lacks a cohesive narrative, with character motivations inconsistent or missing altogether. But no matter: West, dominating the mise-en-scène in a series of perfectly fitted gowns, was all that mattered. For her costar, she had chosen the very handsome Cary Grant, mostly, according to West, because she loved the sound of his voice. These were the early days of Grant's career, far before his image became that of the charismatic, debonair man-about-town, and West did more to establish him as an object of desire than any other star. Across the country, there were reports of audience members "sitting through" multiple screenings, refusing to give up their seats to the West-hungry masses waiting outside the theater. The film was not immune to censorship—several state boards cut scenes—yet as one reviewer explained, "the real wallop emanated subtly from Mae herself."

Suddenly, West was a phenomenon. Her 36-26-36 frame—naturally, the purported measurements of the *Venus de Milo*—incited a craze for curves. In "Curves—Hollywood Wants Them, and So Will You!" the author proclaimed that the "boyish" lines of Joan Crawford, Greta Garbo, and Marlene Dietrich were emphatically *out*. As one fan exclaimed in the "letter of the month" to *Motion Picture*, "She deserves a great BIG hand for making those half-starved ingénues self-conscious about their scrawny figures." Of course, attitudes concerning a desirable body always communicate a tremendous amount about a society's desires and anxieties—so it was no coincidence that the voluptuous figure of West came into vogue at the height of the Depression, when economic conditions made the emaciated female frame a daily reality and reminder of poverty.

Part of what made West so compelling was the utter frankness with which she approached the subject of sex. Sex had long been one of Hollywood's most lucrative narrative forces, but it was almost always *implied*. West may not have been explicit by today's standards, but the way she spoke about sex, especially off the screen, was refreshingly, if a bit terrifyingly, honest. Granted, she never specifically discussed the sex *act*, nor did she divulge, at least at the time, any details of her own sex life. But in print and in interviews, she advocated for a revised attitude toward sex: "Here we are ashamed of it," she told one fan magazine author, "even though it is the most beautiful thing Nature has given us." To her mind, "We can no more eliminate the primary emotion of sex-hunger from our birthright than we can remove our hearts." Sex, to West, was no more vulgar than eating.

Critics affirmed her rhetoric: for all her explicit sexuality, her frankness made her "the antithesis of sin." The *New York Times*, for example, proclaimed her "so sane, so frank, [and] so vigorous" that she offered "the healthiest influence which has reached Hollywood in years." *Motion Picture* asserted that even with its sexual explicitness, there was something undeniably "honest and vital" about the film that made it impossible to be offended. West was espousing an early version of what came, over the course of the 1950s, to be known as the *Playboy* philosophy: sex and sexuality are only dirty when suppressed. Her attitudes were ahead of their time—which is part of the reason they were so compelling and inspired so much anxiety.

But West's frankness wasn't limited to sex: she found "goody-goody women" stultifying, especially since they were usually just covering up something, and in keeping with her philosophy, she loathed hypocrites. She wasn't ashamed of her body, and she had no qualms about advising women on how to keep their men: fib about your age, and even get a face-lift if you need it, as "it's easier to lift a sagging chin than it is to lift the mortgage on a sagging romance." This frankness was, according to *Motion Picture*, befitting the tenor of the times: in the era of Roosevelt, of "directness, honesty, and 'facing things,' it was only natural that a star with a similar attitude towards sex and romance would resonate so strongly."

For all of West's forthrightness, her studio—and West herself—understood that audiences would accept only so much. It was one thing to speak frankly about sex, and even to act out that frankness on the screen, but it was quite another to *live* it. West's "real" life was thus constructed as a paragon of morality—lily-white, absent of any hint of scandal or disrepute. Like Caesar's wife's, her private life was, at least from the outside, beyond reproach. The earliest Hollywood publicity emphasized that West was "oppressively good," a sentiment echoed by countless additional pieces. She never drank or smoked; she went to church every Sunday. And according to West, she worked so much that it was impossible for her to get into any sort of trouble—and when she did have free time, she spent it at the prizefights. As she told one fan magazine, she just loved the fighters—ones with "busted noses and cauliflower ears and scrambled pans, especially." If a different type of star hung out with coarse men at the boxing ring—many of them African American—it would've been cause for immediate scandal. But don't forget: West's *father* had been an amateur boxer; the press thus framed her affection for the sport (and, by extension, its men) as yet another of her "natural" attributes.

But as with any star, no manner of protestation could unyoke West from her on-screen persona. Audiences had only seen her play one very specific sort of character, with attitudes about sex, men, and life in general that seemed like a plausible lifestyle for the independent, unwed star. West and other authors repeatedly and explicitly addressed this conflation: when a fan asked her whether she lived like her character in *She Done Him Wrong*, her answer was "an emphatic *no*. I'll match my life with any woman's." West also saw her clean life in terms of economic imperative: "Just how long do you think my contract would last if I carried on that way in real life?" As she keenly understood, if she started acting like her characters "in real life," audiences would turn on her—they wanted to see immoral fantasies acted out, but only so long as the performance was visible and the lights went up at the end of the hour.

While some doubted the earnestness of West's claims, she was able to maintain her off-screen image, in part, no doubt, because she spent so little time hobnobbing with the Hollywood elite, among whom the gossip columnists usually found their fodder. But West's refusal to join the Hollywood social scene also marked her, from the beginning, as an outsider. Not only was she from New York, associated with Broadway, the author of her own material, and too cool for the Hollywood social clubs, but she was also, suddenly, the most successful star in all of Hollywood. It's like West was the new girl who comes to your high school, refuses to hang out with you, and suddenly becomes the most popular girl in school.

Whether or not other stars felt any animosity, the press understood that brewing feuds made for amazing copy. The first narrative: West was such a threat that she apparently caused Garbo to come all the way back from Europe to defend her box office throne. (No matter that such desperate behavior seemed very, very un-Garbo—everyone loves a feud.) When the Garbo rumors failed to take hold, the next natural adversary was Marlene Dietrich, another sex goddess who was vying for dominance at West's own studio. Their dressing rooms on the Paramount lot were even next to each other—or at least they were according to lore. The feud was exacerbated when Dietrich, questioned about their rivalry, supposedly answered, "I never heard of Mae West."

Paramount and the fan magazines worked to simultaneously diffuse and exploit the feud, explaining that Dietrich had in fact been questioned concerning her opinions of the new Mae West–inspired fashion trends, to which she responded that she hadn't heard of them. But rumors of animosity didn't end there. In October 1933, Paramount hosted a lavish premiere for *I'm No Angel*, West's follow-up to *She Done Him Wrong*, but the stars of Hollywood snubbed it *en force*. A high-profile premiere usually attracted all manner of stars, even those from rival studios. But as reported in *Photoplay*, Paramount had to beg its *own* stars to attend. It wasn't West's fault—or at least the fan magazines worked hard to emphasize as much. Rather, it was the stars, who were jealous: they snuck in to see it after it started, but "they were too jealous to show Mae the courtesy her ability deserves."

The jealousy, however, was warranted: *I'm No Angel*, sold under the luscious tagline "When I'm good I'm very very good and when I'm bad, I'm better," would eventually be seen by more than thirty-six million Americans, more than triple the audience of *She Done Him Wrong*. The script followed a girl who, in West's words, "lost her reputation and never missed it," and served as a variation on the same "down-low" comedic style of *She Done Him Wrong*, featuring an encore appearance by Cary Grant as her love interest. It was the 1930s version of a sequel, and if *She Done Him Wrong* had suggested West's appeal, *Angel* solidified it. At the end of 1933 and the beginning of 1934, the gossip press seemed to be all West, all the time—so much so that Paramount's publicity office, fearful of overexposure, requested a moratorium on West coverage. But her apparent refusal to grant interviews was then used to reinforce her reputation: a *Photoplay* article, pointedly titled "Has Mae West Gone High Hat?," told readers that rumors of her snobbery were unfounded, even as the very title suggested, however implicitly, otherwise. It was the classic Hollywood publicity quandary: West was damned if she talked too much, and damned if she didn't talk enough.

Her popularity and widespread exposure also had a secondary effect—one far more dangerous than Hollywood gossip. The popularity of West, her films, and their explicit attitude toward sex weren't just a fad, or a boon to an industry struggling to make its way through the Depression. They were a flagrant, incendiary violation of common decency, a threat to the morality of the nation, and, most crucially, evidence of the abject failure of the MPPDA and Will Hays to protect audiences from sin in the form of the moving image.

According to popular, reductive history, Mae West single-handedly reinstituted censorship. But as the previous chapter on the anxiety surrounding Jean Harlow and other "kept women" explains—not to mention dozens of incredibly well-researched academic histories—the process was far more complicated. The Hays office had already cracked down on the studios' exploitation of the gangster, which was part of the reason they had resorted to other means of titillation, whether in the form of kept women, West, the anarchistic Marx Brothers, or prison-break films like *I Am a Fugitive from a Chain Gang* (1932). All types of Hollywood films were pushing the boundaries of the written code; West was just doing it with a more visible, remarkable body.

In the summer of 1934, the Hays office decided to "grant enforcement" of the censorship code via the Production Code Administration (PCA) and its very Catholic, very no-nonsense head, Joseph Breen. To briefly summarize a complicated series of events, they got serious. West was the embodiment of all that was morally wrong with Hollywood; it was natural, then, that her next film would be one of the most high-profile test cases. Could she still operate under the new, actually enforced rules of Hollywood—rules that explicitly forbade "first night scenes" and insinuations of women who sell their virtue?

The answer: sort of. Paramount's first action was to change the title of West's upcoming film, *It Ain't No Sin*, to the much less suggestive *Belle of the Nineties* (1934). (The original plan was to simply call it *Mae West's New Picture*—a title that would communicate all it needed to—but the PCA is rumored to have found the suggestion too flip.) West then purportedly acquired her own "personal censor" to sit on set and oversee production; veracity of this claim matters less than what it suggested—namely, that she was cooperating fully, even taking initiative in her own censorship. But the results were lackluster. *Belle of the Nineties* lacked the moxie that had made West's films so compelling. Yet as *Hollywood* magazine explained, it wasn't entirely her fault: "She does the very best anyone could with a picture murdered by censorship."

At the same time, Paramount and the press reinvigorated efforts to disassociate West from her previous characters. Article titles—"Don't Get Me Wrong"; "It's All in Fun"—reasserted that her previous frankness was simply performance. And this time, she was also framed as classy: according to *Motion Picture*, "She always dresses in the best of taste, she speaks in a low, cultured voice, and some of her beliefs would sound less surprising if they came from the lips of a Commencement Day orator." This was a far more subtle, yet equally effective, means of reframing West's image, whose working-class background (She grew up in Brooklyn! She loves fights!) had been so thoroughly established in previous discourse. Through the attribution of specific "natural" behaviors (dressing well, speaking well) the press effectively *re*-classed her, making her decent and respectable. It was a spectacular rewriting of her past and present, with the specific ideological purpose of appeasing the PCA, with the added bonus of making her more sheepish fans feel better—or at least more moral—about their established fandom. Suddenly, West was a guilty pleasure made innocent.

Theoretically, it seems like this strategy would've worked. West was savvy and smart enough to figure out a way to write a compelling character and still be clean. But when *Belle of the Nineties* underperformed—especially in comparison to her previous success—Paramount and West went into disaster cleanup mode. A *Photoplay* piece, supposedly authored by the director of *Belle of the Nineties*, but most likely penned by a Paramount press agent, emphasized that West was no one-trick pony: she was a tremendously skilled actress and could play *anything*, if audiences would give her the chance. To evidence as much, *Photoplay* paired the feature with drawings of West costumed as Catherine the Great, Peg o' My Heart, and Katherine in *The Taming of the Shrew*. The images were intended to suggest West's versatility; in practice, they make her look hilariously out of place. In addition, in anticipation of her next film, *Goin' to Town* (1935), Paramount ran ads for the "new, stream-lined Mae West," who was "versatile" and ready to "set a new standard." West even admitted that *Belle* had been a disaster, mostly because she would write a scene, and *then* have to rework it to fit the censors' demands. For *Goin' to Town*, she had collaborated with the censors from the start, and West promised a more coherent, entertaining result.

Goin' to Town was, indeed, coherent. It was just dull. As the reviewer for the *New York Times*, a self-proclaimed West devotee, explained, West's performance "shows an alarming tendency towards acquiring a serious outlook." Portraying her as a cattle queen, set in the present day, the film had some of the trappings of a West picture, but it cut out its throbbing heart: rather than letting men accumulate at her feet, West even *chased* a man—the most un-Westian romantic tactic imaginable. She may very well have been a versatile actress, but audiences were inflexible when it came to their expectations of the type of role she should play. And it wasn't entirely their fault: West and Paramount had spent two years constructing her image in a very specific way; it was only natural that when they attempted to sell her as otherwise, audiences stayed away.

Just as *Goin' to Town* was about to hit theaters, a long-festering rumor gained traction. Despite her adamant denials, it seems that West *had* been married. Some scandalmongers had unearthed a marriage certificate between Mae West and one Frank Wallace, in Milwaukee, Wisconsin. She claimed it must've been some other Mae West, explaining that she hadn't been to Milwaukee until four years previous. But her denials fell flat: the names of parents listed on the certificate were the same, first and last, as West's own parents. Then there was the matter of the annoying ex-husband, who, once discovered, began advocating for his share of their communal property, revealing that years ago, West's longtime manager had told him, "Mae's going places, and you're not, so you ought to give her a divorce."

In the grand scheme of Hollywood scandals, it was all very bland—just a forgotten teen marriage that lasted the length of a road tour. But the real scandal was the public revelation of West's actual age: if she was married in 1911, and had been eighteen at the time, that put her, in 1935, at right around age forty-two. Granted, West still looked *great,* but there was something about realizing that your sex symbol was an "old" woman that, for many, just didn't sit right—like checking someone out from behind, only to have her turn around and be your mother. Suddenly, West's sexuality, her curves and plumpness, the things that made her so alluring in the first place, seemed somewhat abject—instead of inspiring desire, it was a vague, if subconscious, disgust and shame, the very inverse of the attitude toward sex for which West had proselytized so ardently.

West went on to make three more pictures for Paramount, each less successful than the one before. She faded slowly, the victim of both the empowerment of the PCA and Paramount's unwillingness, especially toward the end of her contract, to spend the money needed to create the sort of picture that could lift her from her slump and restore her to stardom. It wasn't as simple as West going out of fashion; rather, her decline was the result of industrial and cultural shifts, for which she was but one of many catalysts. When her movies became less compelling, it was simple to reconsider her shape, her maturity, and her brazen sexuality, to allow them to become too much of a once-good thing. To allow the industrial imperatives of censorship, in other words, to subconsciously influence cultural tastes.

Which isn't to suggest that with the end of the decade, West somehow faded from public view, a shell of her once robust self. Quite the contrary: she returned to the stage, where, much like Marlene Dietrich, she would spend the next several decades, safe from the strangling industrial norms—and stifling censorship laws—that had hampered her Hollywood career. She maintained her lavish, rococo apartment in Los Angeles, the same one where she had invited so many reporters to "come up and see her sometime." She still went to the fights, she lampooned her own persona, she became even more lurid, more hilarious, more conscious, if possible, of the power of the well-turned phrase. Back on the stage, operating on her own terms, she could be as down low as she desired.

In June 1934, a fan magazine had questioned West whether she, and her particular brand of humor and sex, would last. Her reasoned reply: "The only thing in the world the public hasn't changed is its taste for sex. Since its popularity hasn't waned for thousands of years, I guess I needn't be afraid it will go out of style." West was right: sex doesn't ever go out of style. But at various moments in history, different attitudes toward how it should be contained do, in fact, go in and out of fashion. It's no accident that in the 1960s and '70s, with the rise of camp and the growing visibility, if not actual embrace, of both female and queer sexuality, West became a cult figure, especially as she vocally embraced her gay fans. What's more, various texts and interviews (including her memoir, *Goodness Had Nothing to Do with It*, published in 1959 and reissued in 1970) revealed the extent of her sexual dalliances, including those with African American men and men several decades her junior. It was as if everything fans wanted—and everything moralists feared—to be true of West when the camera stopped rolling had come to light. Depending on your perspective, such revelations were either glorious or proof of the enduring need for censorship. West's tenure in Hollywood was short, but even today, her catchphrases remain, a testament to her wit and startling modernity. And so West, so potent and persuasively sexual, endures, and image becomes icon.

OLD LOVES

The only thing Hollywood loves more than a blockbuster film is a blockbuster romance: the type of star pairing that sparks newfound fervor in fans, who clamor for the details of the stars' courtship, marriage, and everything that comes between. The more investment in the star and his relationship, the logic goes, the more likely the fan is to attend his next movie. Put differently, romances can make the studios a tremendous amount of money.

Which is part of why studio publicity departments, in collaboration with the gossip press, worked so hard to create romance out of the slightest suggestion of affection—but only when the star in question was single, as married stars were strictly off-limits. Or at least publicly—behind the scenes, married stars slept with other married stars, and sham marriages popped up to distract from all manner of indiscretions. Divorce did happen, but it always required a full publicity campaign to soften the blow: the two had grown woefully apart; they were happier this way; it was all for the sake of the children. It was a long, rhetorical slog, with a necessary waiting period until the next relationship could come to light. For some stars, it simply wasn't worth the hassle—they'd prop up their marriages, even when the couple lived apart, and cavort around Hollywood with their new object of desire. And they got away with it—in part because the gossip columnists and fan magazines agreed to keep quiet, usually in exchange for a steady stream of (far less scandalous) information on other stars.

It was a fragile means of keeping open secrets, but it worked. Some dalliances, such as the one between Spencer Tracy and Katharine Hepburn, percolated for decades just under the public radar. But others, like those between (the married) Clark Gable and Carole Lombard and (the married) Humphrey Bogart and (the twenty-five years younger) Lauren Bacall, were exposed to the light, threatening the careers of some of the biggest stars in Hollywood.

But neither relationship resulted in scandal—for reasons that had as much to do with the timing of divorces, gossip column bits, and marriages as the public's desire to believe in the narrative of true love and companionship. The promise of romance—the type of destined love you see in the movies—helped audiences forget to feel scandalized. Indeed, the framing of each relationship was so successful that both couples have become synonymous with Old Hollywood Love, emblematic of the sort of chemistry we just don't see anymore, on-screen or off. But the careful cultivation of these relationships also marked the beginning of the end of an era: by the time of Gable's death in 1961, the age of the studio-protected romance was effectively over, trampled by Elizabeth Taylor and her string of rotating suitors. Yet the stories of these old loves reign supreme, as dramatic and fulfilling as any of the pictures in which the actors starred.

CHAPTER EIGHT

Gable and Lombard: Lumberjack Meets Glamour Girl

When Carole Lombard's plane crashed into a Nevada mountain peak in 1941, the loss was so acute, and so broadly felt, that the United States government named one of its most prominent battleships after her. The madcap, effortlessly glamorous Lombard had been at the top of her career—and all of thirty-three years old. But it wasn't just Lombard's fans who mourned. All eyes were on her husband, Clark Gable, the so-called King of Hollywood: What would he do? How would he cope? Who would hang out on his ranch with him, raising chickens, pulling pranks, driving around in old jalopies? Would he quit Hollywood for good?

After several months of speculation, Gable did quit Hollywood—for the armed forces, requesting to be sent "where the going is tough." When he returned, three years later, it was to an entertainment industry on the cusp of seismic change. After the war, he worked his way through dozens of movies and two additional marriages, but his image never regained the vitality, the utter dominance, that characterized it during his time with Lombard. While the disintegration of the studio and star systems would take nearly twenty years, we can look to Lombard's death—and the events it, along with the war, set in motion—as the beginning of the end for Gable.

Gable and Lombard both became stars during the height of the studio system, with Gable contracted to MGM, the most glamorous and expansive of the studios, which both paved his way to stardom and cleaned up after his multiple potentially scandalous messes. While several of his most famous pictures, including *It Happened One Night* (1934) and *Gone with the Wind* (1939), were actually made with Gable on loan to other studios, he was an MGM man through and through, the quintessential studio system star. Lombard, by contrast, used her star power and the counsel of her agent to leverage tremendous influence and unheard-of control over her projects. While Bette Davis and James Cagney warred with Warner Bros. in the courts, Lombard worked the system, a point that would only further embolden her brazen, iconoclastic image.

Yet years before Gable and Lombard were huge Hollywood stars, before they ever met, fell in love, and managed to trick America into celebrating what was, in essence, a relationship "in sin," they were just humble Midwestern nobodies. Gable grew up in rural Ohio, the son of a farmer father and an "artist" mother, who passed away six months after his birth. He spent the next several years of his life with his grandparents on a farm, but his mother's "artistry," somewhat unsourced, was often utilized to explain how such a strapping, masculine man found his way to the somewhat feminized diversion of the theater. Gable spent the first part of his life *en plein air*, away from people, amusing himself with dirt and sticks and canine companions. According to countless biographical profiles, from that point forward, he would spend the rest of his life attempting to get back to the simplicity and open space of his childhood.

In high school, Gable was good at sports but had no mind for girls or social graces. He was an outdoors boy, more interested in getting away from girls than getting into their pants, a point often used to support the argument that Gable was no feminized "lover," just a naturally handsome guy who was too busy looking out to the horizon to see the girls falling at his feet. He graduated, found solid physical work at a tire factory, and attempted some night classes at the local college, but somewhere along the way he got invited to go backstage at an Akron Stock Company production. He was so smitten with acting, according to one account, that he quit his reliable job and began working as an errand boy for free, just to be near the stage.

The next several years of Gable's life were a mix of physical labor to pay the bills and stock company work to build his talent. He spent time on the oil rigs in Oklahoma with his father; he found work with a stock company in Kansas City; he ended up stranded in Butte, Montana, and, according to conflicting sources, either pawned his suit to buy a train ticket or simply hopped the rails to make his way to Portland, Oregon, where he worked as a logger, at an ad company, and in various theater gigs. In 1924, he met Josephine Dillon, an acting coach seventeen years his senior. Dillon polished his acting skills and taught him how to refine his voice and suit it to different types of masculine roles. She also paid for a new set of teeth, as Gable's were in a state wholly unsuitable for serious acting, let alone Hollywood. Dillon was the first in a string of older women who would function as social and cultural mentors, essentially bankrolling Gable's lifestyle. He was, in many ways, a bit of a kept man, a point that was always neatly elided by emphasizing that he simply loved "sophisticated women."

When Dillon had cultivated Gable thoroughly enough, the pair moved to Los Angeles and got married, while he struggled through bit parts and a failed screen test. He found various roles in traveling troupes, taking him away from both Los Angeles and Dillon, before eventually landing several starring roles on Broadway, where he was lauded for his "vigorous, brutally masculine" turn in *Machinal* (1928). During his tenure in New York, he met Ria Langham, a twice-divorced socialite, also a decade older than Gable. The details of when his relationship with Dillon ended and the one with Langham began are somewhat murky, but by 1931, he was back in Los Angeles for a new play and, in quick succession, obtained a divorce from Dillon and a marriage license with Langham. He did a screen test for Warner Bros., but studio exec Darryl F. Zanuck purportedly declared that his ears were too big and "he looked like an ape."

But Warner's loss was MGM's gain, and after toiling for nearly a decade on the stage and the fringes of Hollywood, Gable signed a contract. At first, he was cast as a heavy—with his dark complexion and well-oiled hair, he fit the part. In 1931, he appeared as a mob boss in *Dance, Fools, Dance*, starring Joan Crawford; it was a supporting role, but Gable was the hottest thing, other than Crawford's legs, in the picture. Over the next several months, MGM cast him in increasingly prominent roles, with the *New York Times* reporting that it was "no secret" that the execs were plotting Gable's path toward stardom.

At this point, Gable's dominant characteristic was that of the *lover*. His seemingly meteoric rise, paired with his glowering stare, naturally encouraged comparisons to Valentino, the last great lover of Hollywood. Like Valentino, Gable sent an "electric shock" through women's hearts simply by appearing on-screen; his physical presence was enough to make women swoon. But it was a specific type of physical presence: as the aptly titled "Why Women Go Crazy About Clark Gable" described, his characters were indifferent, yet asked for "utter submission"—if they couldn't have it, then they'd rather die. It was a stark, exacting, yet somehow romantic understanding of love and passion, and women found it unspeakably sexy.

But Gable—or, more precisely, the publicity team at MGM—also understood that the "lover" image could only get him so far. Sure, women loved him, but he could also incite ire and backlash from male audiences. The solution: a wide-scale campaign to disabuse fans of his "lover" image. To achieve this task, publicity acknowledged that Gable played a particular type of "lover" character on-screen, yet his "real self" was entirely different. He was quoted calling the suggestion of his power over women "a lot o' hooey," admitting that the attention made him blush. "I like women," he told *Motion Picture*, "but they make me uncomfortable unless I know them pretty well." Here, we see the same understanding of Gable at work as in the tales of his time in high school: just because girls were interested in him didn't mean he was some sort of Don Juan. In fact, Gable was so busy being his masculine self, he had no time to learn how to flirt or attract women.

After disavowing the lover image, MGM built an unquestionably masculine one in its place. First task: establish Gable's physicality. In profile after profile, authors emphasized his mighty build, listing his height (6'1" or 6'2", depending on the source) and weight (between 180 and 200, depending on the point in his career). His shoulders were so broad that he could only wear tailored suits, and he drew comparisons to boxing champion Jack Dempsey. He hated wearing neckties and other fancy clothes, opting to spend time in casual sweaters. He gives the same impression of "physical power," according to one fan magazine, "but like Jack, you can't imagine him misusing it."

What's more, Gable was a "tame egg" who never entertained or went out on the town. He claimed that Hollywood was far too civilized, likely to "make a man go soft in a month." His house proved he was a "he-man" both on- and off-screen—there was a "feminine" room for his teenage stepdaughter, but otherwise, it was all male, all the time: a game room and study where he could ash his cigars to his heart's content, with animal heads, all of them shot by his own hand, lining wood-paneled walls. This was certainly no Valentino, with his exotic drapings and slave bracelets—this was Clark Gable, "the last of Hollywood's Great Untamed."

Gable's image was effectively re-centered around stalwart masculinity, but he still wasn't necessarily a star. Numerous biographers claim that he was hot and heavy with Crawford during this period—by 1934, he would've appeared in six films with her—but MGM clearly couldn't publicize as such. While fans always love an all-star couple, both actors were married; what's more, if the two were to start dating in real life, it would further conflate Gable with his lover persona. What he really needed was a charismatic star turn—and not like the one in *Red Dust* (1932), in which his beguiling costar, Jean Harlow, stole the show.

Cue *It Happened One Night*. According to apocryphal myth, in 1933, a very intoxicated Gable had hit and killed a pedestrian while driving home; the MGM fixers cleaned up the mess, arranging for a studio employee to take responsibility and the jail bit. Furious at Gable for the trouble he'd caused, studio head Louis B. Mayer punished him by loaning him to Columbia (a minor studio to MGM's major status), where he was cast in *It Happened One Night* as an affable, no-nonsense newspaperman who tames an unruly heiress via a combination of well-directed spankings and pointed lectures. The film, released in 1934, was a monster hit. It won Gable an Oscar, but more important, it offered an on-screen image to which MGM could wed his "real" (read: masculine) image.

Gable himself underlined the association: as he told *Motion Picture*, Pete was the first character he'd played in which he could really see himself. Pete was him—so much so that Gable even opted to wear his own ten-year-old hat for the role, as both he and Pete were the kind of guys who'd wear a shabby hat into the ground. This "New Gable," according to *Photoplay*, had "cut the apron strings" that had tethered him to his heartthrob image. No longer just an object of female desire, Gable was now a *man's* man. The film's success was the product of an excellent script and performances on the part of both Gable and Claudette Colbert, but it didn't hurt that it was also intensely suggestive, in the way that only thirties movies that actually show no sex can be. Colbert lifted her skirt and showed off her leg in the now iconic hitchhiking scene, and Gable famously took off his shirt to reveal . . . a lack of undershirt. This might seem like a small detail now, but at the time, it was standard sartorial practice for men to wear undershirts at all times. When Gable didn't wear one—and in one of the most popular films of the year, at that—makers of undershirts feared for their business. Regardless of actual, measurable economic effect, it was the narrative that mattered: Gable was the sort of star whose wardrobe choices could influence a whole way of thinking.

For Gable and MGM, the next three years brought one hit after another, usually in films, such as *The Call of the Wild* (1935) and *Mutiny on the Bounty* (1935), that further bolstered his masculine image. Despite attempts on the part of the studio fixers to suggest otherwise, his marriage was in shambles. He and his second wife, Ria, had already separated in 1932, purportedly due to his dalliance with Crawford. To assuage rumors of adultery, especially persuasive given Gable's virile screen presence and Ria's age and relative homeliness, *Photoplay* offered an entire article on "Why Male Stars Marry Plain Girls," suggesting that Ria had "something more than mere physical beauty"—namely, the "charm, poise, and culture" to outshine any gorgeous starlet.

Why, suddenly, were the fan magazines working so hard to uphold the Gable marriage? Maybe because he had impregnated his very young *Call of the Wild* costar, Loretta Young. The fan magazines might not have known as much, but the MGM fixers certainly did—enough to plant strategic distractions in the gossip press. Young, a devout Catholic, had bent her beliefs far enough to have affairs with both Gable and the very married Spencer Tracy, but an abortion—the usual solution for the unwanted results of star affairs during this period—was out of the question. In a scheme that has gone down as one of the most intricate in Hollywood cover-up history, Young embarked on a lengthy European voyage, returning to Los Angeles in her eighth month, at which point MGM arranged for her to be sequestered, far away from roving eyes, with a cadre of MGM-employed nurses. In order to silence rumors of the true cause of Young's "long illness," MGM set up an interview with a fan magazine, given from her bed, with carefully arranged pillows concealing her actual condition. She gave birth in November 1935 and gave the baby up for adoption—only to adopt it herself nineteen months later. The public never knew, and both Gable's and Young's images remained intact. It wasn't until decades later that the secret became public knowledge.

Ria Gable may or may not have known of the affair and its complications, but according to one fan magazine account, when Gable returned from filming *The Call of the Wild*, his first words were, "I want my freedom." Yet with whispers of his potential dalliance with Young in the air, MGM knew it was not the time to complete a divorce. Thus: a separation, with Gable headed to a long-term vacation in South America and a tentative, generous property settlement. It was a breakup in segments. Rumors of unhappiness in the marriage had circulated for so long that it seemed natural; little by little, it became accepted knowledge that Gable was a bachelor in everything but legal name.

A bachelor needed a bachelor image—and for Gable, it wasn't hard to find. If before, his image had been that of a frank, no-frills, masculine guy, now it was that of an übermasculine he-man. If the press narratives are to be believed, Gable never spent a waking moment in Hollywood when he wasn't working—as soon as the makeup was off his face, he was headed to the mountains, the wilderness, the riverbanks, no matter, so long as he could go there in his jeep, overflowing with guns and camping stuff. It was a nice narrative, and it helped distract from whispers of Gable's association with another high-profile Hollywood star, one with whom he'd appeared in one movie, years ago, when their images were just forming. A woman with enough vigor and vitality to match his own: Carole Lombard.

Carole Lombard's early image was like champagne: sophisticated, effervescent, and intoxicating. But Lombard was also madcap and a ballbuster, a proto-feminist who, in the words of film critic David Thomson, "didn't give a fuck and was famous for saying so." Lombard, née Jane Peters, was born near Fort Wayne, Indiana, and despite leaving the state midway through her childhood, her wholesome "Hoosier" background was used to downplay her otherwise progressive image. Her father was injured on the job when she was young, and his resultant fits of anger drove Lombard, her two siblings, and her mother to Southern California. Lombard made her way into young adulthood, eventually, according to legend, catching the eye of a talent scout while playing baseball in the street.

Like Gable, Lombard spent years toiling in relative obscurity before securing a foothold among the Hollywood elite. In 1921, at the age of thirteen, she played a tomboy in *A Perfect Crime*, followed by a string of bit parts that culminated in a contract with Fox in 1925. But before she could make her mark, she was in a serious car accident—so serious that it took her out of action, thus nullifying her contract. But she fought her way back in, earning a spot as one of Mack Sennett's famous Bathing Beauties, which entailed spending a lot of time in a bathing costume and showing off her legs. Her stint with Sennett, along with a bunch of two-reelers for Pathé Studios, would eventually lead to a contract with Paramount, but unlike fellow Bathing Beauty Gloria Swanson, Lombard would never try to deny her past—her body, and her willingness to use it to get what she wanted, was always part of her image.

Lombard's early roles with Paramount were throwaway: she was like a Victoria's Secret model brought to the big screen, used for little more than window dressing. She had beautiful gowns that draped perfectly from her body, but her image was amorphous, indistinguishable from the other comely starlets on the studio lot. Lombard wasn't making much of a mark, but she did find a husband—the daft, mustachioed William Powell, a rising star—while filming *Man of the World* and *Ladies' Man* in 1931. Powell was coming off a divorce and sixteen years older than the twenty-three-year-old Lombard, but no matter: they were likable and in love.

Nevertheless, rumors plagued the marriage from the beginning, in part because the pair appeared so rarely in public. In a 1932 tell-all with *Movie Classic*, Powell attributed their lack of social life to Lombard's apparent yearlong sickness, one that began shortly after their wedding and continued, in various forms, throughout the year. It's unclear what Lombard may have been suffering from—she did, after all, complete five films in 1931, and another five in 1932—or if Powell and his press agent were simply trying to tamp down already brewing rumors of a separation. Lombard herself participated in the publicity process, sitting for a lengthy interview in which she, or someone writing under her name, professed her thoughts on the "seven types of love," including the most important—"Healthy Love," which she shared with Powell.

But in a hilarious publicity twist, the piece was about to go to press when Lombard announced her separation from Powell. The editors hastily added a preface, explaining the apparent fickleness of all seven types of love. But for those reading closely, Lombard's love philosophy—and the potential for divorce—was in clear evidence: according to her, Healthy Love could be compromised when one person outgrew the other, which, in her words, "is why I believe in divorce." Even without the preface, the piece would read like the musings of a woman readying herself for a breakup, a sense that became all the stronger given the reality of Lombard and Powell's separation.

During her marriage to Powell, Lombard's profile had risen slightly. Most significantly, she starred opposite young Clark Gable in *No Man of Her Own* (1932), the only time the two would appear on-screen together. But Lombard needed a breakthrough role—something to texture and embolden her image the same way *It Happened One Night* had done for Gable. That role came by way of Howard Hawks, who was on the hunt for a leading actress for *Twentieth Century* (1934), a comedy based on a popular stage play he was producing and directing for Columbia starring veteran actor John Barrymore. The film, which tracks the antagonistic relationship between a lingerie model turned actress and her Svengali mentor, needed a female star who could project stubbornness and vulnerability, aloofness and absurdity. Dozens of prominent actresses, from Gloria Swanson to Joan Crawford, were considered for the role, but Hawks had someone else in mind.

Months before, Hawks had met Lombard at a Hollywood party, where he became convinced that she had been underused, or improperly used, as an actress. So much for the glamour girl:

Lombard was meant to play comedy. Columbia agreed to cast her, in part, one can be sure, because she was so much cheaper than the other, big-name actresses floated for the role. Lombard was pitch-perfect, oscillating between utter insecurity and total arrogance, the perfect comic foil to John Barrymore's grandiose, constantly mugging performance. With its madcap antics and its pair of mis-matched lovers, *Twentieth Century*, along with *It Happened One Night*, would set the template for the screwball genre that would proliferate over the next decade.

Suddenly, Lombard's career shifted into high gear. She became known as "Hollywood's hostess," celebrated for throwing the best, weirdest parties in town. At one such fete, she hid com-pressed air contraptions all around the house, which would blow up women's skirts and dresses without warning, much to the de-light of the male attendees. She publicly advised her fans to "be modern or else be a wallflower," suggesting that the truly modern girl—which she clearly was—got men, but got them through cul-tivating a variety of interests and skills, from horseback riding to driving a car, from studying up on the latest plays to "going in for sports with zest." Lombard was the most popular girl in town, but despite a celebrated, scantily clad turn in the steamy *Bolero* (1934) and appearances in a half dozen other films, she still hadn't quite made good on the comedic promise of *Twentieth Century*.

At least, that is, until *My Man Godfrey* (1936). When Universal began developing the script for *Godfrey* in 1935, they assigned it to veteran comedic director Gregory La Cava. But La Cava would only make it if he could get Powell—and Powell, in turn, would only make it if they cast his ex-wife, aka Lombard, as the ditzy, well-meaning, somewhat dopey debutante who "discovers" a homeless Powell during a scavenger hunt and puts him to work as the family butler. True love, naturally, ensues. Universal knew it had publicity gold on its hands—Ex-husband and -wife! United at film's end!—and *Godfrey* was a huge hit, in no small part due to the warmth emanating from both its leads. Lombard's performance is hysterical, in both senses of the word; today, it's the role for which she's most remembered and celebrated.

With *Godfrey*, the Lombard image finally consolidated into something spectacular, equal parts sophisticated beauty and madcap playfulness. While she had developed a reputation as Hollywood's Practical Joke Girl as far back as 1934, now, with her new, so-called lunatic persona in place, the press ratcheted it up a notch. According to "Fieldsie," Lombard's secretary and close friend dating back to her Bathing Beauty days, Lombard's new house never slept: the servants didn't know when dinner might be, or what weird accent she would employ the next time she picked up the phone. Fieldsie also warned journalists not to venture into the yard, because it was never clear when Lombard might go out and shoot her BB gun at nothing in particular. If Lombard's first house post–Powell divorce was all sanity, femininity, and sophistication, the new one was a madhouse, and Lombard was the least predictable, most fun girl in town.

Enthusiasm for the madcap persona also directed attention away from the most significant, and potentially most scandalous, development in Lombard's "real" life: her burgeoning relationship with Clark Gable. The story of Gable and Lombard's first "re-meeting" has been heavily mythologized, with no less than three different variations. A summary: on February 7, 1936, a common friend—Jack Whitney? Gable's friend Donald Ogden Stewart? The famed Countess di Frasso?—threw a big afternoon party. According to one account, it had to be in the afternoon because the host's wife, suffering from a nervous breakdown, had been ordered not to attend parties after dark. The easy solution? Throw a party during the day, call it the Annual Nervous Breakdown Party, and make everyone wear white. Another narrative explained that it was merely an "all-white party"; yet another claimed it was simply a wear-formalwear-in-the-afternoon affair.

Whatever the occasion or motivation, Lombard's entrance remained the same: clad in all white, she arrived in an ambulance, only to be carried into the party itself by four strapping young men. Gable found it hilarious, and they spent the rest of the afternoon playing tennis, during which she impressed him with her utter lack of self-consciousness. As *Photoplay* explained, here, at last, was a girl "who didn't seem to care a continental darn whether her makeup wore off or her hair fell out of place." A week later, Lombard arranged for an ancient, rusted-out Ford Model T, "the most disreputable car in all the modern world," to be painted all over with hearts . . . and delivered to Gable's doorstep, just in time for Valentine's Day. Naturally, Gable loved it—and immediately hopped in and headed over to pick her up for a ride around the town.

Whether truth or fiction, the story of their meeting wasn't public knowledge at the time. Instead, the MGM fixers worked to keep their relationship as secret as possible, lest the public respond negatively to tales of the King of Hollywood on the prowl while still officially married to another woman. They were public enough that the gossip columns couldn't *not* report—a bit in "The Talkie Town Tattler," on newsstands in July 1936, reported the two attending a circus, insinuating that one of their names rarely gets mentioned without the other's alongside. But there were still attempts to squelch the rumors: a piece in Sheilah Graham's gossip column declared that Gable and Lombard had decided they were unsuited, even for friendship, given their different temperaments—a sentiment so at odds with their public movements that it reeked of an obvious studio-arranged plant.

But as the relationship endured, MGM realized they needed a way to spin it, lest the truth of the affair emerge outside of the studio's control. A *Photoplay* feature, titled "Clark Gable's Romantic Plight," laid out the "facts" of the situation: Gable was still married, but only on a technicality; and now, for the very first time, he had a girl "whose vitality and zest for life was as strong as his own." To substantiate the claim, the author offers the full-blown narrative of their first meeting, with extra emphasis on the congruity of Lombard's antics with Gable's sense of humor. There was also a nicely timed, fully publicized baptism of the son of MGM star Patrick Moriarty, with Gable and Lombard serving as very responsible godparents; at the same time, fan mag pictorials framed Lombard as "Gable's Girl" and Gable himself as "very much in love." The publicity seemed to be daring the public to find fault: if you did, you were coldhearted, bent on preventing the destined union of a perfectly suited, perfectly beautiful couple.

Somewhat conveniently, the slow rollout of the Lombard-Gable romance coincided with Lombard's own negotiations with Paramount—negotiations that would ultimately win her choice terms that were the envy of Hollywood. Lombard's resistance and self-advocacy was public knowledge, as her "colorful career" was highlighted in the fan magazines as early as 1935. By 1937, with her star value in sharp focus following the success of *Godfrey*, Paramount moved to re-up her long-term contract. But Lombard, with the help of her agent, Myron Selznick, pulled a fast one, leveraging her value toward a nonexclusive deal with both Paramount and Selznick International Pictures.

The terms were unheard of: three pictures a year at $150,000 apiece, along with control over all aspects of the Lombard image. She could choose the cinematographer, the director, even the supporting cast—not to mention her fashion designer and still photographer. She had final say over every publicity still that left the studio lot, plus tight control over the type and number of publicity stories published about her. If it all sounds a lot like a contemporary celebrity contract, that's because it is—and Lombard had it years before the rest of the industry transitioned to the "free agent" model of stardom.

Lombard's new contract was great for her career, but it was also a perfect opportunity to change the conversation about her. While MGM-approved pieces focused on Gable's connection to her, articles on Lombard focused on her achievements: "She Gets Away with Murder" offers the details of her contract, highlighting the ease with which she was able to achieve her demands, with "no suits or sulks on either side"—a stark contrast to the endless, embittered, highly public war between Bette Davis and Warner Bros. But lest Lombard appear too spoiled, the article highlights the regard in which the studio held her: she thought like a producer; she had no time for trifling gossip columns or catty infighting; her only concern was "enhancing her value" by making "consistently good pictures that will make consistently good money."

"How I Live by a Man's Code" further highlighted Lombard's business acumen and status as a "modern Career Girl." Her rules: pay your share, don't kiss and tell, keep a sense of humor, and most of all, *be feminine*. In other words, be every man's dream girl: the smart, savvy woman who can pay her own way, laugh at crude jokes, refuse to gossip with her nosy friends, and still look amazing in an evening gown. While these articles emphasized Lombard's status as the "complete package," they never mentioned Gable's name—even as they drew connections between Lombard and Mary Pickford, another major star who not only took control of her career but successfully weathered a high-profile, potentially scandalous romance to another prominent macho Hollywood star.

The image of Lombard as savvy career woman didn't necessar-

Damning? Not entirely. But it was suggestive enough to incite the wrath of the Hays board. Bad enough, in fact, that *Photoplay* published an uncharacteristic retraction the following month and the stars' respective studios began a forceful push to marry off the unmarried husbands and wives. Suddenly, Ria Gable was headed to Reno, where'd she take up the necessary residency to achieve a divorce. While details of the divorce decree were never made wholly public, rumor had it that MGM forked over more than a quarter million dollars, taken from Gable's future paychecks, to get Ria to go away quietly. With the divorce decree in hand and Gable on a brief break from *Gone with the Wind*, an MGM publicity exec arranged for the pair to be whisked to Kingman, Arizona, where, on March 29, 1939, they surprised a reverend in the early morning hours and returned to Hollywood as man and wife.

There were no declamatory editorials; no incensed public outcries. Just cheery pictures of the happy couple, legally bound at last, morally righteous in the eyes of God and countryman and moviegoer. Their wedding, and its importance to Hollywood, was likened to that of Pickford and Fairbanks—here, at last, were the new reigning King and Queen of Hollywood. Publicity in the months following the wedding was similar to that which preceded the wedding, only amplified: if before, Gable and Lombard liked to play outdoors, now they were going to duck camp together, with Lombard the only lady allowed on-site. They moved into director Raoul Walsh's old ranch, with Gable boasting about his acreage, the crops he was harvesting, and the poultry he was raising—which he sold, naturally, to the MGM commissary. Instead of a pool, they had a swimmin' hole, complete with a tire swing hanging from an old oak. It was a pastoral ideal that just happened to be peopled with two of the biggest stars in the world.

And the jokes! Lombard's image had always been that of the trickster—which, at least according to the popular narrative, is part of what made Gable fall so hard for her. Now that they were married, the gags became the second most important feature of their life together: for Lombard's birthday, Gable arranged for a cake iced with "To Mammy on Her 75 Birthday," while Lombard made a "gallery" titled "World's Worst Photographs," filled with Gable's attempts at artistry, including a choice shot of Lombard with half of her head cut off. Whenever they were separated, even for a day, they would fill the house with gag gifts, from hams to life-size statues. Here was Lombard's madcap personality, rubbing off on Gable and making them all the more self-deprecating and likable.

Gable and Lombard were a publicity dream, offering just enough access to their private lives to satiate public curiosity, while cultivating an appetite for more. They had successfully navigated the maelstrom leading up to their marriage, and now they just had to sit back, sustain their stardom, and rake in the profits— proof positive that true love could, in fact, endure. But when the United States declared war in December 1941, Hollywood was the first to be enlisted for service on the "home front," collaborating with the government in a wide-reaching program that covered everything from the production of training films to slight modifications to forthcoming movies, such as *Casablanca* (1942), to incite broad citizen support for the war. And as had been the case during World War I, prominent stars were put to work touring the country and selling war bonds, one of the primary means of continuing support for the war.

In January 1942, Lombard embarked to do her part, traveling to her home state of Indiana, accompanied by her mother and Gable's longtime press agent, Otto Winkler. After raising an astounding two million dollars in war bonds in a single day, the trio headed home. According to popular legend, Lombard's mother and Winkler wanted to take the train, but Lombard was eager to return to Gable, from whom she'd never been apart for more than a few days, and convinced them to take a plane. The plane departed from Indiana, touched down to refuel in Las Vegas, and took off again—only to crash, a little more than twenty minutes later, into a nearby mountain range, killing all twenty-two on board, including sixteen servicemen. Back in Hollywood, Gable had been waiting at the airport; when the flight was delayed, he was told to go home, where, according to one account, he busied himself readying gags for Lombard's return. When news of the crash reached him via MGM publicity head Howard Strickling, he was decimated by grief.

Whenever a Hollywood star dies young, it's a tragedy. Whenever a Hollywood star dies young while serving her country, leaving behind her much-beloved husband, with whom she had been very publicly and blissfully happy, the tragedy amplifies into something else entirely. Lombard became the first high-profile loss in the war, her youth and vitality a stand-in for the youth and vitality at risk in the war at large. Gable was never one for public emotion, but his absence, from both Hollywood and the screen, was a signifier for the nation's grief. Still in mourning, he returned to work, modeling the expectations for the country; as for the film that Lombard had been about to begin shooting, Joan Crawford took her place, donating her entire $112,000 salary to war relief.

The fan magazines attempted to process the nation's grief vis-à-vis Gable's, offering to answer "What the Loss of Carole Lombard Means" and "How Clark Gable is Conquering Loneliness," detailing his twenty-pound weight loss and the deep sadness in his eyes. But those were just words, few with little more import than any others. What made sense, and what made Gable a hero, was his declaration, weeks after wrapping his film at MGM, that he would enroll in the army, with the ardent request to be "treated like any other soldier." His hand shook as he took the private's oath, and military guidelines called for him to shave his signature mustache. According to his colonel, he took "the bumps and hurdles with the rest." In time, he would be promoted to captain, allowed to regrow his mustache, and shifted away from the war zone to making training films. A star like Jimmy Stewart could fly planes and face actual enemy fire, but the government knew that a Gable death would not inspire the nation's morale, but destroy it.

When the war was through, Gable received a hero's welcome, returning to a Hollywood that, at least on the surface, looked remarkably similar to the one he had left behind—save, of course, the stunning absence of one of its most beguiling comediennes, who, at thirty-three years old, had just been entering the prime of her career. In the years to come, Gable would remarry, and the perfection of his romance with Lombard would come into question. Did he ever truly stop cheating? Were they really as perfectly paired, as goofily happy, as their publicity would have us believe? But such questions are missing the point: what mattered then was that Gable and Lombard evidenced that Hollywood marriage could, in fact, work—even if it took a few bumps in the road to get there. They likewise proved that even sticky romantic situations could be successfully negotiated, especially if the stars played along. What could have been an incendiary scandal, in all sorts of ways—Lombard's unruliness, Gable's constant philandering, her power, his near-bigamy—became a love story fit for the screen, equal parts screwball and passionate romance.

But this love story was also a tragedy. As Gable grew older and his costars grew younger, as he worked his way through one marriage and another, it was difficult to shake the feeling that he, and his image, were never the same again. In *The Misfits* (1961), Gable shares the screen with Marilyn Monroe and Montgomery Clift—

huge stars, but of the next generation of Hollywood, embodying an attitude toward sex, acting, and the management of publicity utterly foreign to the once-reigning king of MGM. Watching the film, you can't take your eyes off him, but that's because you can't figure out the ineffable something he seems to be missing. When Gable died months after filming, it was only appropriate that he was buried, as had long been his intention, beside Lombard. For in 1937, Lombard's ability to set the terms of her stardom heralded the beginning of a new paradigm of Hollywood stardom. Gable's death, nearly twenty years later, signaled the end of the old one.

CHAPTER NINE

Bogart and Bacall:
First Couple of Film Noir

With his weathered face, weary mouth, and wizened flesh, Humphrey Bogart was never young. But with his sardonic wit and mischievous eyes, he was never quite old either. He became a star at forty-one and, over the next fifteen years of his life, made as many canonic films as stars with twice his time in Hollywood. He was the consummate tough guy—he once told a reporter that he'd killed a man on-screen in every way imaginable save throwing acid on his face, and that was only because the Hays board wouldn't allow it—and, according to all accounts, he lived as self-destructively off-screen as he did on. He was unapologetically garrulous; he openly dismissed all women save the one he was with; he was regularly mistaken for a mob boss. He hated phonies and racists and loved lunchtime martinis, elaborate practical jokes, and his motorboat, *Sluggy*. Bogie was either a crotchety ass or a total softy, depending on whom you spoke to, and in the years following his death, he became a symbol of the counterculture and the quintessence of detached cool.

But what set Bogart apart—what made him more than just an iconoclastic villain—was his May-December romance with Lauren Bacall. The two met on the set of *To Have and Have Not* (1944), and the resultant chemistry is on film for all to see—one of many reasons a somewhat hackneyed adaptation of one of Hemingway's lesser works has become a classic. But how did a forty-five-year-old man, still embroiled in his third marriage, manage to disentangle himself and marry a twenty-year-old vixen with nary a hint of scandal? The answer was before every audience member's eyes. Bogie may well have been old enough to be Bacall's father, but that was all forgotten when you saw the heat with which they looked at each other. It may not have been typical, but it was destined—and so their relationship went down as one of the most highly erotic and celebrated couplings in film history.

But that sort of reception would've been impossible without Bogart's image and the tough-guy masculinity it represented. His path to Hollywood was atypical: he wasn't a Midwestern farm boy like Clark Gable or an orphaned jack-of-all-trades like Cary Grant. Rather, he was a bona fide blue blood, born in New York City to a well-to-do surgeon father and an accomplished artist mother, who had originally exhibited in highfalutin French salons. Bogart and his younger sisters grew up in the lap of luxury, splitting their time between their Upper East Side apartment, a lake cottage, and boarding school. As a teen, he was sent to Phillips Academy Andover with the expectation that he'd eventually matriculate with the rest of his class to Yale. But according to Bogart, he accumulated nineteen and a half demerits in his first term. The details of how he finally managed to get himself kicked out vary slightly from article to article, but the rhetorical effect was the same: Bogart was a troublemaker and ne'er-do-well from the start.

With schooling out of the question, Bogart signed up for the navy, serving for several years during the First World War. But he was no model soldier—at least according to him. The narrative of his past sounds like the plot of a Bogart film: he despised authority for authority's sake; he was "tossed in the brig" for a month; he had no idea what he was doing. But being in the military was "the best thing that ever happened to him"—"it put hair on his chest, a sense of propriety in his soul. In short, it made a man of him." The navy did more than make Bogart a man, though—according to studio-generated bios, it gave him his face; more specifically, the distinctive scar above his upper lip, incurred via stray shelling, which gave his face a look of gravitas and menace. The actual provenance of his scar has been contested—some argue it was from childhood; others think it was the result of a barroom fight in the twenties—but the story of the stray shell was much more gallant.

After an honorable discharge from the navy, Bogart set about trying to be a regular working stiff—but as he was eager to emphasize, that life was just not for him. He had always liked clowning around and making up plays with his friends while summering at his cottage, so he got in touch with the father of a friend from that period—William A. Brady, theater promoter and father of famed stage actress Alice Brady—who got him a job as an assistant stage manager. But that was the last bit of paternalism that would come his way: for the next two decades, he would strive, and mostly fail, like any other actor.

It was in his role as stage manager that he met his first wife, stage actress Helen Menken. According to Bogart, the story went something like this: It was opening night of a new show, with Menken in the lead. Yet she quickly grew frustrated with the delays between acts and began to rail at the cast and crew. Bogart, seeing that she needed to be calmed down lest she ruin the show entirely, "slapped her on the fanny," pushed her into her dressing room, and locked the door. It was love at first mild physical abuse, and after a four-year courtship, the pair married, in 1926. But they quarreled incessantly, over things like "whether she should feed the dog caviar when people were starving," and divorced, somewhat amicably, a year after the wedding. This anecdote, first propagated in a *Motion Picture* feature introducing Bogart to the world, worked to establish his attitudes toward women: he expressed himself physically; he loathed displays of emotion; he fought with every woman he loved.

Bogart's first wife was a star, but that didn't make him one. His first real stage role was as a Valentino-like sheik, and he was so proud that he'd walk the streets with his slick, styled hair hoping that someone would mistake him for the star. He also paid his dues appearing as a sporty juvenile—meaning he usually was on the stage with a preppy getup and a sporting item (bat, tennis racket, golf club) in his hand, asking if anyone was up for a round. These romantic parts were, according to Bogart, "the actor's lowest estate"—he found them vapid and laughable, the very opposite of the type of actor he endeavored to be. After his divorce, he fell for another actress, Mary Philips, whom he had first met while costarring in *Nerves*.

The time line's a little contradictory here—Bogart married Wife No. 1 in 1926, but *Nerves* ran in 1924—but studio publicity cares little for precise chronology. Wedding licenses, however, don't lie: about six months after finalizing his divorce to Wife No. 1, he married Philips. Cue the stock market crash and the general decimation of Broadway, with many up-and-coming, hungry actors, Bogart included, making their way west in search of a decent wage in Hollywood. Bit roles, a contract with Fox, and more bit roles followed, but Bogart lacked the acting skills and coherent image to distinguish him from the hundreds of other young male contract players. In the early thirties, Fox was desperate for its own hunky, masculine leading man to compete with Gable, so it attempted to mold Bogart in Gable's image. It was a dismal failure: Bogart was too skinny, too angular; Columbia head Harry Cohn even told him to "go back to Broadway and stay there. We've shot you from every possible angle, and there isn't a single photogenic feature about you."

They tried to make him into a western hero, but he didn't know anything about horses. He was no romantic leading man, no strapping young working-class rabble-rouser. Even in his early thirties, he looked like an old man—or at least like a bad guy. But following the Hays office crackdown in the early thirties, gangster films were, at least temporarily, out of bounds. So he shuttled between Hollywood and Broadway, making ends meet and watching his marriage gradually disintegrate, until a Broadway producer cast him in *The Petrified Forest*—not as a handsome, sporting juvenile, but as a vengeful baddie. He wasn't the lead, but he made his mark.

Petrified Forest ran for a year, with such success that Warner Bros. bought the rights for a screen adaptation. The catch: Leslie Howard, who had starred in the stage production, was already attached as star and producer, and he insisted that Bogart be cast as well. Warner Bros. balked, attempting to put Edward G. Robinson, veteran gangster, in the role. Bogart relayed the information to Howard, who responded by telegramming head of studio Jack Warner: NO BOGART NO DEAL. Bogart got the part, and with his unshaven whiskers and gruff, uncompromising demeanor, he stole every scene he was in, grabbing enough attention that Warner Bros. offered him a contract—a no-frills, no-bonuses, no-options one, but a contract nonetheless.

Over the course of the thirties, Warner Bros. had developed a reputation as the studio of gritty realist films—of Edward G. Robinson and James Cagney—and the new, bad-guy Bogart was a perfect fit. But the studio was also known for its exploitative treatment of stars (against which both Cagney and Bette Davis would very publicly rebel), and it worked Bogart to the bone.

From 1936 to 1941, he starred in six or more films a year with little to no variation from this bad-guy archetype. With his screen persona firmly established, the Warner Bros. publicity office fashioned a profile to accentuate it. Key words: *menacing, independence, frankness,* and *simplicity*, combining to form a dark, urban form of masculinity that contrasted sharply with the likes of Clark Gable and other popular male stars of the day.

To achieve this image, the press downplayed his patrician background in favor of his juvenile delinquent past—getting kicked out of boarding school, being an ass in the navy, the inability to conform to societal expectations or buckle down and get a job. His name also became synonymous with villainy: he was "the outstanding bad man of motion pictures, a "meanie," and Hollywood's "new menacing man." Gossip columnist Grace Wilcox reported that her readers had been asking for months if she knew "Humphrey Bogart, the killer," confessing that she was too afraid to meet him. Fans even began to claim that he looked like famed gangster and "public enemy number one" John Dillinger, a resemblance that was picked up and recirculated in the gossip columns.

Bogart himself regaled columnists with tales of being mistaken for his on-screen persona: he went to nightclubs and was immediately surrounded by mid-level mob men promising to "go to bat" for him; a Hollywood nightspot refused service because his presence was making the other customers nervous. In an article for *Collier's*, appropriately titled "Tough On and Off," Bogart claimed to have taken a cue from one of his on-screen depictions, snatching the cigar of a bouncer who refused him entry, giving it a twist, and plopping it back in his mouth before entering the club, demanding a table for four in the front, and socking the guy who attempted to tell him otherwise, proclaiming "Take dis rat outta here."

Bombast? Likely. But it fit the bill. And given Bogart's avowed dislike of publicity and "phonies," it was easy to believe. But in case you thought he was just a jerk, there was an overwhelming sense of moral decency that underpinned all that frankness: he always defended the underdog and loathed "social injustice" in all of its forms, a point supported by his vocal support for African Americans in Hollywood. He was "proud" to have actress Lena Horne as his neighbor, proclaiming, "In the world of theater or any other phase of American life, the color of a man's skin should have nothing to do with his rights in a land built upon the self-evident fact that all men are created equal." He may have been a tough, but he came down on the side of justice.

And if all that gruffness wasn't masculine enough, Bogart hated everything fancy. He hated the Hollywood social scene; he hated pretense and "sloppy emotions." He called his house Liberty Hall because it was the only place he could get away from the "Hollywood hooey" and loathed dinner parties so fiercely that he removed the dining hall from his own home. He hated formal clothes, instead donning a consistent uniform of slacks, untucked shirts, and "sandal shoes." Even his food had to be straightforward: no gravy, no sauces, and no desserts covered in whipped cream—just well-cooked steak and chops and martinis, because, in his words, "I want to see what I eat."

The terseness bordering on crankiness further confirmed Bogart's on-screen persona. In the movies, he was a cold-blooded gangster with neither time nor sympathy for frivolity, excess, or emotion, and he demonstrated as much by gun or other forms of violence. Off-screen, that intolerance manifested itself in more legal yet equally convincing ways. He might not have had the imposing stature of Gary Cooper or the physical gravitas of Gable, but this was a man's man—a man who got things done, with little tolerance for anything that would distract him or otherwise temper his hard, brittle masculinity.

And you know what really cramped a hard man's style? Women. He hated working with "dames," as they "mess things up." "If I have to make love to dames in pictures I'll do it," he told one reporter, "but only as a business proposition." To his mind, the perfect world would be one where you could shrink a woman down, put her in your pocket, and take her out only when you needed her. He liked individual women—"they're quite necessary to me"—but refused to be tied to them in any way. He never called home with his whereabouts; he refused to say I love you, instead communicating affection by a smack on the behind. Words, especially romantic ones, "have no value to me at all."

How, then, did such a terse, self-proclaimed "ugly" man over the age of forty became Hollywood's leading sex symbol? Over the course of the next eight years, that stoic lack of romance calcified into a palpable, if ironic, hotness. At first, it was just a bit of bad-boy desirability.

The Petrified Forest brought him his early success, but it wasn't until *High Sierra* (1941), with Bogart as a desperate, wild-eyed convict on a doomed final heist, that he became a bona fide star. The same year, he played hard-boiled detective Sam Spade in the film adaptation of Dashiell Hammett's *The Maltese Falcon* (1941). *Falcon* was the first film of John Huston—who had penned the screenplay for *High Sierra* and quickly became one of Bogart's favored drinking companions—and, like *Sierra*, was a critical and financial success, earning three Oscar nominations, including one for Best Picture. It was also one of the first in a genre that would come to be called "film noir"—a black, dirty take on the gangster film, filled with the exact sort of ambiguity and terseness for which Bogart had become known.

Falcon also gave Bogart his first high-profile turn as an object of romance. In the movie, his character, Sam Spade, falls for Ruth Wonderly (Mary Astor), the woman who hires him, embroils him in the mystery of the film, and who, by film's end, is revealed, in classic femme fatale fashion, as a duplicitous, manipulative murderer. Like all film noir, the plot is somewhat emasculating—the hero, after all, is proven somewhat of a dupe. But the film also made Bogart less menacing and darkly handsome, with his trench coat and hat askew. Spade may not have gotten the girl at the end, but the film demonstrated his vulnerability to women—a vulnerability that made him all the more beguiling.

It wasn't as if Bogart had never been cast in a romantic role—among his dozens of gangster turns, he'd been given romantic storylines in "hillbilly musical" *Swing Your Lady* (1938) and *The Wagons Roll at Night* (1941). These were lead roles, but they were in B pictures—and had nothing of the exposure of *Falcon* or Bogart's next hit, *Casablanca* (1942). Today, *Casablanca* is a wartime classic, a film best known for its catchphrases ("Here's lookin' at you, kid") and conversion narrative, in which the resolutely independent Bogart is swayed by the anti-fascist cause. But at the time, it was sold as a "male melodrama"—essentially, a wartime, male-centered version of the female-directed "weepies" à la *Now, Voyager* (1941), in which female characters taste love but ultimately reject it for the greater good (usually family). In *Casablanca*, Rick gives up the love of his life in dramatic, heartrending, self-sacrificing fashion—all in the name of the greater Allied cause. It's "right," but that doesn't mean it doesn't elicit a bucket of tears.

The film was initially conceived of as a routine bit of genre fare, but it evolved into something else entirely. In addition to turning a significant profit and making a star out of Ingrid Bergman, it garnered nine Oscar nominations—including a nod for Bogart—and a win for Best Picture. It also made Bogart a sex symbol, to which he responded with typical candor: "I've been going along for forty-three years and they suddenly discover I've got sex appeal." He had been ascribed with sex appeal before—as early as 1937, *Motion Picture* was reporting that his "volcanic quality" was providing "the intriguing sort of danger with which the female of the species has ever enjoyed flirting"—but this was something different, something bigger, something Warner Bros. knew it could exploit.

Usually, Warner Bros. would've exploited that sex appeal with relationship gossip. But Bogart's home life was more unforgiving gangster and less vulnerable romance. When he was first hired at Warner Bros., he began an on-set romance with costar Mayo Methot. He was still married to second wife Mary Philips, but the two had been long distance for some time—when he spoke to *Photoplay* in the summer of 1937, he reported that the two were on "trial separation," explaining that they had agreed to a "modern marriage"—each was allowed to see whomever they liked, with no jealousy between them. Bogart, however, quickly discovered that he wasn't as "modern" as he thought. The tacit suggestion: he wasn't a philanderer! No matter that Philips had gone to the press claiming that Bogart's excuse for divorce was that he had found married life "monotonous"—all he really wanted was a normal marriage with a normal girl.

After the finalization of his divorce from Philips, he and Methot dated for a year before marrying on August 21, 1938. Methot agreed to give up acting, conceding to Bogart's contention that his former wives' careers had kept them from devoting themselves wholly to the marriage. So far, so romantic. He claimed that she was "perfectly content" to stay home and make house, yet her resentment grew like a cancer. She was obsessively jealous—one gossip columnist called her "the most possessive wife in Hollywood," and she refused to allow Bogart to even see the final cut of *Casablanca*, such was her jealousy of his beautiful young costar, Ingrid Bergman. They fought *constantly*—in public, in private, sober, drunk, and very drunk. A *Life* magazine profile used their fighting as a centerpiece, detailing how Methot, when angry, would regularly pick up a highball glass and throw it at Bogart's head. The brawls between the "Battling Bogarts" were so public, and so frequent, that they eventually became standard filler for gossip columns short on content.

The off-screen Bogart was distinctly at odds with his *Casablanca* image—but he wouldn't be for long. For Bogart, the year after *Casablanca* was filled with films already in production before the revelation of his sex appeal. He was a merchant marine dodging U-boats in *Action in the North Atlantic*, and he beat the Nazis, desert warfare–style, in *Sahara*. *Passage to Marseille*, released in February 1944, was an unmemorable reassemblage of *Casablanca*, reuniting Bogart with the film's director, Michael Curtiz, and the bulk of the remaining cast, save Bergman. The film that came next, *To Have and Have Not*, wasn't a melodrama. It didn't evoke tears or sorrow; it didn't make you feel for Bogart's loss or admire his self-sacrifice. Because Bogart, for the first time, had met his match, both on-screen and off.

Ernest Hemingway published *To Have and Have Not* in 1937. It was a loose, ill-formed book, especially compared with his other work, but Howard Hughes snatched up the film rights, selling them in the early forties to veteran director Howard Hawks, who turned to Warner Bros. to develop the film as a star vehicle for Bogart. After telling Hemingway that the original book was a "piece of junk," Hawks worked with him to significantly overhaul the script, bringing it down to its barest bones (rum running in the Caribbean by a conflicted yet moral hero) and building it back up, adding a backdrop of Vichy-occupied Martinique and other *Casablanca*-esque elements. And, of course, a love interest for Bogart.

According to well-circulated legend, Hawks had provisionally hired another young starlet, name withheld, to play the part. With the film still in the early stages of production, the "pert young thing" was proving difficult—so difficult that Hawks spent a significant amount of time complaining about her to his wife. His wife had a simple solution: ditch her—he could make *anyone* an ingénue. When the exasperated Hawks asked whom, exactly, she had in mind, she reached for the nearest magazine and pointed to the cover model: "Here. Here's one for you." It was the March 1943 cover of *Harper's Bazaar*, and the cover girl was a striking teen by the name of Betty Bacal.

Hawks contacted the magazine, obtained the name of the model, contacted her agent, and forgot about it—until she showed up at his office a week later. Bacal had basically no acting experience—a walk-on role on Broadway; a chance bit part—but Hawks saw something he could shape. He changed her name to Lauren Bacall, put her on personal contract for $250 a week, and went to work. He wanted to make her voice huskier, more distinctive and sexy, and had her read aloud for hours, intermittently screaming at the top of her lungs. He discovered she possessed an "instinctive balance"—the ability to look poised and on point, even when surprised—and taught her the fine points of how to "non-act." More to the point, he was making her into an appropriate foil for the sort of hard-boiled hero he envisioned for Bogart.

When Hawks first introduced Bogart and Bacall, Bogie purportedly told her, "I think we're going to have a lot of fun making this picture together, kid." The legitimacy of the quote matters less than the actual good time they had together, clearly evidenced on-screen. Bogart was forty-three, Bacall was nineteen, but the chemistry between them was crackling and real—a connection that couldn't be taught. She seemed his psychological equal. They were clear-eyed realists, with little tolerance for bullshit. Her character even goes by the masculine, no-nonsense name of Slim.

Mary Pickford writing at her desk, ca. 1918.
(Library of Congress, Prints and Photographs Division, LC-DIG-ppmsca-18840)

Pickford and husband Douglas Fairbanks in an undated photo.
(Library of Congress, Prints and Photographs Division, LC-DIG-gg-bain-30611)

Roscoe "Fatty" Arbuckle
in undated photograph.
(Library of Congress, Prints and
Photographs Division, LC-DIG-
ggbain-33071)

Arbuckle's first manslaughter trial. San Francisco, November 18, 1921.
(Library of Congress, Prints and Photographs Division, LC-USZ62-63393)

Mrs. Wallace Reid in Washington, D.C., attending a narcotics meeting
(with photo of Wallace Reid in the background).
(Library of Congress, Prints and Photographs Division, LC-DIG-hec-43044)

"It" girl Clara Bow.
(Library of Congress, Prints and Photographs Division, LC-USZ62-103883)

Rudolph Valentino in typical finery.
(Library of Congress, Prints and Photographs Division, LC-DIG-ggbain-38782)

Mae West, greeted in New York upon her return from Hollywood, ca. 1933. (Library of Congress, Prints and Photographs Division, LC-USZ62-111081)

Jean Harlow with husband Paul Bern.
(San Diego Air & Space Museum Archives)

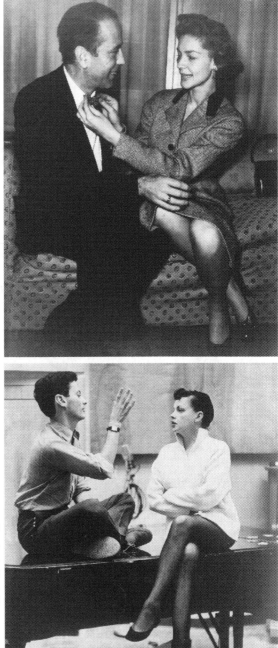

Lauren Bacall
straightens Humphrey
Bogart's tie, ca. 1951.
(Corbis)

Judy Garland rehearses
with Richard Avedon,
ca. 1956.
(Library of Congress, Prints
and Photographs Division,
LC-USZ62-137211)

Dorothy Dandridge, ca. 1954.
(Library of Congress, Prints and Photographs Division, LC-USZ62-109664)

Montgomery Clift and Elizabeth
Taylor in a publicity still
for *A Place in the Sun*, ca. 1951.
(Corbis)

Marlon Brando in the stage
production of *A Streetcar
Named Desire*, ca. 1948.
(Library of Congress, Prints and
Photographs Division, Carl Van Vechten
Collection, LC-USZ62-116614)

In their most famous scene together, Slim instructs Bogart's character, "You know you don't have to act with me, Steve. You don't have to say anything, and you don't have to do anything. Not a thing. Oh, maybe just whistle. You know how to whistle, don't you, Steve? You just put your lips together and . . . blow." Bogart remains seated throughout the scene, but Bacall stands tall, filmed in a manner that emphasizes the power differential—they may be equals when it comes to wit, but Bacall, with her sly, seductive eyes and languorous way of moving about the room, clearly has the upper hand. He was clearly intoxicated by her—an intoxication that spread to the entire audience.

To Have and Have Not was to be a run-of-the-mill release, a war picture of the same caliber as the last three in which Bogart had starred. But when Warner Bros. president Jack Warner saw how people reacted to the two leads, and the palpable connection between them, while the film was in previews, he decided to delay its release until the fall—enough time to build up a massive publicity campaign for the film itself and for Bacall, whose contract Warner Bros. had immediately purchased from Hawks. When the film was released in October 1944, it coincided with an onslaught of publicity, including a close-up of a sultry Bacall on the cover of *Life* paired with a multipage spread on the film. Objectively speaking, the film is somewhat slight—but it's also the kind in which the plot is so clearly secondary to the performances. Warner Bros. announced that a second collaboration between the two actors was in the works, ready to promote them as the next big thing in on-screen pairings.

The only thing that would've made better publicity would've been an actual relationship between Bogart and Bacall. And, indeed, according to later reports, a romance did begin during the filming, with all traces assiduously erased lest it erupt into scandal. Bogart was still very much married to Mayo Methot, and Bacall was inconveniently twenty-three years his junior. In order to clear the way for both the actual relationship and the publicity blitz—and millions of dollars in potential film revenue—that a sanctioned romance could provide, Bogart, Bacall, and the publicity office took several carefully orchestrated steps.

First, just a week after the release of the film, Bogart announced his intent to seek a divorce. Given the extensively chronicled disputes between him and Methot, it was no great surprise; indeed, the *Chicago Daily Times* headlined the divorce as the end of a "six-year battle." At this point, some must have speculated about the timing, especially in light of the way he seemed to be interacting with his young costar on-screen—not to mention the fact that Bacall had started appearing at his side at various Hollywood nightclubs—but the press remained mum. An October profile of Bacall, published in *Collier's*, admitted that Bogart had been kind to her on the set before being blown away by her acting, while a gossip columnist reported that he thought a "great deal" of Bacall's abilities and was thrilled to be working with her a second time. But there was no mention of a relationship, burgeoning or otherwise.

Bogart allowed several months to pass, assuring gossip columnist Sheilah Graham that the divorce was "definite" on January 15, 1945, before retreating to the Ohio farm of a longtime friend, Louis Bromfield. By that time, the rumor engine had garnered steam: Hedda Hopper playfully reported that while Bogart was headed east with Bromfield, Bacall was likewise headed east with Howard Hawks, leaving it ambiguous as to whether or not they were headed east to the same location. Two weeks later, Bogart told the press that he had "signified his intentions" to Bacall. The next day, both stars were in New York—they'd arrived on separate trains, but they were staying in the same hotel, albeit on separate floors. As the *Boston Globe* reported, the press found Bogart "sitting disconsolately alone in his shirt-sleeves," admitting that he had nothing to say until Bacall made the next move.

It was all very un-Bogart, but it had the ring of a man desperately in love. Bacall never made an official statement as to whether she'd accepted Bogart's "intentions," but during their time in New York, she gave more than sixty interviews, satiating the press, keeping them on her side, saying a lot while revealing very little. Bogart made sure that the couple was never photographed together; when one lucky photog caught them outside a function for navy veterans, Bogart personally visited the navy publicity offices and ensured the photo never saw the light of day.

The two absconded to Bromfield's farm, where they hid out for three weeks before the gossip hounds arrived during the second week of March 1945. Two months later, with the divorce from Methot finalized, the pair were wed in a simple, three-minute ceremony on the farm, with Bogart reportedly greeting his wife with, "Hello, baby," and Bacall sighing, "Oh goody!" after the pair's first wedded kiss. They seemed the picture of wedded bliss. He gifted her a bracelet with a whistle, evocative of their famous exchange from *To Have and Have Not*, attached; when the two stepped off the train after their honeymoon, reporters begged her to blow it. "Shall I, honey?" asked Bacall. "Oh, that's Van Johnson stuff. But go right ahead." And the fans *loved* it. Hundreds of screaming bobby-soxers awaited their train, and two months after the marriage, Bogart's fan mail had increased 38 percent—one of the studio's primary indicators of fan approval, tantamount to an official sanction of his relationship with Bacall. Apart from a bit of squawking from Bacall's long-estranged father, who claimed it was a "cheap publicity stunt," there wasn't a whiff of scandal.

The lack of scandal can be traced to the ways in which the relationship—and its buildup—was "naturalized" by both *To*

Have and Have Not and extratextual publicity. Because Bogart and Warner Bros. had kept evidence of the affair under wraps until his divorce from Methot could be announced, his relationship with Bacall seemed to develop naturally—the *result* of their on-screen chemistry, not the cause of it. Bogart's vulnerability, their cross-country adventures, the will-they-won't-they turned the discourse around their romance into its own romantic comedy, complete with quips from Bogart and a wedding at the end. As for concern over the gap in their ages, it's not that it went unmentioned—in February, Hedda Hopper quipped, "If Lauren Bacall eventually becomes Mrs. Bogart, there'll only be a little matter of twenty-six years between them." If the two had met in Hollywood and started dating, it would've been a different situation, one that reeked of lechery and could have permanently affected their images. Instead, their introduction as a couple was within the narrative of a film—a film in which they seemed not only believable but, again, *natural* as a couple.

Bacall's character in *To Have and Have Not*, Slim, was clearly meant for Bogart's character. Publicity thus had to frame the "real" Bacall as equally meant for the "real" Bogart—no insignificant task, given the well-established tenets of his image. Yet she was a complete unknown; her image was raw material, just ready to be shaped in a manner complementary to Bogart's. While several Bacall profiles were published before their relationship went public, all were shaped by Warner Bros. publicity, with the knowledge of the secret relationship and the possibility of it becoming public.

Like Bogart, she was a native New Yorker; unlike Bogart, she was from the Bronx, the child of immigrants, with little of the privilege that accompanied his childhood. Her father left the family, and Bacall and her mother formed a close bond and survived on their own. She attended drama school, which is how she landed her walk-on bit in a Broadway play, but she attracted no special attention. An editor at *Harper's Bazaar* purportedly spotted her "prowling gracefully" into a speakeasy and gave her a modeling job; she spent the next three years bumping between modeling gigs and agitating for parts in plays that never came. People were seldom nice and were more often dismissive—which, at least according to *Life*, is how she developed her tough exterior. Circumstances made Bacall into a survivor—she paid her dues, just like Bogart, even if it was for slightly less time.

From the start, Bacall was framed in sexual terms. She was the female counterpart to Bogart's noir hero—the femme fatale, a woman who uses her sexual power to inveigle the men around her. Her body is described in exotic language brimming with connotations of danger: her eyes are "slanted" or "half-mast," her movements are "slinky" and "sultry"; she's a "cinema siren," a "glamorous menace," "provocative," "insolent," and "dripping with intrigue." At least four articles penned during the lead-up to their marriage place her as the latest in a long, distinguished line of cinematic vamps—women like Theda Bara, Marlene Dietrich, and Hedy Lamarr—who used sex appeal to milk their men dry. Even her studio-given nickname, the Look, was intended to evoke the insinuating way in which she stared men down.

Bogart and Bacall's next film together, *The Big Sleep* (1945), was a critical and popular success, wiping away the memory of her less-than-stellar performance in *Confidential Agent* (1945). They starred in two additional films together—*Dark Passage* (1947) and *Key Largo* (1948)—solidifying the suggestion that they brought out the best in each other. Both proved equally insubordinate to Jack Warner, refusing to star in material they believed unworthy: Bogart's record-breaking twelve suspensions were topped only by Bacall's thirteen. Bogart was an unspoken opponent of red-mongering; Bacall was, too. When the pair went to Washington,

D.C., to protest the House Un-American Activities Committee scrutiny of Hollywood, both weathered the backlash, both apologized, and the 1948 *Photoplay* article "I'm No Communist," penned by Bogart, featured a picture of him alongside Bacall.

Instead of fighting, they joked around, complimented each other, and made babies. Bogart praised Bacall's independence, honesty, sense of humor, and lack of jealousy—attributes that he had long emphasized as essential components of his own personality. Bacall, fashion model, turned into Bacall, down-to-earth mother, preferring simple clothes in grays and blacks, even in summer, and refusing to wear makeup at home. They had big boxers, with whom they regularly posed for pictures, and a lengthy *Saturday Evening Post* profile posed them making faces and joking around on their front steps. In 1951, Bogart wrote an editorial for the *Los Angeles Times* claiming "Love Begins at 40!" while Bacall told *Look* "Why I Hate Young Men," complete with ten examples of why the only men who interested her were "all born at the turn of the century."

Bogart had always hated the social scene, so with Bacall at his side, they made their own—their Holmby Hills house was in the fancy section of town, but it was still "as informal as the Bogarts," clearly designed to be lived in, and lived in well. Around 1955, whether of their devising or the press's, the Bogarts and their tight group of neighbors—Judy Garland, her husband Sid Luft, David Niven, Frank Sinatra, and a rotating cast of others who loved to drink and be not fancy—became known as the Rat Pack, with Bogart as their unofficial leader and Bacall as their "den mother." They were "fun-loving bohemians," according to the press, "who lived the kind of life actors are supposed to live."

Today, "the Rat Pack" has become shorthand for the drunken antics of a group of men behaving like children; then, it was a way of distinguishing Bogart, Bacall, and the rest of the "pack" from the over-manipulated, overly Hollywood likes of Debbie Reynolds, Rock Hudson, and the other young stars who Bogie crankily described as "all alike . . . I see 'em all the time and I can't tell one from the other." They drank, they sang, they made ruckuses at nightclubs, they played practical jokes on one another, and when Bogie was too far gone on whiskey, Bacall was the only one who could keep him in check. The endurance of their marriage, and their apparent contentment and continued compatibility, was a testament to the legitimacy of their publicity. Even though neither would've ever said it aloud, the press suggested it for them: their love was *destined*.

When Bogart died on January 14, 1957, from cancer of the esophagus, it was tragic, but it was also to be expected—more than any other star of the period, he refused to hide his hard-living ways. And while he left behind a young, beautiful wife and two small children, going out in his prime seemed, in many ways, a fitting end for the man who despised sentimentalism and rejected artifice. To the end, Bogart was riffing on the press reports on his illness and trading barbs with everyone around him; his last words to Bacall, before slipping into a coma, were "Good-bye, kid." It was a narrative of death that matched his narrative in life, and when journalist Alistair Cooke penned his remembrance, his words pinpointed the Bogart appeal: he "lived in a town crowded by malign poseurs, fake ascetics, studio panders, the pimps of the press. From all of them he was determined to keep his secret; the rather shameful secret, in the realistic world we inhabit, of being a gallant man and an idealist." Bogart had played the role of cranky old man, but for anyone with eyes to see—his wife, his children, his friends, the most perceptive of his fans—he was generous, fiercely moral, and even a romantic, albeit a reluctant, recalcitrant one.

Who knows what Bogart's image would have become without

Bacall? No other woman, save perhaps Katharine Hepburn, played as magnetically beside him. No one made him seem more desirable, more young and vital. Without the third act of his life, he'd lack the softness that fatherhood brings, the freshness that attends a renaissance of love. Which isn't to suggest that Bacall made Bogart a sucker or a sweetheart, or, in all truthfulness, altered his image in any substantial way. Rather, she accentuated it, deepened the myth, and helped transform the story of his life from one of grit and suffering to one of intrigue and revelry. Without Bacall, Bogart was just another gangster; with her, and the story of their romance, their names, forever linked, became iconic: *Bogart and Bacall*, the First Couple of Film Noir, and the standard against which all other attempts at filmic chemistry would be forever measured.

BROKEN BY THE SYSTEM

At the peak of the studio system, Hollywood stardom was engineered to be every girl's fantasy: the glamour, the clothes, the handsome costars. And that dream was the studio's most valuable product, as the desire that underpinned it could be funneled directly into the purchase of movie tickets. There wasn't much to disprove that dream—even the faded stars of the silent age, such as Mary Pickford and Gloria Swanson, still seemed resplendent in their spoils, as glamorous as ever. With the vivid exception of Clara Bow, the Hollywood of the 1930s seemed to be a healthy, happy place to be, a giant playground for Shirley Temple and a sprawling dance floor for Ginger Rogers.

But as World War II drew to a close, the studios began to transform. The so-called Paramount Decrees, issued by the federal government to uphold antitrust practices, required the major studios to divest themselves of the theater chains that had helped them monopolize the industry. Over the next ten years, the studio system would disassemble itself and, in so doing, forever alter the way movies were made, funded, and distributed, as well as how the stars of those movies were groomed, cultivated, and maintained.

Amid this process, the veneer of the perfect, glamorous Hollywood—and its perfect, happy stars—began to crack. It wasn't just that the stars were fooling around or, like Robert Mitchum, smoking dope; it's that the studio itself was revealed as a factory, its workers miserable, overworked, and broken. The most dramatic proof of this unseemly underbelly was Judy Garland, who effectively grew up on the MGM lot and whose continual struggles with drugs, alcohol, and men were framed as the direct result of overwork and psychological abuse at the hands of her employer.

But the reorganization of Hollywood wasn't all bad—it made way for independent productions, including those that targeted "niche" audiences, paving the way for the first wave of African American stars, including Harry Belafonte, Sidney Poitier, and Dorothy Dandridge. With her role in *Carmen Jones*, Dandridge rocketed to fame, only to watch her stardom dwindle to nothing over the course of the next four years. Like Garland, Dandridge was broken by the system that built her, only in ways shaded with insidious racism and systemic forms of discrimination. When Garland died at the age of forty-seven, she was trumpeted as a survivor; when Dandridge died at forty-two, she barely made the papers. Her story, paired with Garland's, provides a lucid picture of an industry that was the stuff not of dreams, but of nightmares—a sentiment that would make it easy to celebrate the stars' emancipation from the studios and tolerate the bloated salaries and extravagant demands that followed.

CHAPTER TEN

Judy Garland: Ugly Duckling

If Humphrey Bogart was seemingly never young, then Judy Garland was never old. She began her Hollywood career at age thirteen, played one of cinema's most iconic girls at age seventeen, and became MGM's top female star before the age of twenty—and there she stayed in the world's imagination, a perpetual adolescent, overflowing with emotion, angst, self-doubt, and bad decisions. Forever "the little girl with the big voice," Garland was a singular talent: a triple threat who could sing, dance, and act. But in a studio filled with glamour girls, Garland was always the ugly duckling—unsexy, ungainly, and always too fat or too skinny, or so the studios, and the press, told her. She was one of the first public figures to be openly analyzed—by gossip columnists, by fans, by ex-lovers—in the newly fashionable style of Freud, and her mercurial rises and falls, romances and breakdowns, provided press fodder for more than two decades.

Was her tragic life the fault of MGM? Her overbearing, manipulative mother? Or the studio system and fame at large? Garland was the first public victim of stardom—and certainly not the last. It isn't that other stars of the era weren't turned neurotic or psychologically damaged by the process of stardom—it's that no star did so as publicly, and as sympathetically, as Garland did. As MGM and the golden era of Hollywood faded to a memory, Garland, aged beyond her years, held together by sheer tenacity, was evidence of its dark underside.

Garland's rise to stardom coincided with the general surge of "juvenile" stars in the late thirties, a group that included her constant film companion, Mickey Rooney, along with soprano singing sensation Deanna Durbin, teenage glamour girl Lana Turner, and Shirley Temple, the cherub who, at least according to popular narrative, single-handedly rescued Fox Studios from the Depression. But none of those stars parlayed their teen stardom into quite the career, or success, that Garland did, in part because Garland's talent was never rooted in her appearance on the screen so much as the sheer power of her voice. But due to her longevity in Hollywood, the story of her youth, discovery, and early life at MGM were told and retold to the point of mythology.

According to this mythology, Garland was born, like many of her characters, "in a trunk"—a showbiz way of saying that her parents were entertainers and constantly on the road. In actuality, Garland, given name Frances Gumm, wasn't born on the road, but she was born to a family of entertainers—her mother was an actress, singer, and pianist, while her father owned the theater in the small Minnesota town where her family had settled. When Garland was three years old and the rest of her family were appearing in an amateur night, she chose a song, "Jingle Bells," to sing in front of the crowd. According to well-worn legend, her public debut was quite literally pitch-perfect. But after singing through the song once, she just kept going, eventually working her way through five verses and three choruses before being ushered off the stage. With this story, Garland is framed, from the start, as both a natural talent and a tenacious artist with uncharacteristic endurance.

The rest of her early childhood was spent as part of a traveling act with her two sisters, going by the unflattering moniker of the Gumm Sisters. Sometimes they'd seem to be on the brink of making it—they even appeared in a series of Vitaphone film shorts in the late twenties—only to find themselves with one egg and a loaf of moldy bread with no funds to travel onward. They were continually rejected—by crowds, managers, critics—which, depending on the gossip columnist, was either how Garland acquired the thick skin necessary to make it in Hollywood . . . or how she first developed the inferiority complex that would plague her for the rest of her life.

At some point in the mid-thirties, the Gumm Sisters became the much more pleasant sounding Garland Sisters. The family, at this point settled in California, took a vacation to a resort on Lake Tahoe, where Garland eventually ended up singing for songwriter Lew Brown (some stories have it as Harry Axt) and a chance agent, who helped set up a screen test for her at MGM. According to one version, the agent asked Garland's mother, then and there, why she hadn't put her daughter in pictures before—to which she replied, "I've never thought she was pretty enough." The anecdote is clearly fabricated, as Garland, at this point, had already appeared on-screen in the Vitaphone shorts, but the import remained: even her own mother didn't believe she had a face for the big screen.

But the magnitude of Garland's talent made her face somewhat inconsequential. A week later, when called to the MGM lot, she captivated the audience. She was fresh, natural, and most of all, enthusiastic—so much so that studio head Louis B. Mayer was called in to listen. Mayer signed her on the spot, making her the only star, at least according to legend, to ever be signed without a screen test. Of course, MGM most likely had access to her prior on-screen footage, but the story, along with reports that she'd had only a single singing lesson her entire life, was so much more Hollywood: Judy Garland, the girl whose talent was so profound it didn't even need refining.

Garland's "first" on-screen appearance was in the short film *Every Sunday* (1936), alongside opera wunderkind Deanna Durbin, who, at that point, was under contract to MGM. Mayer was apparently trying to figure out if he needed two girl singers on the studio's roster, and the film was meant as a sort of barometer—but by the time he'd made the decision to keep both girls, the option on Durbin's contract had lapsed, leaving her to take a lucrative deal with Universal. Durbin rocketed to fame, yet MGM struggled to find Garland's niche. She made a mark in *Broadway Melody of 1938* (1937), but her career was nothing in comparison to Durbin's tremendous and immediate success.

In 1937, MGM paired Garland with fellow trouper—i.e., ex-vaudevillian—Mickey Rooney in the B film *Thoroughbreds Don't Cry* (1937). The pair proved excellent foils for each other, and Garland was slated for the next in the popular *Hardy Family* series, *Love Finds Andy Hardy* (1938). Crucially, love didn't find Rooney and Garland; instead, she played the permanently friend-zoned sidekick while Hardy fell for the comely Lana Turner. In a theme that would stretch through other *Hardy* appearances and pervade the rest of her films, her songs are all lovelorn: "Nobody" (*Strike Up the Band*, 1940), "But Not for Me" (*Girl Crazy*, 1943), "I'm Always Chasing Rainbows" (*Ziegfeld Girl*, 1941).

Garland's status as undesirable ugly duckling on-screen mirrored stories of her "real life" awkwardness: an article in *Silver Screen* reported that at parties, Garland was a continual outcast; as she related to her mother, "I heard one of Deanna Durbin's friends say, 'She'll never be an actress! She just thinks she can sing. She's too fat. Imagine her being a movie star!'" She was called ungraceful and Little Leather Lungs, the butt of the joke and forever on love's sideline. With *Love Finds Andy Hardy* and the press that followed, Garland's ugly duckling status became a ground note of her image and yet another method for authors to explain her difficulties with love and life in general.

While her contemporaries were gradually transitioning into teenage roles, Garland was cast in the role that would define her for the rest of her career, as Dorothy in *The Wizard of Oz* (1939). The character of Dorothy is what we'd now call a "tween"—the awkward age right before pubescence, emphasized by her gingham frock, braids, and unadorned face. The part was much younger than Garland's actual age, but she fit so perfectly—and acted the fears and emotions of a curious, fearful, yet brave child so winningly—that she won an Academy Award for Best Performance by a Juvenile. *Oz* also featured her rendition of "Over the Rainbow," a song that would become her signature piece in the onstage performances that dominated the second half of her career. For all its hopefulness and poignancy, "Over the Rainbow" would forever link Garland to the image of yearning girlhood.

After shooting *Oz*, MGM re-paired Garland with Rooney for *Babes in Arms* (1939), essentially a *Hardy Family* picture by another name. As press for *Oz* built, the studio sent Garland and Rooney on a nationwide tour to ballyhoo *Babes*, attracting mobs of bobbysoxers wherever they went. The movie made $3.3 million—even more than *Oz*. When the nation's exhibitors voted on the most profitable stars of 1940, Rooney came in at number one, with Garland at number ten. It might seem a dubious honor, but she was one of only two female stars in the top ten, second only to Bette Davis—all before her twentieth birthday.

The fan magazines and gossip columnists ate it up. Garland—or her handlers at MGM—provided excellent, mercurial, impassioned copy, much more exciting than the staid, controlled narratives of adult Hollywood stars. According to press portraits from the period, she was a stereotypical female teen: she *loved* boys and felt every emotion acutely. But just in case the public thought that the young Garland was oversexed, publicity framed her as thoroughly unsexual. A crush, like her reported admiration for Bob Hope and Laurence Olivier, was one thing; physical action was quite another: she told one interviewer that she "hated" necking, another that she didn't even *believe* in it. When Sheilah Graham brought up the topic, Garland shuddered, exclaiming, "Girls look so unattractive after a necking session! I've seen them with lipstick all over their faces and mascara running down their eyes. It looks awful!" In some interviews, she'd vow that she wasn't even interested in boys; in others, she'd admit that she goes on friendly dates, where she might receive a good-night kiss, but if a boy went in for a second, she'd refuse to see him again. She didn't go to nightclubs or gallivant around town—according to Garland, boys came to her house, where they sat in her music room and listened to symphony records: "Now that's real fun!"

All this studio-approved publicity was, at least in part, intended to make Garland appeal to the lovesick teens of America—the same teens who had made her such a moneymaker. The problem, however, was that once she was firmly established as a stereotypical, desexualized teenage girl, it proved nearly impossible to separate her from that image, even as the "real" Judy Garland decided to get around. She had publicly admitted her affection for handsome bandleader Artie Shaw, and Shaw seems to have encouraged it, but the two were by no means a couple. But then he eloped with fellow MGM star Lana Turner in February 1940, and it was like *Love Finds Andy Hardy* all over again.

At the same time, Garland was in the early throes of what would be a lifelong, thoroughly publicized battle with her weight. In November 1939, Graham reported that Garland's lunch was a meager three spoonfuls of soup; without regular assurance that she was, indeed, looking slimmer, she refused to eat anything at all. Of course, Garland was never fat—she had a big chest with a big diaphragm, and doctors assured MGM that she was as "strong as a small horse." But she was never stick thin, and the camera added poundage; studio minders, including Mayer himself, insisted that she "reduce." When she attempted to order a normal lunch at the MGM canteen, the waitress would bring her a bowl of soup and a plate of lettuce.

These aren't hidden anecdotes, revealed years later—they were in the press *at the time*. In other words, Garland watched as the world watched her, scrutinizing every appearance. The gossip columnists only fueled the process: in 1940, Graham reported that Garland wasn't feeling well, with a look in her eyes that said "no more dieting." Graham noted that she hoped Garland would stick to that maxim, yet persisted in reporting on her weight on nearly every encounter. A piece in the *Washington Post* used the headline JUDY REDUCES, THEN CELEBRATES to trumpet her "new sylph-like figure," while the *Los Angeles Times* outlined her "one-day liquid diet" to lose weight fast. Years later, it would become public knowledge that MGM was giving Garland, Rooney, and other teen stars amphetamines to keep up their energy during demanding, exhausting shoots—and then barbiturates to help them sleep, fueling borderline drug addiction that would only further amplify Garland's issues with her weight. At the time, though, she was just the plump ugly duckling who couldn't get her body under control.

After the disappointment of Artie Shaw, Garland rebounded with another bandleader, ten years her senior, named Dave Rose. Rose was bad news from the start: his divorce from comedienne Martha Raye, finalized in May 1940, had culminated in Raye's front page declaration of Rose's "extreme cruelty" during their marriage. The divorce was too fresh, Rose was too old, and MGM worked arduously to shut down the romance—or at least prevent public knowledge of its existence. A plant in Cal York's gossip column, on newsstands in October 1940, claimed that MGM was "breathing relief" over the end of their romance, but a month later, Graham reported that Garland was "saving her dances" for Rose, admitting that her crushes on Oscar Levant and Robert Stack had been just as "violent."

The public reacted poorly. These rumors began circulating just a year after Garland's turn as Dorothy—it was like watching your kid sister go on a date for the first time, only that date was with a much older, divorced guy. But Garland couldn't stay single forever. A *Movie-Radio Guide* article chided upset readers, instructing them to "get over the idea she's just a little girl" and actually compare her dating activities to those of other eighteen-year-olds. In light of this reaction, MGM demanded that Garland and Rose wait a year to marry. The studio couldn't delay the seemingly inevitable, but it could try and shape her image away from Dorothy and toward adulthood.

The results were awkward. Garland's first on-screen kiss, in *Little Nellie Kelly* (1940), was "most embarrassing," according to her costar, George Murphy, who said it felt like being "a hillbilly with a child bride." And her first attempt at quasi-glamour, in *Ziegfeld Girl*, fell flat. At this point in Hollywood history, the notion of glamour was strongly linked with sexuality and womanliness. A girl can't be glamorous, but a woman can—and all the so-called glamour girls of Hollywood (Joan Crawford, Hedy Lamarr, Lana Turner) were also stars whose images were defined by sexuality. But Garland was publicly established as the antithesis of glamorous: she pined for it, telling Graham, "All my life, I've wanted to be a glamour girl. Is there any hope for me?"

With an image so firmly linked to notions of innocence and girlhood, the answer was no. In *Ziegfeld Girl*, Garland played the role of a chorus girl hopeful alongside Lamarr and Turner. Lamarr and Turner were hired for their looks; Garland was hired for her vaudeville ability. While Lamarr and Turner got gorgeous gowns and sexy plot lines, Garland, by contrast, was clearly still a girl: she lived with her father, and her costumes remained childlike. She and her potential love interest behaved like little more than friends, going off for milk shakes while the other two stars slunk around the nightclub with glasses of champagne. Presumably prompted by the studio, Sheilah Graham asserted that Garland "stole" the entire film, claiming her legs were "the prettiest in town." But proof otherwise was on the screen for all to see.

On May 29, 1941, Garland and Rose announced their engagement, but the wedding was still on hold while MGM enlisted the most moralizing of the gossip columnists, Louella Parsons, to sanction and sanitize the romance. Parsons insisted that rumors of Garland's role in the separation of Rose and Raye were completely unfounded, claiming that Raye's recent remarriage proved as much. She likewise painted the first of many portraits of companionate romance: Rose liked Garland because she was "fresh and unspoiled" with "great sweetness," while Garland loved Rose's dignity and the fact that, as an older man, "he talked sense instead of the slang of the young generation." It was all a bit suspect—Rose, for one, sounded somewhat lecherous, and Garland sounded like a square—but the ugly duckling had found love at last.

Yet on July 28, 1941, Garland and Rose surprised (and infuriated) the studio by eloping in Las Vegas. The studio passive-aggressively responded by refusing to allow Garland a honeymoon, insisting she return to the set to continue filming. But Garland was unfazed: as she told the press, "This is no ordinary Hollywood marriage. It is the result of a wonderful romance of two years and it's the real thing." No matter that that statement dated their romance to before Rose's divorce from Raye—now they were man and wife, and the studio would have to promote them accordingly.

The MGM publicity office thus begrudgingly changed gears, flooding the fan magazines with pieces singing their praises and promise as a couple. *Modern Screen* trumpeted their "common language" of music, emphasizing, in a bit of revisionist history, that their relationship had, to the point of their marriage, been so honorable that they "shamed gossip-mongers into silence." Rose, as *Screen Guide* suggested, was kind of a weird guy—but that only made him more of a match for Garland. Their love was "a true rarity."

Over the next two years, MGM continued its attempts to navigate the line between the on-screen Garland (cute, awkward, unsexy) and the off-screen Garland (married, "grown-up," implicitly sexual). In the weeks immediately following the wedding, she was back on-screen with Rooney in *Life Begins for Andy Hardy* (1941). This time, she and Rooney were both ostensibly "grown-up," but the *Hardy* narrative automatically reasserted her as a childlike kid sister, certainly no object of desire. The dissonance was so acute that the *Washington Post* published a piece titled "Judy Garland Is Two Persons, More or Less, Since Marrying," claiming that by day, she played the role of a high school girl, complete with "puffy sleeves" and "puppy quarrels" with Rooney, while by night, she "puffs at a cigarette," goes to the nightclubs dressed in furs and silks, and hangs out with Lana Turner.

MGM was forced to give up the dream of a forever-young Garland. *For Me and My Gal* (1942) was touted as her first adult role—she even "got" Gene Kelly's character at film's end—but it was a worn-out claim, as her turns in *Love Finds Andy Hardy* and *Strike Up the Band* (1940) had both been publicized similarly. She was given the "glamour treatment" in *Presenting Lily Mars* (1943), with a visibly made-up face and dyed hair, but her overall look remained stubbornly childlike. It's no accident that the most memorable performance in the film—"Caro Nome"—is a hilarious send-up of the exotic, over-the-top nightclub performance. She was winsome and charismatic and a pleasure to watch, but a glamour girl she most emphatically was not. It was in the overexcited way she walked, the ebullience of the performance: she keenly experienced the world around her, which put her clearly at odds with the cool, composed sexuality of her glamorous contemporaries.

Amid all this confusing image manipulation, overwork, on-and-off again MGM-facilitated drug use, and yo-yo dieting, Garland found herself pregnant in the fall of 1942. When the *Los Angeles Examiner* asserted as much in a November gossip column, it set the MGM machinery in motion. The brief mention wasn't necessarily scandalous—columnists hinted at pregnancy constantly, much in the manner of our contemporary "baby bump" watches—but MGM's stance was firm: Garland could not have a baby. In addition to making future adolescent roles implausible, a pregnancy would take her out of production for a year. The MGM fixers, in collaboration with Garland's mother, arranged for her to have a behind-doors abortion before she even had the chance to tell her husband.

Of course, none of this was common knowledge, but it took its toll on Garland's young marriage. Rumors of marital unrest had been swirling since the summer of 1942, and on January 25, 1943, Garland and Rose announced their intention to separate. The separation would last more than a year. Even when she announced her intention to file for divorce, on January 10, 1944, the press still hinted at a potential reconciliation—but these plants were likely a means of shielding speculation surrounding Garland and very married director Joseph Mankiewicz, whom, according to legend, Louis B. Mayer fired from MGM in order to put a stop to their dalliance.

By the time the divorce from Rose went through, Garland was already filming *Meet Me in St. Louis* (1944), a musical set amid the buildup to the 1904 World's Fair, directed by Vincente Minnelli. Minnelli had been hired by Arthur Freed, head of the famed Freed Unit at MGM and responsible for the studio's trademark musicals, in which Garland featured prominently. Minnelli had first encountered Garland while directing a music number for *Strike Up the Band* in 1940, but *Meet Me in St. Louis* was only his second film as primary director. Garland told Freed she didn't want to do the picture, as her character seemed a clear regression to more childish, less glamorous parts. Even after she was convinced, she quarreled on set with both Freed and Minnelli.

But the results were magnificent. *St. Louis* went on to gross more than any other MGM film to date, save its stake in the coproduction of *Gone with the Wind*. It washed away any unpleasantness surrounding Garland's divorce, but even more important, the film itself made Garland look *stunning*. Dressed in high-necked turn-of-the-century costumes, Garland didn't look glamorous, per se, but with the rich Technicolor and Minnelli's deft direction, she looked, at last, womanly, and at home in her own skin.

At some point during the filming, Garland realized as much: she was "so taken by [Minnelli's] sensitivity and understanding," according to *Modern Screen*, that she "couldn't help but fall in love." She insisted that Minnelli take over for Fred Zinnemann as director of *The Clock* (1945), her first dramatic, non-singing role, and kindled (or rekindled, depending on the source) a romance with him. This time around, the romance was wholly sanctioned by the studio: Minnelli was a known and reliable commodity, and when the pair married on June 15, 1945, Mayer was there to give the bride away. After a long California honeymoon, the pair returned to the set, where Garland was slated to begin production of *Till the Clouds Roll By* (1946). She discovered she was pregnant, but the studio had a solution: they'd simply have Minnelli, with whom she worked the best, direct all of her scenes and musical numbers, ensuring that the film would wrap before her pregnancy stalled production. The plan worked, and Garland gave birth to a daughter, Liza, in March, while *Clouds*, released in December, was a runaway success.

As the film's release approached, rumors of Garland's ill health began to percolate. Decades later, it would become obvious that she had been suffering from postpartum depression, but at the time, she was simply reported as faint and weary in public. In June, she met with *Los Angeles Times* columnist Edwin Schallert to defuse the building rumors. In the months after Liza's birth, she simply hadn't been "up to snuff," but now she was the happiest she'd ever been. But the production of her first film post-pregnancy, *The Pirate*, costarring Gene Kelly and directed by Minnelli, was turbulent. Whereas Minnelli's direction had once been a balm to Garland's anxieties, now they inflamed them—the two warred over her reliance on prescription drugs, a point that was, at this time, not public. The studio couldn't hide that the production was behind schedule, with Garland missing more than half of the scheduled shooting days.

In July 1947, she suffered the first in a series of high-profile nervous breakdowns. On July 17, Hedda Hopper opened her column with the blunt announcement that Garland's breakdown-induced absence would leave a huge hole in the MGM production schedule. A month later, she reported that Garland was "resentful" about her forced trip to a New England sanitarium, making claims that she wasn't sick, then or in the past. Hopper's terse comment: "Well she certainly was the last time I talked to her."

It was the beginning of Garland's long downward spiral. She

muscled through *Easter Parade* (1948) but broke down again during the filming of *The Barkleys of Broadway*. MGM replaced her with Ginger Rogers, put her on suspension, and let it be very publicly known that she was on doctor-prescribed three-month rest. Garland made it through the production of *In the Good Old Summertime* (1949), featuring the first appearance of then-three-year-old Liza, without major incident, but she was using drugs, including morphine, drinking heavily, and suffering from debilitating migraines. Her marriage was in shambles, and MGM was barely holding the pieces of her stardom together. And yet she was still enormously popular: in a time when MGM was attempting to figure out a formula for the future, Garland, for all of her problems, was a surefire moneymaker. She was difficult, but she was worth it.

That changed during the filming of *Annie Get Your Gun* (1950). MGM slotted Garland as the star and Busby Berkeley as her director, but Garland, who had endured Berkeley's exacting, arguably cruel directing style in the *Babes* trilogy, refused to work with him. MGM stood firm and the film began production, but Garland protested by being habitually late and quarrelsome, and periodically refusing to show up at all. When, on May 11, 1949, she was chastised for yet another late appearance, she stormed off the set and refused to return. MGM suspended her yet again. This time, however, Hopper was on her side. On the front page of the *Los Angeles Times*, she emphasized Garland's "great strain" during the six weeks of filming, attributing her animosity toward Berkeley to his lack of care for her scenes, and her rapid weight loss of twenty pounds, which left her, at the time of her suspension, at ninety pounds, "a mere shell of the healthy little Judy of 'Over the Rainbow.'"

MGM was at a crossroads: they'd already filmed too much to simply replace her. But Garland was also clearly not in working condition, at least not with the setup as it stood. The suggestion that Betty Hutton replace Garland began to circulate, but Garland believed she might still be reinstated—as Edwin Schallert rather dramatically declared, "There has seldom been a more colossal situation in moviedom." By May 25, Hopper was shutting down the rumors, declaring that Hutton had officially signed on for the part, and two days later, Garland was en route to the East, accompanied by her manager, Carleton Alsop, and his wife.

Garland's eastern tenure was a small public relations marvel. It's unclear whether Alsop or MGM was supervising the publicity, but it was sympathetic, generous, and boldly recuperative—a theme that would run through the majority of Garland's press from that point forward. According to these reports, Garland wasn't a problem child on set; she simply suffered from migraines. As for her dramatic weight gain and loss, that was all the fault of the studio: she had been too skinny, so the Alsops had fed her their "best viands" whenever possible. In truth, when she presented herself for *Annie Get Your Gun*, the studio insisted she lose the weight, resulting in a crash diet that took its toll on her physical and mental health. Of course, Garland had been causing problems for weeks, but the mediation of her breakdown, and the weeks immediately following, painted her a "little tragic figure," a victim of the studio's brash decision making.

As Garland regained her strength and returned to Hollywood, her manager penned a melodramatic tale of her breakdown and recovery for *Photoplay*. In "Judy's Singing Again," Alsop claimed that the so-called mysterious malady was just exhaustion. And Garland's exhaustion stemmed from working so hard to make the pictures that you, the reader, loved: getting up for a five a.m. studio call, going through constant wardrobe fittings, interviews, photography sessions, and makeup tests, not to mention being nice, smiling constantly, and all while singing and dancing without showing any measure of fatigue. "You can't slip out of your girdle and take off your shoes and sprawl," Alsop explained. "You must dance! You must sing! You must act!"

Alsop's piece, along with similar ones in other leading fan magazines (choice title: "Why Hollywood Prays for Judy"), helped accumulate enough sympathy that when the *Los Angeles Times* reported that MGM had nearly suspended her yet again, for showing up for *Summer Stock* "overweight" and ignoring an earlier "order" to reduce, it was the studio, not Garland, with the problem. In January 1950, Hopper countered rumors that Garland had been problematic on set, claiming that her own cast members claimed she'd been nothing but cooperative. Over the course of the spring, Garland wrapped *Summer Stock* (1950) and was slated for *Royal Wedding* (1951) with Fred Astaire, but yet again, repeatedly failed to report to the set. On June 18, the studio suspended her for the third time in as many years.

Two days after her suspension, the front page of the papers reported that Judy Garland had slashed her throat in what appeared to be a suicide attempt. In years to come, Garland and others would testify that she had merely grazed herself with a glass shard, creating a wound superficial enough to be covered with a Band-Aid. At the time, the event was mediated in a way that was careful not to suggest actual danger while simultaneously painting Garland as a woman who was clearly unwell. Headlines did not proclaim, GARLAND ATTEMPTS SUICIDE; instead, she had "slashed" her throat or been found with a "throat wound." MGM issued an official statement, claiming that Garland had been "under nervous strain" since her suspension and had been "thrashing out" the problem with Minnelli and her personal secretary when she became "hysterical," rushed out of the room, and locked herself in the bathroom, where she broke a water glass and "rubbed" the edge against her throat. When Minnelli begged her to unlock the door, she opened it immediately, "weeping and remorseful." The doctor who had treated Garland, undoubtedly under MGM supervision, officially declared the wound "superficial," claiming it had been the result of an "impulsive, hysterical act."

The press release, like anything else that came out of the MGM publicity department, was crafted with extreme care; each word was there for a reason. According to MGM, Garland was thrashing, impulsive, and hysterical (twice over); her actions were superficial; her reactions weeping and remorseful. She may have been under nervous strain, but the studio or her work schedule (not to mention her MGM-sanctioned drug addiction) are never mentioned; even the passive phrasing of "she was suspended" elides MGM's role in the breakdown. Two days later, Garland was heavily sedated in order to prevent another attack, with MGM mournfully admitting that she might never make another movie.

Over the course of the next four years, Garland retreated to Europe with Minnelli and their daughter, negotiated an amicable release from her MGM contract, and announced her intent for a prolonged screen absence. She and Minnelli separated shortly thereafter, and Garland began appearing in public with Sid Luft, a somewhat questionable man-about-town with a questionable past. Luft became her de facto manager and encouraged her to return to the stage—the site of her first passion for performance. She appeared to great audience acclaim in London, blew everyone away in New York, and was credited with single-handedly reviving vaudeville, breaking all previous records for attendance and consecutive shows at the famed Palace Theatre. After such a public collapse, Garland seemed wholly revived by her return to the stage. She married Luft, gave birth to a second daughter, and seemed to be on the path to a career renaissance. With Luft by her side, she produced and starred in *A Star Is Born* (1954), her first non-MGM film, to tremendous acclaim. She lost the Academy

Award to Grace Kelly, but Garland was the toast of Hollywood: she had, indeed, come back.

While her comeback was remarkable—*A Star Is Born* is arguably her best, most important film—what's more compelling is the way her previous breakdowns, as well as recurrent issues on set and onstage, were dissected and explained. From the early fifties until her death, to write about Garland was tantamount to a therapy session, with the author as analyst. This wasn't a wholly novel tactic—Freudian concepts were infiltrating the zeitgeist and roundly applied to other stars' romantic woes. Because Garland had grown up on-screen, fans had a firsthand take on how the specifics of her childhood would have, at least according to some pop Freudian psychology, resulted in her adult neuroses. Garland had been working since she was first conscious of herself as a person, thereby robbing her of a "normal" childhood and psychological growth: she was overworked at fourteen; an exhausted workhorse by nineteen.

As a child and teen, Garland had rebelled against that work the only way she could—by eating. In a story that would become common profile fodder throughout the fifties, the fifteen-year-old Garland had taken solace in food, "sneaking double malts between scenes," until she became notably plump. Louis B. Mayer called her into his office, telling her, "You look like a hunchback. We love you. But you look like a monster." Garland herself told this story to Hopper, and its accuracy matters less than the portrait of the cruel, regimented girlhood it painted. Mayer's admonishment came to function as the very root of her lifelong struggle with weight. Crucially, it also painted Mayer as an unsympathetic villain—and Garland as his naive victim.

Mayer might have been horrible and MGM a factory, but the person responsible for putting her there, at least according to popular understanding, wasn't Garland herself, but her mother. In the weeks immediately after Garland's suicide attempt, some began to speculate that she hadn't received "proper care and loving treatment" during her childhood. Ethel Gumm was quick to shoot down such allegations, but at that point, she and her daughter had been estranged for several years, somewhat undermining her denials. The real demonization of Ethel Gumm didn't manifest until after her death, when a high-profile *Saturday Evening Post* piece, suggestively titled "The Star Who Thinks Nobody Loves Her," explained that Garland had grown up with MGM as a father . . . and a mother who would threaten her that she'd "tell the studio" on her if she misbehaved. Later in life, Ethel became petty and vindictive, publicly shaming her daughter for not caring for her in her late age, even though Ethel had failed to save money for Garland throughout her career as a child star. Stories of Ethel's surprise at Garland's stardom ("I thought she wasn't pretty enough") were suddenly shadowed with connotations of abuse. The not-so-subtle suggestion: not only had Garland been overworked, but she had lacked the motherly care and compassion Freud posited as essential to normal development.

And so Garland remained a girl. Her inability to grow up onscreen had long been an issue, but discourse throughout her rise to fame, young motherhood, and breakdowns textually maintained her juvenile status: at eighteen, she was "one swell kid"; at her twenty-second birthday, she cried "like a baby—but a pretty one"; in 1947, she was "the rainbow girl"; in 1949, Alsop claimed she was "everyone's little girl"; her suicide attempt was "childish"; when she lost the role in *Royal Wedding* "the little girl" couldn't take it anymore; she was alternately MGM's "problem child" and "golden girl"; she told the *New York Times* that she wasn't the "bad girl" everyone said she was, just "a very tired girl." Even after her comeback, when Garland was over thirty years old, she was "the little girl with the big voice," "the girl with the velvet brown eyes," who behaved "like a child" if you criticized her performance and who spoke as frankly of her past "as a kindergartner asking the way to the bathroom." And while women are often colloquially referred to as "girls," the sheer frequency with which Garland was aligned with childishness speaks not only to the resilience of her Dorothy-era image but to her behavior, and the way the public conceived of it, in the years that followed.

Considering how Garland was psychologically stuck in adolescence, her emotionality, boy troubles, and debilitating lack of self-confidence—what Garland herself termed an "inferiority complex"—suddenly made sense. But that very emotionality was also the wellspring of her talent: her "emotional intensity" made her a great actress; her vitality and sensitivity were what made her songs "convey so much." *A Star Is Born* director George Cukor explained that on the set, Garland's capacity to play hysterical was so precise that he was able to print the very first take. For the scene when James Mason's character slaps her, she did it dozens of times until they got it perfectly right, telling Cuckor, "I feel nothing." It was an artistic catch-22: her neuroses, and the manifestation thereof, were both what made Garland so beloved and what made her private life so very difficult.

Her fans may have begun to understand, or at least *thought* they understood, the complicated motivation for her behavior—but that didn't mean that she stopped behaving that way. Through the duration of the 1950s, she weathered the peaks and valleys of stardom, cycling in and out of success and failure, retreats and triumphant returns. In 1959, she was diagnosed with hepatitis and told she had five years to live and that she might never sing again—only to return to rave reviews at Carnegie Hall, the recording of which topped the charts and garnered four Grammy Awards. She was nominated for an Academy Award for Best Supporting Actress for her turn in *Judgment at Nuremberg* (1961), a nod widely agreed to have been industry recompense for years of slights.

Garland spent the majority of the 1960s in and out of debt, battling a host of health and addiction problems that had, at that point, plagued her for more than twenty years. She remarried and divorced and married once again, and it was her fifth husband, Mickey Deans, who discovered her in her bathroom dead, at the age of forty-seven, from an accidental overdose of barbiturates. In her final months, Garland looked like a woman twenty years older, a puffy, jaundiced, weary semblance of the vivacious girl who had so charmed the world.

It was the predictable end to a tumultuous life—Garland had in essence been writing her own obituary for years. But what hadn't made sense, what defied analysis, was her indomitable resilience. She had been drugged and battered, overworked and manipulated, verbally and psychologically abused. And yet she continued, always searching, in the mode of her most popular songs, for a life of peace, happiness, and enduring love. It sounds hokey—or, at the very least, it sounds like the yearnings of a sad teenager—but such was the tenor of Garland's image, from her most childlike roles to the bittersweet ending of *A Star Is Born*. That pureness of emotion, the pitch and fall of yearning and self-doubt, is precisely why Garland's image connected so powerfully with so many. And the resilience, as star theorist Richard Dyer has so thoroughly and convincingly argued, functioned as the foundation for her status as gay icon.

Garland was the quintessential Hollywood creation: a major star at the most major of the studios. But her slow decline, and the pervasive analysis thereof, didn't make MGM or the studio system it emblematized look glamorous or, as the system unraveled itself over the course of the 1950s, like that was a loss to be mourned. Garland wasn't the only victim of Hollywood—indeed, the 1960s came to resemble a graveyard of tragically beautiful female stars, physically and psychically decimated by their studios and the enduring scars they inflicted. But Garland's scars were the most visible. Today, she remains one of Hollywood's most enduring stars—and the most compelling reminder of what our affection for the idols on the screen, and the machinery that feeds it, does to both body and mind. Her life suggested hope and despair in equal measures, begging you to love her and damning you for doing so. And that, more than anything else, is what has always made Garland so difficult to ignore and so impossible to forget.

CHAPTER ELEVEN

Dorothy Dandridge vs. the World

Dorothy Dandridge's life wasn't that different from Judy Garland's. Both were born to mothers who were entertainers; both spent their earliest, most formative years on the road, touring with groups composed of their sisters. Both struggled during their initial years in Hollywood; both were ultimately better singers than actors. Both were subject to intense press scrutiny, only by different sections of the press. Both endured a string of affairs with men who would not or could not love them in the open, forced abortions, and marriages to men who would abuse and manipulate them. Both died of drug overdoses before their fiftieth birthdays. But one star became an icon, starring in dozens of films, while the other became a footnote in film history. The straightforward reason: Dorothy Dandridge was black. The press agreed that she was beautiful, glamorous, and ineffably sexy, but in 1950s Hollywood, she fought tirelessly, and with only intermittent success, for roles that didn't cast her as a slave or a stereotype. She spoke openly about her desire for better roles for African Americans, but that struggle, and her hesitance to accept degrading roles, would ultimately destroy her career.

Dandridge was born in Cleveland, Ohio, in the early 1920s,

the child of an entertainer and a cabinetmaker-minister, whom her mother left before she was born. By age five, Dorothy and her older sister, Vivian, were performing at local "kiddie" revues as the Wonder Children, singing, reciting, and performing acrobatic stunts, and traveling the so-called chitlin circuit. By the late twenties, the Depression had dried up most of the gigs, and the family left for California, where, at some point in the early thirties, the Wonder Children added a family friend, Etta Jones. As the Dandridge Sisters, they traveled to Hawaii in 1935, followed by a European tour and an appearance at New York's famed Cotton Club. Dandridge learned endurance, poise, and how to handle the road—but she also lacked almost any form of schooling, having spent much of her time away from her mother, who was busy furthering her own career. In profiles of Dandridge and her success, those details, along with any specifics of her father, would be neatly pushed to the side. Like Garland, Dandridge was a trouper, born into the business with a genetic disposition toward entertaining.

While the sisters were touring with Jimmy Lunceford's band, Vivian ran off with the trumpet player, effectively ending the Dandridge Sisters' run. But it was a surprise blessing: when Dorothy returned to Hollywood, she found scattered film work, appearing in Warner Bros. shorts, guesting at high-profile nightclubs, and working in a string of B pictures for Republic Pictures. She wrote a feature for *Afro-American* on "How I Crashed the Movies" and was touted as Republic's newest "sepia find." In 1942, the twenty-year-old Dandridge married Harold Nicholas, half of the famed Nicholas Brothers dancing team, and gave birth to a daughter, Harolyn, a year later. When Harolyn was only a few months old, Dandridge realized she was quiet, unresponsive, and somehow different from other babies; doctors diagnosed her with brain damage, likely caused by a lack of oxygen during birth. In later years, Dandridge would speak openly about her daughter's condition, emphasizing that her hard work was, at least in part, in order to provide the best care for her daughter. At the time, however, Harolyn stayed hidden, a source of recurring guilt.

By 1947, the bit parts had slowed to a trickle, but Dandridge wasn't giving up. Instead, she refocused her efforts on a career as a singer, refining her vocal talents and learning how to move her body and better communicate with the audience. Eventually, she won a chance gig filling in for the vocalist in the Desi Arnaz Orchestra at the Mocambo. She split from Nicholas and began working with famed bandleader Phil Moore to further refine her act, improving her "song styling and tone phrasing," and investing in a set of dazzling new costumes. In 1951, this "new" Dorothy Dandridge opened at the Mocambo to great fanfare, with the *Los Angeles Times* encouraging readers to catch the "impish, beautifully gowned" Dandridge before she set forth on a European tour—her first review in a major mainstream publication.

Dandridge's real break, however, came several months later, when *Life* ran a picture of a shimmying Dandridge dressed in a gorgeous strapless, body-fitting gown, under the headline SHY NO MORE. *Life* declared her "the most beautiful Negro singer to make her mark in nightclubs since Lena Horne," thus establishing a characterization that would follow Dandridge throughout her career. Working with Moore—the same man who had mentored Lena Horne—Dandridge had apparently shed her inhibitions and natural shyness; now, she'd "wriggled and sung her way" to nightclub stardom. The piece was accompanied by a pictorial spread of Dandridge's career trajectory, from Wonder Kid to nightclub vixen, but the real charm was in the piece's closing line: "'Somehow,'" she said with surprise, "'people just like to look at me.'"

With a spread in *Life* and a chorus of raving critics, Dandridge quickly became a national figure. From San Francisco to St. Louis, she was trumpeted as a huge success, opening at La Vie en Rose, the swankiest of swanky New York clubs, and appearing on Jackie Gleason's *Cavalcade of Stars*. But you weren't someone in café society until you made your way into Walter Winchell's column—which Dandridge managed on December 3, 1951, when the acerbic gossip columnist crowed that she and Phil Moore were "beyond control."

At this point, Dandridge had been in the national spotlight for three years and an entertainer for nearly twenty. Even without any major film roles, her star image was coming into focus. Its central and most enduring tenet: *beauty*. From the beginning of her adult career, Dandridge's name was paired with beauty, usually quite literally: she was "pretty Dorothy Dandridge," the "pretty wife" of Nicholas, "Dorothy Dandridge, pretty and talented actress," "glamorously beautiful Dorothy Dandridge," and dozens of iterations thereof. It was her most defining feature—akin to Garland's "big voice," Bacall's sultry look, or Bogart's scowl—but it was a specific type of beauty: a columnist for the *Pittsburgh Courier* said that you "take a big hunk of honey, mold it into a lovely figure, add the face of a goddess and you have Dorothy Dandridge." She was, to put it bluntly, light-skinned, with "Anglo" features that matched the African American beauty ideal, which was itself a knotted ideological construction of Caucasian and African American values.

You didn't have to be light-skinned to be a star—Hattie McDaniel, the first black woman to win an Oscar, was dark-skinned, as were Paul Robeson and Bill "Bojangles" Robinson. But at this point in time, you did need to have light skin to be a sex object, especially outside the realm of the black entertainment circuit. It's no accident that the two most significant black female performers of the forties and fifties were Dandridge and Lena Horne, two women who didn't precisely look alike but shared the same petite, slender build and straightened black hair. As one black columnist explained, "Dorothy Dandridge was one-half of what every white man thought every beautiful Negro woman looked like. The other is, of course, Lena Horne." Dandridge would be compared with Horne for the rest of her career, and while Horne was probably the better singer, the constant pairing accentuated the qualifications for black female stardom.

Female nightclub singers built their names on the sultriness of their performance, and Dandridge was no different. The *Life* feature established her as a subject of the gaze, now able to court others' eyes upon her. A female columnist for the *Los Angeles Sentinel* declared that Dandridge had hit stardom with "every ounce of her sexy curvaceous body"; she was named one of the *Pittsburgh Courier*'s Ten Sexiest Women in Show Business, with a body that "could make a burlap sack look like a bikini." She was "shapely," "tantalizing," with "one of the oomphiest voices" out there.

And after her training with Moore, she had that ineffable something that connected her with audiences: not only did she have the look, but she could "sell" a song—make every audience member think she was singing to them. In interviews, Dandridge declared herself "more of a psychologist than a singer," working to figure out the precise delivery to elicit the strongest response from her audience. And it worked, at least according to the press: "If you've never been in love, she makes you want to be; if you're a cynic, she makes you want to try again, and if you're already in love, she makes you want to stay that way."

In the years to come, Dandridge would repeatedly emphasize that the nightclub act had always been intended as a means to an end: a way to get the studios to notice her. By the summer of 1952, it was clear that the strategy had worked, as MGM cast her as a demure schoolteacher opposite up-and-coming Harry Belafonte in the "all-Negro" production of *See How They Run*, prompting her to cancel seventy-five thousand dollars in night-club bookings in order to refocus on her film career.

The film featured Dandridge as a sweet, rural schoolteacher who helps a struggling child. Her natural beauty was on display, but it was a far cry from her nightclub persona—which might have explained at least part of why *See How They Run*, renamed *Bright Road* (1953), proved a box office failure, despite lauds from the black press for its avoidance of stereotypes. The other reason: MGM failed to push it. And this wasn't just some behind-doors gossip—Hedda Hopper stated it plainly in her column, adding that she thought the film "excellent."

Both Hopper and Winchell, who continued to drop Dandridge's name in his column, were nationally syndicated columnists—meaning that even if Dandridge never went to your small town, or her movie never came to your theater, her name was becoming familiar. 20th Century-Fox was willing to take a gamble on Dandridge—perhaps because it had just agreed to fund Otto Preminger's all-black adaptation of Georges Bizet's famed *Carmen*. They signed her to a three-picture contract, and Dandridge set about advocating for the lead in *Carmen*. But Preminger, who had apparently only seen *Bright Road*, thought her too soft and sweet for Carmen, one of the best known sirens in theatrical history. Preminger had tested every established black actress save Dandridge, and when she showed up to change his mind, he thought she wanted to role of Cindy Lou, the mild-mannered girlfriend of the man Carmen seduces. Preminger told Dandridge she was "too regal" for the part of Carmen, but Dandridge knew better: when she showed up the next day, she was wearing a short skirt and suggestive blouse, and burst into Preminger's office breathless, with her hair tousled. Preminger's response: "It's Carmen!"

The heavily circulated anecdote emphasizes several themes of Dandridge's image moving forward: First, she was stubborn and willing to fight for the role she wanted, just as she would continue to do. Second, for Dandridge, sexiness was an "act"—something she could put on for an audition or a role, something she could use to get what she wanted, but not her "true" self. Forget all that *Life* magazine stuff about the "suppressed sultriness"—the "real" Dandridge studied philosophy and psychiatry, with a quiet, serious demeanor and a "fine, thoughtful mind" that "sees below the surface of things." She wasn't a nerd, necessarily, but she wasn't a harlot: as she told the *Boston Globe*, when it came to acting, "it doesn't matter to me whether I'm a saint or a sinner . . . it's just acting, not being that way in private life."

But once the revelation of Dandridge as Carmen hit screens nationwide, no matter of testimonials to her bookish seriousness could disentangle her from that role. Within the first ten minutes of the film, Dandridge, dressed in a diaphanous black blouse and a form-fitting red skirt, burns the film to the ground. Harry Belafonte is handsome; Pearl Bailey is gregarious; but the film is all Dandridge's. Ironically, neither she nor Belafonte sang their parts, as their natural voices were deemed too low for the operatic score. Today, that score seems a bit melodramatic and off, but at the time, it was a smash, raking in six million dollars and seemingly proving that an all-black cast could pull far beyond the all-black audience.

Suddenly, Dandridge was everywhere—most visibly, dressed in her Carmen outfit on the cover of *Life*, peering over her shoulder and beckoning to the reader in a pose usually reserved for pinups. Louella Parsons called it one of the best musicals to come out of Hollywood, and Hopper got so excited during the picture that she burned a hole in her dress, but the real fanfare, at least in the mainstream press, was for Dandridge herself. Gossip columnist Dorothy Kilgallen reported that previewers were "raving" about Dandridge's beauty and talent; Parsons declared her a new "glamour star"; Winchell wrote that *Carmen Jones* was filled with "fiery music and blazing passion," with Dandridge as "its loveliest flame." London's *Daily Express* even placed her above Jane Russell and Marilyn Monroe, claiming she had a personality "as hot as an oven door" with an "emotional kick like a mule." They even gave her a new nickname: Heatwave.

Carmen Jones was roundly praised in the black press, but its success was met with somewhat tempered optimism: the reviewer for the *Atlanta Daily World* underlined that even though the film was beautiful and well acted, "it is not everything social progress demands with its All-Negro cast." It was one thing to have black characters make love, fight, and otherwise engage within a hermetically sealed, all-black world on-screen; it would've been quite another for those black characters to interact with—and have meaningful, non-servile relationships with—white characters. Even the film's male lead, Harry Belafonte, was tepid when it came to the film's overarching value for the black entertainer. When asked if *Carmen* would lead to a more sensitive treatment of his race, his answer was a definitive *no*—with the caveat that it could function "symbolically," proving that black actors could play all facets of human drama, not just the stereotypical roles to which they had been relegated. Hollywood, to his mind, was inherently conservative when it came to race. The only solution was independent producers, such as Otto Preminger, who were willing to press boundaries.

It was this symbolic wave that Dandridge hoped to ride, and over the months to come, change did seem distinctly possible. Fanfare for Dandridge escalated, hitting a fever pitch with her Academy Award nomination for Best Actress. But her competition was tough: Garland was nominated for *A Star Is Born*, along with Hollywood darlings Grace Kelly and Audrey Hepburn. What's more, as Dandridge herself pointed out, the Academy didn't go in for "sexy" roles—and her role wasn't just sexy, but ultimately unsympathetic. She also refused to use her nightclub appearances to lobby for the award: "If I can't stand on my own," she told the *Chicago Daily Times*, "I'd better give up." Dandridge would lose to Grace Kelly, but earlier in the night, she presented the award for Best Editing. It was the first time a black actor had presented an Academy Award, a landmark Dandridge acknowledged onstage, declaring, with tears in her eyes, that the moment meant as much to her as it did to the person to whom she was about to give the Oscar.

Opportunities for Dandridge began piling up: Hopper included her in the "Top Stars of 1955" year-end pictorial, and the *Afro-American* reported that twelve "all-tan features" were in the works. Dandridge also became the first black person to appear at the storied Waldorf-Astoria, in New York, where the crowd included a who's who of New York café society, from Winchell to hotel owner Conrad Hilton. There were reports that Dandridge had negotiated an antisegregation clause in her Fox contract, intended to ensure she was cast in integrated films. With both Belafonte and Dandridge in apparent demand, it was easy to feel optimistic: on the micro level, for black stardom; on the macro level, for what black stardom might mean for race relations.

Rumors floated of all sorts of roles for Dandridge, from onscreen as one of Moses's wives in *The Ten Commandments* (1956) to on Broadway in a revival of Oscar Wilde's *Salome*. But the choice offer—what Hopper called "a honey of a role"—was as one of Yul Brynner's wives, Tuptim, in *The King and I* (1956), a big-budget spectacular. The highly sympathetic role of Tuptim would've brought Dandridge worldwide recognition, but it was also the role of a slave. In the spring of 1956, she declined the role,

Fox head Darryl Zanuck convinced her to take it, and then she rejected it again, this time under the advisement of Otto Preminger, who assured her that more choice roles, *lead* roles, would come her way soon.

After declining the role in *The King and I*, Dandridge waited for the offers to roll in, but Fox had nothing to give her. While waiting for her next move, she toured, she made money, she brought down the house, but there was no sign of the starring role she desired. In April 1956, a year and a half after the release of *Carmen Jones*, Louella Parsons remarked how surprising it was that Dandridge, who was about to wrap four triumphant weeks at the Savoy, in London, was still without a new role. She'd turned down another part, in *The Lieutenant Wore Skirts* (1956), this time because the role was too small. The African American–directed *Chicago Defender* explained that she had been waiting for a "suitable part," but the fact remained: she had been the hottest new thing in Hollywood, and then she had disappeared from the screen entirely.

And Dandridge knew it. She agreed to appear in *Island in the Sun* (1957), an ensemble piece based on the popular novel of the same name featuring her, Belafonte, Joan Fontaine, James Mason, and Joan Collins. Unlike in the all-black *Carmen Jones*, both Dandridge and Belafonte would be paired with white love interests— exactly the sort of progressive narrative that Dandridge had hoped for when she turned down *The King and I*. But her role in *Island* was clearly a supporting one: she had waited too long, and now she was billed third. By the time the film hit theaters, she'd been off the screen for a startling two and a half years.

The film was a success, grossing more than five million dollars on a budget of $2.5 million. But it also underlined enduring anxieties over interracial relations. Belafonte and Fontaine weren't allowed to kiss or otherwise act on their sexual tension; even for that, Belafonte received hate mail for 'making love' to a white star. And general gossip around the film wasn't kind: in an article titled "Dorothy Dandridge Learns Her Lesson," the author outlines Dandridge's history of aloofness, snubbing reporters from various African American press and angering the mainstream press both for avoiding them and for refusing the role in *The King and I*. According to this article, Dandridge figured out that she had to be nice—but two weeks later, Dorothy Kilgallen was reporting that Dandridge was "pulling a Garbo," avoiding all members of the cast and speaking to as few people as possible. Her reputation, in other words, was quickly becoming that of a snob.

A snob and, in short order, a trollop. Three months before the release of *Island in the Sun*, *Confidential* ran a cover story with the suggestive title "Only the Birds and Bees Saw What Dorothy Dandridge Did in the Woods," detailing a tryst between Dandridge and white bandleader Dan Terry that supposedly took place *en plein air* while the band was playing at Lake Tahoe. By 1957, *Confidential*, which pledged to "tell the facts and name the names," had been terrorizing Hollywood for three years, using a complex network of tipsters to obtain scandalous details of the stars' theretofore hidden, sordid lives. Most of what *Confidential* printed was true—or at least rooted in truth, backed up by affidavits, which is one of the reasons it had managed to avoid libel prosecution for so long.

But Dandridge understood what allegations of a sexual dalliance with a white man would do to her already oversexed image. Before the *Confidential* issue hit stands, she had filed suit against another pulpy scandal rag, *Hep* magazine, for an article titled "Dorothy Dandridge—Her 1000 Lovers." When *Confidential* published its piece, she filed suit yet again, employing a somewhat ingenious tactic. Instead of filing suit against the magazine's publisher alone, she expanded the suit to include the California distributor of *Confidential*. If the case went to court, the distributor would be required to name every retailer of the magazine—drugstores, newsstands, etc.—on the public record. *Confidential* sold like crazy, but it was also incredibly lowbrow, and few merchants would want to have their store name publicly linked with *Confidential*'s. To avoid losing their entire California distribution network, *Confidential* offered a ten-thousand-dollar settlement and promised to print an apology in an upcoming issue.

But the apology never came. Before they could print it, the California attorney general brought *Confidential* and its publishers to court on charges of conspiracy to publish criminal libel. The high-profile case became known as the Trial of the 100 Stars, because at least a hundred Hollywood stars were the subject of the magazine's supposed libel and could thus be called to the stand as witnesses for the prosecution. As the trial started, dozens of stars fled the city, hoping to avoid testifying. It wasn't just that they didn't want to be in a courtroom—if they were called to the stand, the jury would also have to hear a reading of a libelous article in which they had been named. *Confidential* had a circulation of more than twelve million, but the contents of this article, including summaries of dozens of other *Confidential* narratives in question, would reach the eyes of everyone who read the newspaper. Even if the stories weren't true, the star's name would be linked, in national press, with scandalous behavior. It was a public relations nightmare.

In the end, only two stars were called to the stand: Maureen O'Hara, who supposedly took a "tumble" with a "Latin Lothario" in the back of a movie theater, and Dorothy Dandridge. But neither side of the case knew that when Dandridge took the stand, she would offer an incisive indictment of the enduring racial politics in America. For her defense against the story was simple: she couldn't have fornicated with a white man outside, because the prejudice against black people in Lake Tahoe was so strong that and today, most people familiar with Dandridge know of the affair and its ramifications on her career. Over their four-year affair, Dandridge would become pregnant with Preminger's child; when it became clear that he would not leave his wife, she was forced to abort the baby or end her career. The choice was a stark one—especially given her guilt over her first child's brain damage. But a marriage of that sort, at that time, under those circumstances, would've effectively blackballed her from Hollywood.

Dandridge managed to extricate herself from her relationship with Preminger, and starting in October, rumors began to circulate concerning recent dates with a "white-haired headwaiter" at one of the Vegas casinos. Dandridge discreetly dated this headwaiter, Jack Denison, for the next year, likely conscious of how a high-profile romance with a white man would affect her career following the *Confidential* story and trial. Following the release of *Island*, Dandridge completed two oddball pictures. The first, an Italian production called *Tamango* (1958), featured Dandridge as a slave, but due to its interracial relationship, it struggled to find an American distributor. The second, *The Decks Ran Red* (1958), was a high seas thriller—and clearly a B picture. Dandridge's role, if not her performance, was lauded, in part because it was what, in today's parlance, we'd call "color-blind," aka absent any specific discussion of race or race dynamics. Neither film bombed, but they were a far cry from the A-picture trajectory of *Carmen Jones*.

So Dandridge did something that she would have categorically refused just a few years prior: she agreed to play Bess in *Porgy and Bess* (1959). On its face, the role was everything Dandridge had been looking for—its producer, Samuel Goldwyn, was known for his high-budget, supersuccessful films. The story of the wayward Porgy and Bess had been enormously successful as a book, a play, and an opera, and with the director of the opera already on board, it seemed like a natural hit. The problem, then, was its characterization of African Americans. Dandridge's character was a drug-addled prostitute, and the rest of the characters in the film were various iterations of black stereotypes: drug dealers, ne'er-do-wells, rapists, murderers, and beggars. Harry Belafonte turned down the role of Porgy, and Sidney Poitier attempted to, before his manager promised to get him to reconsider, prompting Goldwyn to claim that they'd had an "oral agreement." Sammy Davis Jr. was the only actor in Hollywood willing to play the role of Porgy's drug dealer, Sportin' Life. But Goldwyn told Dandridge she was the only actress he could imagine in the role of Bess: she *had* to accept.

The role seemed like Dandridge's last chance at legitimate stardom. If *Porgy and Bess* succeeded, she could restart her career; even at the age of thirty-seven, she still looked young. But the film was embroiled in turmoil from the start. On the first day of rehearsals, a flash fire burned through the soundstage, destroying millions of dollars in sets and costumes. The reason for the fire was never determined, but rumors of arson began to spread, exacerbated by vocal protests of the film's negative depiction of African Americans. While the sets were being rebuilt, long-running disagreements between director Rouben Mamoulian and Goldwyn reached a tipping point, culminating with Goldwyn kicking Mamoulian off the picture and replacing him with Otto Preminger.

What Goldwyn did not anticipate, however, is how a personal dispute would turn into an industry-wide confrontation. Following Mamoulian's dismissal, Leigh Whipper—one of the main supporting actors, who had also worked with Mamoulian on the stage adaptation—resigned from the picture, publicly stating that he would not participate in "any project that may prove derogatory to my race," which he claimed Preminger's adaptation would be. Whether it was simply a matter of loyalty or not, Leigh was also the head of the Negro Actors Guild of America, and declared that the guild's twelve hundred members would have no association with the film.

But none of the major actors were enrolled in the guild, and Pearl Bailey and Sammy Davis Jr. went so far as to issue public statements in support of Preminger. Even the head of the NAACP voiced his confidence that *Porgy and Bess* would be in "the best of taste and with utmost regard for the dignity of the Negro people." As for Dandridge, she had no comment—perhaps because if she had known that Preminger would be her director, she never would've signed on to the picture. As filming resumed, she was miserable. Preminger had long been known for his harsh manner on set, and now, vindictive toward Dandridge, who had been the one to sever things for good, he ratcheted up his harshness, regularly bringing her to tears.

The poster for *Porgy and Bess* promised "a new era in motion pictures." But it was not to be: despite its six-million-dollar budget, its big-name producer, and its months in postproduction refining the score, the film was an unmitigated flop. Poitier had films lined up for miles and Davis had the Rat Pack, but for Dandridge, it was a disaster. In the months leading up to the film's release, she had quietly wed Jack Denison. He had pursued her for years, sending her flowers in the earliest days of her post-*Carmen* club appearances. In him, she had found a man with whom she could share "a wonderful understanding." As Dandridge explained to the press, Denison didn't begrudge her her fame or independence, and had no desire to live a high-profile life. The charged subject of their "mixed marriage" seemingly concerned everyone but them.

But this was before the turn in Dandridge's career. After the disappointment of *Porgy and Bess*, she struggled to find work, appearing in lowbrow European productions and performing for free at her husband's floundering Sunset Strip nightclub, rumored to be funded on Dandridge's earnings. When a group of reviewers from the black press screened *Tamango*, finally released in the United States in September 1959, it was, as one critic remembered, "one of the worst movies any of us had ever seen." At the post-screening celebration, held at the Denison-owned nightclub, they found a desperate, melancholy space, with less than a half dozen paying customers.

There were rumors of a comeback, as there always are with faded, crumpled stars: a biopic of Billie Holiday; a television show with Nat King Cole. But none of them came to pass. As she told the *Los Angeles Times*, Hollywood had finally gotten past stereotypes when it came to black performers—but now, "too many producers are afraid to use us at all. Rather than do wrong, they do nothing." Some of the work she refused on principle: when offered a gig at the halftime of a Redskins game, she publicly declined, citing the team's refusal to hire an African American player. One day, her marriage was reported "a bust" after a hysterical fight over dinner; the next, she was telling a gossip columnist that she and Denison were considering a double adoption, one Greek child, one black child.

By August 1962, Dandridge had dropped off the national radar. When she abruptly quit her gig as a supporting player in a Chicago performance of *West Side Story*, she was reported to have been suffering from "severe exhaustion." A writer for the *Chicago Defender* articulated the unspoken worry: since Marilyn Monroe's death just weeks before, "sick," especially when applied to troubled stars, augured something tragic. Two months later, Dandridge filed for divorce, revealing that Denison had stuck her violently on several occasions. The black press had never fallen over itself to sanction the wedding; now, the *Philadelphia Tribune* spoke freely, claiming that the marriage had been a "three year masquerade" in which Dandridge played the part of contented wife, while Denison treated her "as his meal ticket."

When Dandridge declared bankruptcy four months later, she was confirming what everyone had expected. No longer able to afford her daughter's personal care, she was forced to place her in a state mental home. She took on embarrassing gigs, and then no gigs at all. She disappeared into her tiny Sunset Strip apartment until, over the summer of 1965, she began plotting a comeback with the help of her longtime manager, traveling to Mexico and signing a contract for a smattering of film roles and appearances. But on September 8, 1965, when her manager arrived to arrange for a costume fitting, he found Dandridge, naked save a blue scarf around her neck, dead in the bathroom. Cause of death: an overdose of depression medication. Dandridge was forty-two years old. She had two dollars in her bank account.

In the end, Hollywood forced Dandridge to embody one of the stereotypes she loathed so fiercely: the tragic mulatto, a woman accepted in some ways by both the black and white communities but rejected in other crucial, heartbreaking ways. The white community loved her "white" beauty, the hazy allure of her sexuality, but refused to let her act on it—at least not on-screen, and certainly not with a white man. Dandridge saw this clearly. "America was not geared to make me into a Liz Taylor, Monroe, or a Gardner," she explained. "My sex symbolism was as a wanton, a prostitute, not as a woman seeking love and a husband, like other women."

Just a decade after her death, Dandridge may have found parts, as Sidney Poitier did, in pictures that helped spark conversations about race, integration, and interracial marriage. Twenty years later, she could've been a blaxploitation queen. Thirty years later, she could've been a cross between Beyoncé and Kerry Washington. Yet Dandridge's life, and its parallels to the present, illuminates how far our society has come—and how far it hasn't. Fifty years after her death, the vestiges of discrimination, prejudice, and sexual stereotyping remain. To be a mainstream black female star in Hollywood is to inhabit a circumscribed world. Whitney Houston could do little more than kiss Kevin Costner in *The Bodyguard*; Halle Berry was roundly criticized for taking a hyper-sexualized role in *Monster's Ball*, which, according to some, is the reason she was awarded an Oscar—a win she dedicated to Dandridge. Viola Davis, Octavia Spencer, Jennifer Hudson, Mo'Nique—none of them can get a leading role in a major Hollywood picture, much less a romantic leading role. "If I were Betty Grable," Dandridge wrote, "I would capture the world." That race still holds that much weight today, more than fifty years after her death, speaks to the true tragedy of Dorothy Dandridge's life: that of unspoken, insidious, enduring prejudice.

THREE ANGRY MEN

In the years after World War II, a combination of pride and depression, valor and self-doubt, stoicism and vulnerability characterized the national emotional landscape. If stars are manifestations of conflicting societal and cultural impulses, then no one embodied those conflicts more than Montgomery Clift, Marlon Brando, and James Dean.

On-screen, they yelled and wept, lost themselves and refused to be found. Beautiful, supplicating women surrounded them yet offered little solace. With each performance, these men unraveled American masculinity a bit more, tangling it to the point that it could not be reassembled without breaking threads. Their work transformed our understanding of acting, of manhood. When they entered a scene, the world seemed to pulse with them.

Off-screen, they broke all the unspoken rules. Brando and Clift refused to sign contracts. Their approach to acting challenged Hollywood's conceit of performance, and the way they lived was an affront to the entire industry. None of their actions were singularly scandalous; rather, their *images* were scandalous. Their very existence—and the breathless reaction to them on the part of the audience—was the scandal.

Clift, Brando, Dean, and the emotive rebelliousness they represented, were one of the catalysts that transformed Hollywood in the 1950s. Their success encouraged the production of cerebral, morally ambiguous drama—drama that incorporated elements of the European art cinema to which thousands of troops had become accustomed before returning home. They startled audiences out of postwar complacency, giving structure to a brewing anxiousness most didn't know how to name. Disillusioned, proud, and pleading, these three angry men, and the scandal of their on- and off-screen performances, broke Hollywood's implicit rules of stardom, and in so doing, encouraged a new generation of stars to do the same.

CHAPTER TWELVE

The Long Suicide of Montgomery Clift

Montgomery Clift had the most earnest of faces: big, pleading eyes, a set jaw, and the sort of immaculate side part we haven't seen since. He played the desperate, the drunken, and the deceived, and the trajectory of his life was as tragic as that in any of his films. A car crash in the prime of his career left him in constant pain, and he drank himself to an early death, creating an aesthetic of suffering that has guided the way we think about him today. But for twelve years, he set Hollywood aflame.

Like Brando and Dean, Clift was a child of the Midwest, born, along with a twin sister, to a well-to-do family in Nebraska. Unlike the other two stars with whom he's so often grouped, his family got out of the Midwest almost immediately—first to Chicago, then to New York, where Clift's father worked as a stockbroker, making enough money to send Clift and his siblings to Switzerland for boarding school. It was an odd childhood, a mixture of schooling abroad and long vacations to winter in Florida with the family, creating massive gaps in their schooling, to be filled by private tutors. But it was in Florida, during one of these winters, that Clift, age fourteen, happened upon a community rehearsal of *As Husbands Go*, ending up with a bit part. The next summer, a family friend, who just happened to be a Broadway producer, offered a letter of introduction to the casting director of a stock company in Stockbridge, Massachusetts. The future was sealed.

But Clift was no blazing talent, at least not at first. He was kept on, according to the director, because he was "quiet, well-bred, and knew the lines." But it was enough to recommend him for another part, and others after that, eventually making him the top juvenile performer on Broadway. He didn't have a high school diploma, but he won the lead in *Dame Nature*, a major Broadway production, before the age of eighteen. He was in a string of Pulitzer Prize–winning plays, turning down offers from Hollywood, including what would've been a high-profile role in the hugely successful wartime drama *Mrs. Miniver*.

Clift was *discerning*—a characteristic that would become a cornerstone of his image. He didn't act for glory or money; he acted because it was *art*. Or at least so went the narrative, and the explanation for why he was who he was and did what he did. To him, Hollywood, at least at in that era, seemed the antithesis of art. But his principled stance wasn't always enough to pay the bills. Despite a decade of accolades, he'd found himself on unemployment when, in 1946, he was offered a role in the Howard Hawks western *Red River* (1948), opposite John Wayne.

In 1946, the attachment of Hawks and Wayne was industry shorthand for "big deal." This wasn't some run-of-the-mill western; it was a "psychological" western, with the same darkness and depth that characterized the Hawks oeuvre. Somewhat hilariously, Clift couldn't ride a horse, and had to go to intensive schooling in "horsemanship" and "whipping out six-shooters"—a point that would be well covered in the press as a means of emphasizing his patrician background. But the acting part, he had down. His performance as the adopted son of Wayne who leads a rebellion against him is understated and complex, perfectly in tune with the revisionist tone of the film.

But for various reasons, *Red River* was delayed for two years. By the time it was released, Clift had already appeared in *The Search* (1948), a Holocaust survivor drama, mostly forgotten today, that won him his first nomination for Best Actor. *Red River* finally hit theaters six months later, and suddenly, Clift was a phenomenon, winning *Movieland*'s poll for the hottest new star and bringing in loads of fan mail to *Photoplay*. He was the hottest thing out there, with his choice of projects—and a face that brought fans to tears.

And so the twin pillars of Clift's career began to manifest, coalescing around the themes of talent and beauty. While Clift, like Brando and Dean, is commonly associated with the performance style known as the Method, his skill was, in fact, an amalgamation of acting styles, a "synthesis," according to film historian Amy Lawrence, of "multiple and radically different approaches to acting" that he encountered over his theater career. He worked with the old guard and the new, the legendary and the experimental, before attending the Actors Studio in the late 1940s.

Clift used this synthetic approach to lose himself in the character—so much so that when he appeared in *The Search*, audiences and critics alike believed that he was an actual GI the director had found on the streets of Germany. Clift slaved over the role, corresponding constantly with director Fred Zinnemann, working to refine the character into something that was less stereotypical and simple, more psychologically complex and believable. Zinnemann told Hedda Hopper that Clift never posed. "Sometimes," he explained, "I think he doesn't act at all. He behaves as the character would."

Clift was breathtakingly handsome, but there was something else, something poignant and ineffable about him. Elizabeth Taylor said that the first time she saw him, her heart stopped. When photographer Richard Avedon saw him on-screen in *The Search*, he cried. Clift had that sort of visceral effect on people, the result of the intensity of performance and immaculate face. People *loved* him, but as a *Saturday Evening Post* article explained, they had very little reason to, at least on-screen: over the course of those first two, crucial films, he had but one "perfunctory clinch" with a costar. Why all the excitement, then? He was "a whole of an actor." Talent, in other words, was supremely sexy.

From the start, Clift was framed as a rebel and an individual. When he first arrived in Hollywood, he didn't sign a contract, waiting until after the success of his first two films to negotiate a three-picture deal with Paramount that allowed him total discretion over projects. It was unheard of, especially for a young star, but it was a seller's market. If Paramount wanted him, they'd have to give him what he wanted—a power differential that would go on to structure the star-studio relationship for the next forty years.

Clift's first film for Paramount was *The Heiress* (1949), a big-costume adaptation of Henry James's *Washington Square*, in which he played a suave, debonair man-about-town opposite Olivia de Havilland's shy, quasi–ugly duckling of an heiress. While filming, Clift became obsessed with making the script, the acting, *everything*, better. He thought de Havilland's lines were horrible and gave him little to respond to, so he rewrote them; he thought she was too compliant with director William Wyler, and he told her so. Clift was a perfectionist, fixated on his own performance and the performances of those around him. And with a 1948 *Life* spread of him watching himself in *The Heiress*, that self-scrutiny became part of his public image: it's impossible not to see the weight of self-judgment so abundantly apparent in his eyes and posture.

When the press talked about Clift, they talked about the skill and the beauty, but they also talked about what an offbeat, weird guy he was. He insisted on maintaining his residence in New York, spending as little time in Hollywood as possible. His apartment, which he rented for ten dollars a month, was described by friends as "beat up" and by him as "terrific." He survived on two meals a day, mostly combinations of steak, eggs, and orange juice, and he eschewed nightclubs, instead spending his spare time reading Chekov, classic works of history and economics, and Aristotle, whom he praised for his belief in happiness, or the "gentle art of the soul." When he wasn't reading or exhausting himself in preparation for a part, he liked to go to the local night court and attend high-profile court cases just to watch the humanity on display.

Clift cared nothing for appearances: the *Los Angeles Times* called him the "Rumpled Movie Idol"; he infamously owned only one suit. When he came to visit storied fan magazine author Elsa Maxwell at her home, she had her maid darn the elbow in his jacket. His beat-up car was ten years old, and his best friends were all outside of the movie business. He was, in his words, nothing more than an "ordinary, second-class wolf."

These anecdotes, and dozens like them, would establish Clift, along with Brando, as the embodiment of fifties youth culture, rebelling against conformity and all that postwar Americans were supposed to embrace. Yet Clift would come to hate the image that constrained him, just as he hated the suggestion that he was a slob, unfriendly, or loathed in Hollywood: after the story of his bare closet came out in the *Saturday Evening Post*, he worked arduously to set the record straight, underlining the ways in which publicity takes a kernel of the truth and expands it into legend. In his words, "I learned that most writers don't need interviews to write about me. They seem to have their stories all written out beforehand."

Clift's private life was boring—he didn't date, he didn't flirt, he didn't hang out in public. His image was, more than anything else, *confusing*—unmalleable to Hollywood's preexisting star categories. But he was handsome and beguiling on-screen, creating an appetite for confirmation of that same Clift off the screen. So the fan magazines got creative: the August 1949 cover of *Movieland*, for example, featured a grinning, suited, respectable-looking Clift paired with the tantalizing headline "Making Love the Clift Way." But when readers looked inside the magazine, all they found was a two-page spread of stills from *The Heiress*, featuring Clift in various stages of flirtation with de Havilland, extrapolating that Clift's kissing style was "soft yet possessively brutal; pleading, but demanding all. . . ."

It was a flimsy speculation built on shaky evidence, but with no sign of any "real" lovemaking in Clift's life, it was all the fan magazines had. Indeed, it was his apparent lack of romantic attachments that confounded the gossip press the most. He had a close friendship with a woman named Myra Letts, whom the gossip columnists tried arduously to frame as a love interest. But Clift's rebuttal was firm, emphasizing that they were neither in love nor engaged—they'd known each other for ten years, she helped him with his work, and "those romantic rumors are embarrassing to both of us." He was also close with stage actress Libby Holman, sixteen years his senior, who had become a notorious feature in the gossip columns following the suspicious death of her wealthy husband, rumors of lesbianism, and her general practice of dating younger men. Clift was so protective of Holman that when offered the plum role of the male lead in *Sunset Boulevard*, he turned it down—reportedly to avoid any suggestion that Libby Holman was his own delusional Norma Desmond, using a handsome young man to pursue her lost stardom.

Clift was unperturbed by his apparent lack of a love life: he told the press that he would get married when he met a girl he wanted to marry; in the meantime, he was "playing the field." When another columnist asked him if he had any hobbies, he replied, "Yes, women." But as the years passed, it became more and more clear that Clift wasn't just picky. He was, at least in the press, something approaching asexual—the title of a *Motion Picture* article, "authored" by Clift, declared simply, "I Like It Lonely!"

The unspoken truth was that Clift was gay. The revelation of his sexuality did not emerge until the seventies, when two high-profile biographers, one endorsed by his close confidants, revealed as much, rendering him a gay icon within the span of two years. Today, it's impossible to know the specifics of Clift's sexuality: his brother, Brooks, would later claim that his brother was bisexual, while various writings from within Hollywood indicate that Clift's sexuality wasn't entirely a secret. In Truman Capote's unpublished novel *Answered Prayers*, for example, the author imagines a dinner party between Clift, Dorothy Parker, and flamboyant stage actress Tallulah Bankhead:

> ". . . He's so beautiful," murmured Miss Parker. "Sensitive. So finely made. The most beautiful young man I've ever seen. What a pity he's a cocksucker." Then, sweetly, wide-eyed with little girl naïveté, she said "Oh. Oh dear. Have I said something *wrong*? I mean, he is a cocksucker, isn't he, Tallulah?" Miss Bankhead said: "Well, d-d-darling, I r-r-really wouldn't know. He's never sucked *my* cock."

Other testimonies to Clift's gayness abound: early in his film career, he had purportedly been warned that being gay would ruin him; he was so conscious of being seen as feminine or fey in any way that when he ad-libbed a line in *The Search*, calling a boy "dear," he insisted that Zinnemann reshoot the take.

Clift's sexuality, like those other fifties idols Rock Hudson and Tab Hunter, was carefully concealed from the public. But that didn't mean that the gossip press didn't hint at something different, something *queer*, in the broadest sense of the word, about him. Just look at the fan magazine titles: "Making Love the Clift Way," "Two Loves Has Monty," "Montgomery Clift's Tragic Love Story," "Is it True What They Say About Monty?" "Who is Monty Kidding?" "He's Travelin' Light," "The Lurid Love Life of Montgomery Clift," and, perhaps most flagrantly, "Monty Clift: Woman Hater or Free Soul?" Benign to most but, in hindsight, highly suggestive.

Whatever relationships Clift may have had, he was circumspect. Unlike Rock Hudson, whose affairs were very nearly exposed to the entire nation by *Confidential*, Clift never made the pages of the scandal rags. He was "lonely," yet with the help of his refusal to live in Los Angeles or participate in café society, he was able to keep his private life private.

After the success of *The Heiress*, Clift signed on and signed off of *Sunset Boulevard* (1950), opting instead for *The Big Lift* (1950), shot on location in Berlin, a clear attempt to emulate the Italian neorealist style that was sweeping the art houses. The film was somewhat forgettable, but no matter: his next film, *A Place in the Sun* (1951), was anything but. An adaptation of Theodore Dreiser's *An American Tragedy*, it would costar Clift opposite Elizabeth Taylor, then hot off of *Father of the Bride* (1950).

A Place in the Sun marked the beginning of Clift's lifelong friendship with Taylor, a relationship that would structure the remainder of his career in ways both surprising and tragic. After the success of *Place* and their electricity on-screen, audiences thought that he and Taylor were an item—a rumor that MGM, Taylor's studio, did little to suppress following the disaster of Taylor's annulled marriage to Conrad "Nicky" Hilton. The rumors were greatly exaggerated, but the two did become very, very close friends: he called her Bessie Mae; she called him Monty.

The two of them in this film are like perfection orbiting perfection. Their performances established Taylor as a sex siren and further textured Clift's existing image: he wasn't just a heart-throb; he was a tortured, emotive, working-class heartthrob—an archetype that would become even more salient when Brando tore through *A Streetcar Named Desire* (1951), released just a month after *A Place in the Sun*.

The performance in *Sun* is classic Method: Clift didn't just spend time in the jail to get a sense of what it would be like; he *slept* there. His emotional connection with his character was so intense that after a take, swimming in his own concentration, he'd be drenched with sweat. And his face at the end of the film is just *ruinous*. It ruined Brando, too: when both he and Clift were nominated for Best Actor, Brando supposedly insisted on voting for Clift. (Clift, in turn, voted for Brando.) Charlie Chaplin, he of faint and sporadic praise, called *Sun* "the greatest movie made about America." Brando and Clift lost Best Actor to Humphrey Bogart, nominated for *The African Queen* (1951)—a poignant reminder that the Academy's selections are conservative and favor the aging star. These two virile, emotional boys were just too much.

Clift next played a priest with prurient desires in Alfred Hitchcock's *I Confess* (1953), angering the Catholic Legion of Decency and repulsing the majority of the moviegoing public. But Clift was unfazed, in part because he was busy filming *From Here to Eternity* (1953), arguably the best postwar-about-war film of the entire period. Today, most associate the Fred Zinnemann–directed film with the image of Burt Lancaster and Deborah Kerr's embrace on the beach, yet it has so much more to recommend it: Donna Reed as a prostitute, a jaw-dropping performance from Frank Sinatra, Clift as an obstinate, honorable, self-loathing soldier. *Eternity* encapsulates the conflicted sentiments of soldierdom—and how to reconcile the masculine drive for freedom with the equally masculine desire to serve and protect one's country.

The part was taxing, asking Clift to run the emotional gamut. And his reputation as a powerful, demanding actor was already such that Burt Lancaster was apparently so scared of being outacted by Clift that he couldn't stop shaking during the entirety of their first scene together. And as Clift himself explained, "When you become angry, tearful, or violent for a part . . . it takes a tremendous toll on the performer emotionally and physically. . . . I either go all out or I don't accept the picture." It's unsurprising, then, that *Eternity* marked the point when Clift's drinking began to get serious. Where his letters to Zinnemann during the filming of *The Search* were introspective and detailed, during *Eternity*, they were scribbled, incoherent messes.

Clift earned yet another Best Actor nomination, and when he lost—this time to William Holden in *Stalag 17*—his position in Hollywood seemed clear. Like Brando, he was an outsider, refusing to submit to any attempt to craft a "star" image, and the rest of the trade disliked him for it. Certain Hollywood sets shunned Clift, Brando, and their tagalong little brother, James Dean, because they saw how good they were, saw how clearly they threatened the way that Hollywood had operated and conceived of acting for the past thirty years. These young men were the future of American film, and they terrified those still clinging to the past.

So what did Clift do? He dropped out of Hollywood entirely. For nearly three years, he was absent from the stage and the screen. When asked what he had been doing during his self-imposed exile, Clift's answer was simple: he'd been reading scripts. Nothing met his standards. In December 1955, he signed a three-picture deal with MGM, agreeing to costar in the Civil War melo-drama *Raintree County* (1957). The script wasn't necessarily that special, but it would give him a chance to reunite with Elizabeth Taylor, and that, it seemed, was enough to pull him out of semi-retirement.

Taylor had married British actor Michael Wilding in 1952, but by 1956, their marriage was in decline. During the filming of *Raintree County*, Clift and Taylor seemed to have rekindled their is-it-or-isn't-it relationship; according to one of Clift's biogra-phers, "Some days he would threaten to stop seeing Elizabeth Taylor—then, the thought would make him burst into tears." Other apocryphal legend has Taylor sending Clift piles of love letters, which he then read aloud to his male companion at the time. It's impossible for us to know what happened—or if the two even had a relationship that went beyond the platonic—but it was returning from a party at Taylor's house, mid-filming for *Raintree County*, that he smashed his car into a telephone pole.

Moments after the accident, actor Kevin McCarthy, driving in front of Clift, ran back to check on him, seeing that "his face was torn away—a bloody pulp. I thought he was dead." McCarthy ran to fetch Taylor, Wilding, and Rock Hudson and Hudson's wife, Phyllis Gates, who all raced to the site of the accident. What hap-pened next is somewhat fuzzy: one version has Hudson pulling Clift from the car and Taylor cradling him in her arms, at which point Clift started choking and motioning to his throat, where, it soon became clear, two of his teeth had lodged themselves after coming loose during the accident. Taylor opened his mouth, put her hand down his throat, and pulled out the teeth. True or not, the resilience of the story is a testimony to what people wanted to believe about the bond between the two stars. According to this version of the story, when photographers arrived, Taylor an-nounced that she knew each and every one of them personally—

and if they took pictures of Clift, who was still very much alive, she'd make sure they never worked in Hollywood again. Regardless of the veracity of this story, one thing remains true: there's not a single picture of Clift's broken face.

According to Clift's doctors, it was "amazing" that he was even alive. But after an initial flurry of coverage, he retreated from public view entirely. Months of surgeries, rebuilding, and physical therapy followed. Production resumed on *Raintree County*, which the studio feared would fail following Clift's accident. But Clift knew the film would be a smash, if only because audiences would want to compare his long unseen face from before and after the accident. In truth, his face wasn't truly disfigured. It was, however, much older—by the time *Raintree County* made its way to theaters, he'd been off the screen for four and a half years. But the facial reconstruction, heavy painkiller use, and rampant alcohol abuse made it look like he'd aged a decade.

And thus began what Robert Lewis, Clift's teacher at the Actors Studio, called "the longest suicide in Hollywood history." Even before *Raintree*, the decline had been visible. Author Christopher Isherwood tracked Clift's decline in his journals, and by August 1955, he was "drinking himself out of a career"; on the set of *Raintree*, the crew had designated words to communicate how drunk Clift was: bad was *Georgia*, very bad was *Florida*, and worst of all was *Zanzibar*. "Nearly all his good looks are gone," Isherwood wrote. "He has a ghastly, shattered expression." And it wasn't just in private record: in October 1956, Louella Parsons reported on Clift's "very bad health" and Holman's attempts to clean him up. His decline was never explicitly evoked, but with his visage in *Raintree County*, it was there for all to see.

While filming his next picture, *Lonelyhearts* (1958), Clift lashed out, proclaiming, "I am not—repeat *not*—a member of the Beat Generation. I am not one of America's Angry Young Men. I do

not count myself as a member of the ripped-sweatshirt fraternity." He wasn't a "young rebel, an old rebel, a tired rebel, or a
rebellious rebel"—all he cared about what re-creating a "slice of
life" on the screen. He was sick of being a symbol, a symptom, a
testament to something.

In *The Young Lions* (1958), released just two years after the accident, the pain and resentment seem almost visible. It'd be his
only film with Brando, even though the two barely shared the
screen. Taylor, at last free from her long-standing contract with
MGM, next used her power as the biggest star in Hollywood to
insist that Clift be cast in her new project, *Suddenly, Last Summer*
(1959). It was a huge wager: since everyone knew how much
booze and pills Clift was on, he was virtually uninsurable on set.
But the producer, Sam Spiegel, decided to go forward, no matter
the risk.

The results were not pretty. Clift couldn't get through longer
scenes, having to split them up into two or three chunks. The
subject matter, which involved him assisting in the cover-up of a
dead man's apparent homosexuality, must have sparked mixed
emotions. Director Joseph Mankiewicz tried to replace Clift, but
Taylor and costar Katharine Hepburn defended and supported
him. Hepburn was reportedly so incensed by Mankiewicz's treatment of Clift that when the film officially wrapped, she found the
director and spat in his face.

The decline continued. Clift appeared in *The Misfits*, a revisionist western best known as the final film of Marilyn Monroe
and Clark Gable. The director, John Huston, supposedly brought
in Clift because he thought he'd have a "soothing effect" on Monroe, who was deeply embroiled in her own addictions, with her
own personal demons. But even Monroe reported that Clift was
"the only person I know who is in even worse shape than I am."
The pictures from the set are as poignant as they are heartbreak-

ing: it's as if all three were meditating on their respective declines, and there's a sad, peaceful resignation at the difference between what their bodies could do and how people wanted to remember them.

But 1961 audiences were too close to the day-to-day deterioration of its stars to see the meditative genius of *The Misfits*. It was also a dark, melancholy film: as a review in *Variety* pointed out, the "complex mass of introspective conflicts, symbolic parallels, and motivational contradictions" was so nuanced as to "seriously confound" general audiences, who were likely unable to cope with the philosophical undercurrents of the Arthur Miller script. Or, as Bosley Crowther, taking the populist slant in the *New York Times*, explained, the characters were amusing, but they were also "shallow and inconsequential, and that is the dang-busted trouble with this film."

Whether morally repulsive or philosophically compelling, *The Misfits* bombed, only to be recuperated, years later, as a masterpiece of the revisionist genre. Looking back, the film had a legacy of darkness surrounding it: Gable died of a heart attack ten days after filming; Monroe was only able to attend the film's premiere with a pass from her stay at a psychiatric ward. She wouldn't die for another year and a half, but *Misfits* would be her last completed film. As for Clift, the shoot was incredibly taxing, both mentally and physically: in addition to acquiring a scar across his nose from a stray bull's horn, severe rope burns while attempting to tame a wild horse, and various other rough-and-tumble injuries, he also performed what has widely come to be regarded as one of his best scenes, a stilted, heartbreaking conversation with his mother from a phone booth. Even if Clift himself was already spiraling out of control, playing a character that did the same only amplified the psychological toll.

Following *The Misfits*, Clift's disintegration continued. He was such a mess on the set of *Freud* (1962) that Universal sued him. While filming a fifteen-minute supporting role as a mentally handicapped victim of the Holocaust in *Judgment at Nuremberg* (1961), he had to ad-lib all of his lines. But something of the old talent remained—or at least enough to earn Clift a nomination for Best Supporting Actor, playing, in the words of film critic David Thomson, "a victim irretrievably damaged by suffering." Plans for Clift to play the lead in the film adaptation of Carson McCullers's *The Heart Is a Lonely Hunter* fell through, in large part due to his uninsurability on set, and promises of a fourth collaboration with Taylor, this time with producer Ray Stark, never came to pass. Between 1963 and 1966, he faded from public view, emerging only to film a final performance in the French spy thriller *The Defector* (1966). But before the film could be released, Clift passed away, wholly without fanfare, at the age of forty-five, succumbing to years of drug and alcohol abuse. Taylor, caught up in filming with Richard Burton in Paris, sent flowers to the funeral. The long suicide was complete.

Many Hollywood stars have committed versions of the long suicide. Biographies of Clift posit that he drank because he couldn't be his true self, because homosexuality was the shame he had to shelter within. But if you look at his own words, his testimonies about what acting did to him, you'll see the culprit. His perpetual question to himself, as he once scribbled in his journal, was, "How to remain thin-skinned, vulnerable, and still alive?" For Clift, the task proved impossible. Clift once said, "The closer we come to the negative, to death, the more we blossom." He took himself to that precipice, but he fell straight in. And so he remains frozen in the popular imagination, circa *From Here to Eternity*—those high cheekbones, that set jaw, the firm stare: a magnificent, proud, tragically broken thing to behold.

CHAPTER THIRTEEN

Marlon Brando's Dirty Dungarees

Forget what you know about Marlon Brando. Forget Vito Corleone, forget cotton balls stuffed in cheeks, forget the unspeakable things involving butter in *Last Tango in Paris* (1962). Forget the obscured, bald specter of *Apocalypse Now* (1979), and certainly forget the hulking embarrassment of *Superman* (1978). Instead, think of Brando in *On the Waterfront* (1954)—walking with the swagger of a boxer, of a man who works with his body every day, yet realizes that his way of life, his code of ethics, is disintegrating beneath him. This was Brando at the height of his powers—when something burned behind his eyes, when his entire body seemed to undulate with energy like a live wire. This is when you could not take your eyes off of him, when the alchemy of his physical and emotive presence threatened to immolate the film on which it was printed.

Brando never entered into a long-term studio contract or had the benefit of publicity fixers, and he was never embroiled in a single large-scale scandal—unless, that is, you count doubling your weight, retreating to your own South Pacific island, sending a Native American to accept your Academy Award, or having three children with your housekeeper scandalous. But that was all

Middle- and Late-Stage Brando. Early Brando was never thrown in jail like Robert Mitchum or denounced on the floor of the Senate like Ingrid Bergman. Along with Dean and Clift, he didn't *break* societal rules so much as *bend* them. In this way, Brando changed not only what audiences expected of a "good performance" on the screen, but the type of behavior they'd accept off of it.

The story of Brando's upbringing was well trod in the press, in part because he was so peculiar and childlike. Descriptions of his parents and the specifics of his adolescence were thus a means of using the past to explain the present, with a little pop-Freudianism thrown in for good measure. According to his family, Marlon— known exclusively as Bud to his intimates—was always serious and determined, but had a distinct flair for drama. At a moment's notice, he would "shimmy up on the mantelpiece," said his sister, "and pose there like a general, clutch his heart as if shot, and topple like a corpse to the floor."

He was the baby brother to two older sisters, and they made a contest out of everything—eating, lying, doing homework the fastest. They ran away from home. They wore weird costumes. They were artistic, imaginative, rambunctious kids, and they were that way, at least according to the press, because their parents were artistic, imaginative, rambunctious adults. Brando's father provided for the family as a businessman, but was, in truth, a "frustrated actor." His mother was an actress at the community playhouse, described as a "volatile, active woman" who regularly brought artistic types from across the nation into the Brando home. Young Brando was embarrassed that his parents weren't "like other parents"—they "played undignified games" and his mother was fascinated by the bizarre, the exotic, the esoteric. Brando didn't act, at least not formally, as a child, yet the descriptions of his childhood make his tremendous, unique talent seem like the natural byproduct of an artistic home.

With such a childhood, it was no surprise that Brando turned into a troublemaking teen. He hated authority and loved pranks, a combination that got him kicked out of a slew of schools. His family was solidly middle class—his grandmother told a reporter, "Don't let him fool you—he never did a stroke of manual labor in his life"—so they carted him off to a military boarding school in southern Minnesota. But according to Brando, he just couldn't reconcile being forced to show respect to those he didn't. He loathed the school clock tower, which chimed on the quarter hour, because it seemed to regiment his entire life. So he climbed the tower, worked the clock loose, and buried it in the ground. The prank wasn't what got Brando expelled—for that, he had to set off firecrackers at a teacher's door—but the stories of an unruly, petulant, nonconforming boy made his behavior once he arrived in Hollywood more understandable. Once a rebellious kid, always a rebellious kid.

After the last expulsion, Brando returned home to Illinois, where he found work with a drainage company, essentially running pipe and digging lines for long hours in the sun. He found the work unconscionably uninteresting—"it was dull and dirty"—but endured six weeks before quitting to follow his sister to New York City, where, according to a well-circulated anecdote, he gave a bootblack his last four dollars simply because he looked like he needed it more than Brando did. Like the tales of young Brando regularly bringing bums home for his mother to feed, the story painted him as a man of impulse, yet with a moral code that bent toward justice.

Once in New York, Brando enrolled in the New School. While waiting for classes to start, he'd sit on the sidewalk and learn to mimic: accents, gestures, dispositions. He was a self-described "village rat," hanging around Greenwich Village, finding himself very impressed with "men with beards who painted" and wiling away the nights talking art and culture with other earnest twentysome-things. He found a spot in the stock company of a theater on Long Island and made his way to the Actors Studio, where he learned the Method from Stella Adler and appeared in some mediocre plays that earned him some good notices.

In *Truckline Cafe*, he caught the eye of Elia Kazan, and when casting began for Tennessee Williams's *A Streetcar Named Desire*, Kazan suggested Brando read for the part of Stanley, for which producer Irene Selznick had been conducting an exhaustive, un-successful nationwide search. Brando read in front of Selznick and Kazan, but he still needed the approval of Williams, who was summering in Provincetown, Massachusetts. So Brando up and hitchhiked his way over—only to arrive in the middle of a storm that had cut off power to the Williams home. Brando fixed the lights, read the part, and got the job; Williams later recounted that thirty seconds into Brando's reading, he knew there would be no other Stanley.

With his good looks and emotive style, Brando had caught re-viewers' eyes before. But as Stanley Kowalski, he was magnetic—a force to behold. As famed *New Yorker* film critic Pauline Kael would recall years later, the first time she saw him onstage, "I looked up and saw what I thought was an actor having a seizure onstage. Embarrassed for him, I lowered my eyes, and it wasn't until the young man who'd brought me grabbed my arm and said, 'Watch this guy!' that I realized he was *acting*."

Brando regularly incited this type of response. Hedda Hopper would later say that when she first saw him onstage, he revolted her. Audiences had never seen anything like what he did on the stage—a startling mix of emotional realism that contrasted sharply with the mannerly school of acting that had become the norm. He and Clift bulldozed Hollywood in the early fifties not because they were handsome but because the way they "got at"

acting—and their characters' emotion—was so profoundly different from the great actors that had come before. The Method calls
for the actor to go *inside* the character, whereas the traditional,
British style of acting—think Laurence Olivier—had the actor
approach the character from the *outside*. It may seem like a fine
distinction, but the results could, as evidenced by Kael's response,
be astonishing.

Brando and his sister, a fellow student at the Actors Studio then
appearing onstage in *Mister Roberts* with Henry Fonda, made the
pages of *Life*, which likened his turn in *Streetcar* to the debut of
storied actor John Barrymore. *Life* also pinpointed two of the hallmarks of Brando's performance and overarching image. First, he
had an "oddly compelling way of speaking"—a way that would
quickly become known as the "Brando mumble" and approxi-
mated, according to him, the actual speech of his characters. The
mumble would become so associated with Brando, in fact, that he
would later take a role in *Julius Caesar* (1953) simply to prove that
he had other modes of diction. But as *Life* noted, the mumble made
him compelling, made him different—made you stop and *listen*.

The *Life* article also included a spread of Brando reading to his
young nephew, a familial tableau that would be reproduced in
dozens of Brando profiles over the years to come. He looks completely at ease, and the four-year-old's foot is in the air the way
four-year-olds do when they're comfortable. But the book was
Bambi, and as Brando read, he became so overwhelmed by the
death of Bambi's mother that he was brought to tears. Whether or
not he cried (or, more likely, whether or not the *Life* staff writer
was there to witness it), the story, along with the article's description of his "deeply meant acting," established Brando, to a national audience, not only as emotionally wrought, but with the
sensitivity of a child—a theme that would undergird much of the
publicity of his early career.

Brando played the role of Kowalski for two years, amassing enough accolades that he could essentially have done whatever he chose. He had his pick of Hollywood scripts, but young Brando was vocal in his principles: he wanted to act, not become a star. But while off exploring Europe, he received a brief treatment of the script for *The Men* (1951) and accepted the role on the spot. For *The Men*, he would play a paraplegic veteran, the exact sort of psychological and physical challenge he craved.

And so Brando went west, with a plan to make a film, prove his worth, and return to the stage in a move meant to suggest where real, serious art should reside. To prep for his role in *The Men*, he stayed in a paraplegic hospital for four weeks, spending all his waking hours in a wheelchair. He made fast friends with the other residents; one night, when they went out drinking, a half-drunk woman came up and lectured the group on the power of positive thinking. Brando, in his wheelchair like the rest of the men, listened attentively, then began to slowly rise from the chair, effectively blowing the woman's mind. Stories like this, with their unique combination of earnestness and rascalry—would become a mainstay of the Brando image.

The Men was a middling film, remarkable mostly for Brando's studied performance. But he had already agreed to repeat his role as Stanley for the film version of *Streetcar* (1951), a move that would turn a noteworthy performance into an iconic one. Before, most of America could only read about what Brando was doing differently; with *Streetcar* on the big screen, they could *feel* it. Stanley may have been a plodding asshole, but he—or, more precisely, Brando's performance of him—was also explosively sexual. As one producer explained, "When femmes saw him in *Streetcar* they crawled right up the theater walls. They say there's a large shot of masochism in every dame. I wouldn't know. I do know that they shivered and wriggled at the way he talked, although some nights you could hardly hear him past the tenth row."

That sort of animal sex appeal—*that* was what made Brando a star. If he had just been talented, he'd most likely have stayed on the stage. Mainstream Hollywood supports many things, but serious, experimental art has not historically been one of them. But Brando was also spectacularly, ruinously handsome. And while he certainly inspired no small amount of teen squeals, he was not a teen idol like James Dean. Brando was the kind of handsome that gives grown women shivers, with a sort of physical imprint that lingers in the back of your head for days.

The excitement concerning Brando's maleness was, in truth, over the *working-class* maleness he seemed to embody. This was due in part because the roles that would make him famous were so clearly marked as such (Stanley Kowalski; road biker; longshoreman), but also because the way he comported himself off the screen so precisely matched that image, all dirty dungarees and T-shirts rolled over the biceps. Hedda Hopper called him "Hollywood's New Sex Boat," recounting how, when she mentioned his name over coffee, it "instantly spread over my living room like a flash fire. 'Marlon Brando? He's exciting! Marlon Brando! He's coarse, he's vulgar! Marlon Brando, *he's male!*'"

Brando never made it back to the stage, but he didn't change his attitude toward Hollywood. He wore his opprobrium on his sleeve, refusing to make friends with the gossip columnists or submit to interviews with the fan magazines. When Hopper called upon him, he sat in silence for fifteen minutes, grunting twice; he commonly referred to her as "the one with the hat" and Louella Parsons as "the fat one." When asked to pose for the cover of *Life*, he answered, "Why would I want to do that?"

Like Clift, Brando cared little for money or other trappings of the Hollywood elite. He lived like a bum, in filthy, cluttered apartments. In 1951, he ran an advertisement in *The Saturday Review of Literature*: "Apartment Wanted—Any Old Thing." A *Photoplay* article scornfully described his "habitual costume of Levi's, a T-shirt, and moccasins without socks," a radical statement in an era when male stars were still wearing uniforms of finely tailored trousers. He didn't like "glamour girls" or Hollywood starlets, ignoring them in favor of the "homeliest waifs." And his hobbies skewed to the eccentric: he loved to play congas and marimbas, and specialized in playing the recorder with his nose; he owned a pet raccoon; and he was known to make an entire meal out of peanut butter. (When asked why he didn't fall for *Desire* costar Jessica Tandy, his answer: "She doesn't like peanut butter.")

Brando, at least at this point, wasn't mean-spirited: he was like Rousseau's natural man, a child of nature who simply followed his whimsy. He was "utterly without malice," with the same sort of dogged concentration—and easy distractibility—that typified boyhood. And it wasn't just the pet raccoon—he loved to play pickup sticks and tag; he'd regularly spend a whole afternoon throwing snowballs in the park, analyzing his tactical mistakes on the way home. As a "close friend" explained, "I don't believe a water-pistol has been invented that hasn't been fired in Marlon Brando's apartment." But he wasn't pure id either—he loathed that others presumed he was like Stanley Kowalski in real life. The real Brando was the antithesis of Kowalski: "I despise that type of human being."

Brando's proclivities were doubtless exaggerated. He was an odd guy, but at a certain point, you couldn't find a profile that didn't emphasize his peculiarities. In some ways, it was his fault: since he refused to sit for interviews or provide other means of copy, writers simply found an angle and ran with it until his weirdness consumed the story. Brando had a press agent, but he didn't have anyone telling him what to do, whom to date, what not to say, whom to respect—and if they did, he would've ignored them.

Brando got away with this type of behavior on the amplitude of his stardom. After smoldering his way through *Streetcar*, he donned full "brown face" as Mexican revolutionary Emiliano Zapata in *Viva Zapata!* (1952), proved he could do Shakespeare as Mark Antony in *Julius Caesar*, helped solidify the leather biker look while riding his own motorcycle in *The Wild One* (1953), and made "I coulda been a contender" into a timeless catchphrase in *On the Waterfront*. He earned four Oscar nominations in as many years, finally winning for *On the Waterfront*. In these films, Brando's performances made people feel something that modern viewers can't quite understand, as contemporary Hollywood is peppered with actors who either adhere to the Method (Robert De Niro, Daniel Day-Lewis, Meryl Streep, Christian Bale, Sean Penn) or bastardize aspects of it to "go ugly" and win an Oscar (Charlize Theron, Nicole Kidman).

But back in the early fifties, Brando was operating on an entirely different level than everyone around him. In these films, there's Brando and then there's everyone else succumbing to his gravity. Take, for example, his role in *On the Waterfront*, and the way he interacts with his love interest, played by Eva Marie Saint. What Brando does with Saint over the course of the film is subtle but spectacular: she plays a woman made of Catholicism, shrillness, and buttoned-up jackets who suddenly becomes sexy before the audience's eyes. Part of the transformation can be credited to good directing, lighting, and costuming, but as Brando falls in love with her, the lustful way *he* looks at her somehow becomes the way the audience looks at her.

By 1955, Brando was arguably the biggest star in Hollywood, with his choice of roles. But he was also psychologically exhausted, and in early 1954, he disappeared, failing to appear on set to begin shooting Fox's costume drama *The Egyptian*. He turned up in New York City under the care of a psychoanalyst, who reported that Brando was sick and confused and would be unable to report to the set for at least ten weeks. Fox head Darryl Zanuck tried to work a deal—he'd pay for the analyst to come to Los Angeles; he'd have a phone line between the two open at all times—but Brando balked. Fox sued for breach of contract, but even the language of the two-million-dollar lawsuit underlined Brando's enduring worth: he possessed "unique, unusual, and extraordinary skill and ability." He was, in other words, irreplaceable.

Brando was indeed undergoing analysis, but as he'd later reveal, his real problem with *The Egyptian* was that he hated the material. "Who," he asked, "could act with 50,000 camels? It was nothing but a camel opera." But with a two-million-dollar lawsuit hanging over his head, he made a deal: he'd take the Napoleon role in *Désirée*, Fox's other big-budget costume drama, and split the costs of the filming delay on *The Egyptian*.

Désirée proved to be Brando's first misstep. It made back twice its budget, but the star seems wooden, miscast, distinctly un-Brando. It also marked the beginning of a new period in his public and private life, as he seemed, at least ostensibly, to put away childish things. Here was a new, "domesticated" Brando to replace the old, petulant one: according to the *New York Times*, as soon as his analyst helped him realize that he was play-acting at Kowalski as a means of avoiding "facing himself," he was set free. He wore a tux to accept his Best Actor Oscar win, even posing happily with Best Actress winner Grace Kelly and giving her a chaste peck on the cheek. "That Mad Man Marlon," as one fan magazine had labeled him, was seemingly growing up.

As if to authenticate the claim, Brando proposed to Josanne Mariani-Berenger, the daughter of a French fisherman who'd come stateside to nanny. It was a classic Brando move: with hundreds of thousands of girls fawning over him, he opted for the least likely choice. This wasn't his first high-profile romance: there was a fling with Shelley Winters, an extended to-do with Movita Castaneda, and a dalliance with Rita Moreno. A scandal rag even declared him the "World's Worst Lover" for his predatory Don Juan tendencies. But the details of Brando and Mariani-Berenger's whirlwind courtship made him sound like a bit of a romantic: in "How Marlon Brando Proposed," the type of story usually reserved for the likes of Debbie Reynolds, *Modern Screen* detailed Brando's care and affection for Mariani-Berenger. He invited her to the set, protected her from reporters, and was, according to a friend, "really gone on her," traveling to her hometown in the South of France to meet her parents and announce their engagement.

The fan magazines also constructed Mariani-Berenger as Brando's match: she was a realist, she was tolerant, and most important, she expected Brando to be "moody, quixotic, and unconventional." She was also exotic—which, as evidenced by Brando's high-profile romances with Castaneda and Moreno, he seemed to like. And as she told the press, she didn't love Brando because he was a star, but as a man like any other. Plus, she was a "sloppy dresser" with "odd manners," and the two had first met at his analyst's office—clearly, they were meant for each other.

But Brando's ardor could only last so long. As Castaneda commented upon the announcement of their engagement, "There is a big difference between getting engaged and getting married. We shall see." She was right: less than six months after the engagement, gossip columnist Sheilah Graham reported their engagement had turned into the "long-term-don't-see-each-other-very-often" variety.

The problem, as Mariani-Berenger later recounted, was the publicity. After Brando visited her parents' home, in Bandol,

France, he was the one who encouraged her mother to run the wedding announcement in the local paper. But after the press descended, he grew angry with Mariani-Berenger, claiming that she and the press had goaded him into an engagement. This anger was part of a newly energized antipathy toward the press. He had never been shy about his disdain—in 1953, he had claimed that Hollywood writers asked "such dull, such stupid, such irritating questions"—but while filming *Guys and Dolls* in 1955, he issued an official ban on all fan magazine stories and pictures, informing the film's producers that he'd only agree to publicity stills if they weren't handed over to the gossip press.

The magazines were predictably indignant: *Photoplay* divulged the "secret" of Brando's policy, rallying its readers to send in an attached coupon to voice their anger. In the editors' words, "Marlon's too big to be invisible—and too big a star to be ignored." *Photoplay* was right: Brando's presence had simply become too *big*. He overpowered every role; his turn in *Guys and Dolls* was overshadowed by the knowledge that you were watching Marlon Brando's ardent attempts to sing. And with the new realities of Hollywood, he could choose whatever role he wanted, date whomever he pleased, get paid whatever he desired. With effectively no oversight and enormous demand for his services, Brando began to indulge: in women, in food, in his own vanity. The films after *On the Waterfront* are successively more bloated and embarrassing, and a 1957 *New Yorker* profile, written by Truman Capote, made it clear that Brando was not only fatuous, but perhaps even a dilettante.

The decline steepened. In October 1957, he surprised everyone, including still-technically-fiancée Mariani-Berenger, by marrying Anna Kashfi; a son, Christian, was born seven months later. A year after their marriage, Kashfi filed for divorce, citing Brando's generalized indifference and persistently strange lifestyle. Yet she found herself pregnant once again, and when she lost the baby in January, she reported that Brando had been missing for months. "He loves the adulation of a mob sitting as his feet," she explained, "drooling over him for endless hours." In a custody trial a year later, Brando admitted, without shame, to spanking, slapping, and tying up Kashfi. But, as he equivocated, it was always in self-defense—a response to when she tried to call the police, came at him with a knife, or threw herself on the bed and starting biting him. No manner of recuperative publicity could take the knowledge of that story, with its stinging malice, away.

Brando's first production as a director, *One-Eyed Jacks* (1961), spiraled out of control, a morass of grand vision, hubris, and inexperience. Before production wrapped, he grew so frustrated that he walked away entirely, leaving the studio to pick up the pieces of an unfinished film. He became a political firebrand, denouncing the behavior of the so-called ugly American abroad and marching in antisegregation protests, but never taking up one cause for long. Interviews were replete with unfulfilled promises to quit acting entirely, and when he bought a Tahitian island in 1966, his descent into high-profile megalomania seemed complete.

And so Brando turned rancid. He repeatedly claimed he had no respect whatsoever for acting—it was a "bum's life" that culminated in "perfect self-indulgence. You get paid for doing nothing and it all adds up to nothing." In fact, the only reason he kept acting was that it paid for his psychoanalysis. Which explains his choices in the post-*Godfather* period: a smattering of bad roles in forgettable films for big paychecks. His turn as Jor-El in *Superman* (1978), for which he was paid a staggering $3.7 million, was little more than a glorified cameo. Nonetheless, once the film became a global blockbuster, Brando sued for $50 million in additional profits—a perfect manifestation of the "pure self-indulgence" he'd evoked twenty years before.

Looking back, there is no doubt: Brando was an emotional genius, capable of channeling an astounding intricacy of experience into each performance. The true scandal, then, was that a talent so promising would so predictably succumb to its own hubris. His decline was far more tragic than any illicit affair or recreational drug use, as it betrayed what fame and adulation could do to the actual bodies and psyches that compose our popular images. Indeed, for all Brando's gravitas in *The Godfather* and *Last Tango in Paris*, both performances lack the vibrancy and vitality of his work in the early fifties. Instead, they seem to spring from a well of shame and despair, appealing to the audience to mourn an ideal of masculinity gone to seed.

Brando had an entire generation's desire pulsing under his finger, with a gravity that drew the world to him despite his repeated efforts to repulse it. But the lesson, it seems, is that no one can wield such power on his own. Not a king, not a movie star, not even a brilliant actor in dirty dungarees.

CHAPTER FOURTEEN

James Dean:
Entombed in His Own Myth

James Dean's entrance into the American psyche was in full color: blazing blue eyes, wounded and searching; a crisp red leather jacket that popped off the screen in *Rebel Without a Cause*, suggesting an ironic confidence that his character so tragically lacked. There was a distinct tiredness to his face, as if the pain of living was just too exhausting, and it was this wounded quality that would, over the course of three years, attract a cult of feminine devotion. Dean had the shortest career of any major Hollywood star, spanning but three films, two of which were released after his death in a head-on collision en route to a car race. It could've been a scene in one of his movies—which, of course, is part of the reason for its mythologization. Like Marilyn Monroe's, Dean's image has been flattened, reproduced on posters, and used as a stand-in for youthful rebellion and the tragedy of lost potential. But in the mid-fifties, Dean meant something far more nuanced—much more the sum of his *Rebel* parts.

Dean was seven years younger than Brando, eleven years younger than Clift—the classic kid brother, caught in a constant strain to match what they had become. The earnest transparency of his affection was almost pitiable: Brando and Clift humored him intermittently, but the press was ruthless. He was a poor man's Brando, constantly compared to his Method antecedents; the praise he was given for his performances often invoked Brando and Clift. But Dean was playing a different sort of character: he stood for those who were too young to serve in the war, but whose formative years were spent under its shadow; who emerged into the 1950s lacking the sense of gravity and experience of their elders. These men and women, and the nervous, restless energy they emitted, would eventually coalesce into the various social revolutions of the sixties.

But in 1955, Dean and the characters he played suggested something new in the same way that Clift and Brando had four years before. He was the next wave in the same emotional tide: a part, yet apart. Today, his performance reads as dangerously close to over-the-top, brimming with self-revulsion and despair. But to a generation of fans, he was articulating a new language of confusion and conflict that they would appropriate, elaborate on, and, over the course of the next decade, use as a weapon of protest.

Before Dean became an icon, he was just a young boy from a broken Indiana home. His father was a dental technician at the local VA; his mother kept house, but the Dean family had "worked Indiana land" for more than two hundred years. It was, at least according to the press, "in Jimmy's blood." As proof, even when Dean and his family moved to Los Angeles when he was six, he still wore his farm clothes, hung out with animals, and spent his time outdoors. But his mother died when he was nine, and his father sent him back to Indiana to live with his aunt and uncle.

As a child, Dean had been an accomplished violinist, but gave up music when his mother died; as a teen, he was president of the thespians club and won the state oratory competition. But he was never one for the whimsical or the flowery; from the start, his vision bent toward the macabre. For the state competition, he chose a piece of Dickens that was, in his words, about "a real gone cat who knocks off several people. It also begins with a scream. I really woke up those judges."

After graduation, Dean moved to Los Angeles to live with his father, starting out at Santa Monica Junior College as a PE major and spending his spare time announcing for the FM radio station. He enrolled in a prelaw class at UCLA and attempted to join a fraternity, but "busted a couple of guys in the nose" and got the boot, a story that sounds suspiciously like something out of Brando's playbook. He dropped out of school, found himself an agent, and managed to get cast in a smattering of bit parts, the evidence of which would be neatly passed over to celebrate his "screen debut" several years later in *East of Eden* (1955).

The bit parts were unsatisfying, so he followed a friend's recommendation to move to New York, where he enrolled in the Actors Studio and, like Brando, embraced the Method. Once Dean was in New York, famed casting director Marion Dougherty saw something in him, championing him for parts in several televised anthology dramas, which led to his casting as a mentally handicapped boy in *See the Jaguar*, a play so "arty and experimental" it closed after five performances. But it was that role that attracted the attention of powerful agent Jane Deacy, who signed Dean to a personal contract and helped him land the role of a devious, queer "native houseboy" in *The Immoralist*. The *New York Times* complimented his "insidious charm," and *Theatre Review* named him, along with Harry Belafonte and Eva Marie Saint, one of the twelve most promising actors of the year.

His performance also caught the eye of Elia Kazan, fresh off of *On the Waterfront* and in search of stars for his upcoming adaptation of *East of Eden* for Warner Bros. He had discussed having Clift and Brando play the Cain-and-Abel-esque brothers in the film, but both were busy with other projects. Kazan saw something in

Dean, and with a little push from Deacy, that something was enough to get him back to Hollywood, where he, unlike Clift or Brando, signed a contract—nine films over six years for Warner Bros. In a letter sent to his on-again, off-again girlfriend, Barbara Glenn, from his father's house, Dean oscillated between despair and sexual frustration:

> I don't like it here. I don't like people here. I like it home (N.Y.) and I like you and I want to see you. Must I always be miserable? I try so hard to make people reject me. Why? [. . .] I DONT KNOW WHERE I AM. Rented a car for 2 weeks it cost me $138.00. I WANT TO DIE. I have told [Redacted] and 5 others like her to kiss my ass and what stench, spineless, stupid prostitutes they were. I HAVENT BEEN TO BED WITH NO BODY. [. . .] Wow! Am I fucked up. I got no motorcycle I got no girl. HONEY, shit writting [sic] in capitals doesn't seem to help either.

Dean was a nobody in Los Angeles; he was poor; he was back with his father. Yet his eyes remained set firmly on both Clift and Brando—he signed the letter "Jim {Brando Clift} Dean."

In Brando's memoir, he remembers visiting Kazan on the *East of Eden* set, where he first met Dean. "He had a simplicity I found endearing," Brando recalls, and "he was nervous when we met and made it clear that he was not only mimicking my acting but also what he believed was my lifestyle. He said he was learning to play the conga drums and had taken up motorcycling, and he obviously wanted my approval of his work." The press picked up the similarities between the two even before *Eden*'s national release: a *Life* spread from March 1955 declared him the "most exciting actor to hit Hollywood since Marlon Brando," while the

New York Times highlighted "a lively controversy over [Dean's] histrionic kinship with Marlon Brando" and Hopper declared him "more versatile and better looking than Brando."

Dean may have been the poor man's Brando, but he was younger and more sullen and clearly took far less pleasure in his well-cultivated "individuality" than his freewheeling idol. *Life* commissioned Dean's friend, Dennis Stock, to photograph him in his "formative landscapes" of Indiana and New York, and the results, including an iconic shot of a rain-drenched Dean in Times Square, hands deep in his pockets, cigarette hanging from his mouth, were published the week before *Eden*'s release. The spread's title: "Moody New Star."

That moodiness, combined with an "unvarnished individuality" dating to his performance in *The Immortals*, would ground Dean's image for the duration of his career. The *Times* compared him to a reckless Booth Tarkington hero, while *Life* reported his "militantly independent" behavior off the screen and Brandoesque disregard for the rules of Hollywood, along with his dragracing habit, were making his studio very, very nervous. When Hopper first saw him in the Warner Bros. commissary, he was hunched over the table, looking around the room with brooding eyes, declaring his membership in what she termed the "dirty shirt school of acting."

Dean was "beautifully nuts," capable of making you love and loathe him in the span of one conversation. "I'm a serious-minded and intense little devil," he admitted. "Terribly gauche and so tense I don't see how people stay in the same room with me. I know I wouldn't tolerate myself." He also didn't tolerate fan magazine writers and gossip columns, with the noted exception of Hopper, whom he managed to summarily charm (and who, after his death, would become the guardian of the "true" James Dean story).

Dean's romantic life read like an overwrought scene from one of his movies. While filming *East of Eden*, he met the young, beautiful Italian starlet Pier Angeli and, in the words of one fan magazine, his "wordless longing" was over. They dated for only a matter of months, but candid photos from the time show a couple with an indelible charisma—or at least something quite true in the way Dean looked so lovingly upon her. But Angeli's mother never approved of Dean: his moodiness, quirkiness, and aimlessness, his sloppy clothes and disregard for Angeli's curfew, and most crucially, his lack of Catholicism made him an inappropriate match for her wholesome daughter. The two continued to date, and Dean even escorted her to the premiere of *A Star Is Born*, allowing cameras to capture them in clear coupledom.

But a week later, Angeli announced her engagement to crooner Vic Damone. Her mother was gleeful: there were "no religious differences" between Damone and Angeli; plus, he was a good Italian (American) boy. But Dean was wrecked. When the couple exited the church after their wedding, he was waiting across the street, sobbing. Or at least that's what the "cult of Dean" came to understand in the months following his death, and it was enough to enlist them against Angeli: as the sixteen-year-old president of the James Dean fan club later put it, Angeli "jilted Jimmy. I hate her. A girl friend of mine found out where she was staying in New York. My girl friend tripped her in the lobby for what she did to Jimmy."

But this sort of fanatic protection of Dean was still more than a year in the future. At the time of the actual breakup, he was still an unproven, if highly anticipated, talent, following a blueprint for stardom suspiciously similar to Brando's from five years before. Before and after his courtship of Angeli, he spent his time daredeviling around on bicycles and in fast cars, wearing old trousers and T-shirts. He held Hollywood in low regard, broadcasting his plans to return east and return to high art. In one interview, he was set to direct an expressionist film; in another, he'd direct a one-act opera at Tanglewood. And all this publicity before *Eden* even opened wide.

Reviews for *Eden* were mixed. Bosley Crowther, the cantankerous *New York Times* film critic, was scathing:

> Dean scuffs his feet, he whirls, he pouts, he sputters, he leans against walls, he rolls his eyes, he swallows his words, he ambles slack-kneed—all like Marlon Brando used to do. Never have we seen a performer so clearly follow another's style. . . . Whatever there might be of reasonable torment in this youngster is buried beneath the clumsy display.

Brando himself recoiled at the performance, purportedly stating that while he had great respect for Dean's talent, in *Eden*, he appeared "to be wearing my last year's wardrobe and using last year's talent." It's unclear whether Dean took such a critique as criticism or praise—he was not, after all, cagey about his drive to emulate Brando. And apart from the grumbling comparisons, the rest of the press was generally effusive. Hopper declared that she couldn't remember a time when a newcomer had "aroused as much excitement" as Dean had with his debut—an excitement that she, having finally seen *East of Eden*, had come to share, labeling him a "young genius."

But Dean didn't have time to dwell on reviews: a week after *Eden*'s release, he started production on Nicholas Ray's *Rebel Without a Cause* (1955). *Rebel* crystallized the generational conflict that would retrospectively define the decade. Dean's Jim Stark loathes his parents and what they represent but craves their approval; his mother is domineering and his father is shamefully passive: in a crucial scene, he even dons an apron. Stark rebels not because he's immoral, but because he's bored, numb, yearning to feel something. He's hopelessly misunderstood, and it's that feeling, not a desire to harm others, that powers his recklessness. Given the way the press had been framing Dean—and how Dean, for that matter, had been framing himself—it's easy to see why he was cast, and why his performance, and its seemingly immaculate reflection of his "real" life, became so powerful for so many.

Dean finished with *Rebel* in May 1955, moving on to the Texas oil drama *Giant* (1956), with Elizabeth Taylor and Rock Hudson. Instead of a self-loathing teen, Dean played a self-loathing, villainous oil baron; as Brando and other critics would later note, *Giant* was the first time that Dean stopped trying to play Brando and started to play something of his own creation. Even the crotchety Crowther would praise his performance, calling it the "most tangy and corrosive in the film," with a "stylized spookiness and a sly sort of off-beat languor and slur of language—that concentrates spite."

Giant wrapped filming in late August, and Dean, whom Warner Bros. had banned from racing cars until the end of the shoot, was ready to cut loose. With mechanic Rolf Wutherich, Dean set out for the Salinas Road Races in his newly purchased Porsche 550 Spyder—one in a long line of sports cars Dean had purchased or traded for since arriving in California. According to legend, he had shown the car to actor Alec Guinness, who supposedly called the car "sinister" and told Dean, "If you get in that car, you will be found dead in it by this time next week."

Exactly one week later, on September 30, 1955, the twenty-four-year-old Dean collided headfirst with a Ford coupe, killing him and severely injuring Wutherich. He had been pulled over below Bakersfield, California, at 3:30, and was killed at the California Route 466/61 junction at 5:30 P.M.—meaning he covered

150 miles in two hours, with an average speed of seventy-five miles an hour. Accounting for natural slowdowns, he was likely driving between ninety and a hundred miles an hour the entire time. It was details like this—along with a PSA against driving too fast on the highway, made during the filming of *Giant*—that made the death seem so eerie and fated, even cinematic.

And so man became myth. Recall that at the time of his death neither *Rebel Without a Cause* nor *Giant* had been released. Dean was, at this point, a handsome, sudden star with one movie to his credit. But with the gossip press and Warner Bros. both eager to exploit his death, it took very little to turn him into a cultural touchstone. It's not that the fan magazines or Warner Bros. were acting maliciously—they simply recognized how the death of a promising young star could benefit them, particularly one who seemed to resonate with an elusive yet coveted demographic, a demographic that went to fewer and fewer movies and bought fewer and fewer movie magazines.

By the time *Rebel Without a Cause* opened in late October, Dean was everywhere. The major fan magazines all devoted special "exclusive" sections to him, mining the depths of his family and acquaintances for any semblance of a unique revelation concerning his childhood, romances, moody years in New York, or "death drive." Dozens of "one-shot" magazines delved even deeper, providing psychoanalysis, fan art, and the 1950s version of fan fic. It became a sort of macabre feedback loop: the more Dean information emerged, the more readers clamored for more. Plus the similarities between his death and the tragic drag-race finale of *Rebel Without a Cause* were too uncanny to be ignored. The details leading up to the accident were meticulously reconstructed, with various anecdotes, explanations, and retrospective theorizations weaving together to form a portrait of Dean that, just weeks after his death, already bore the marks of the mythic.

In mainstream magazines and newspapers, the so-called hysteria surrounding Dean's death became yet another symptom of the undisciplined youth culture. In a one-shot titled *The Real James Dean Story*, fans testified to "the star they'll never forget." One girl hated fan clubs of all kinds, but made her own kind of club with two of her friends, sitting around, looking at pictures of Dean, talking about how wonderful he was, and playing a record called "James Dean (the Greatest of All)," crying fiercely as they listened. Others reported seeing *Rebel Without a Cause* over and over again, weeping from beginning to end, and legions of fans wrote in with poetry and tributes memorializing his short life.

Riding that wave of emotional energy, *Rebel Without a Cause* grossed $4.5 million at the box office—an impressive figure for a relatively low-budget teen film. Dean won the 1955 Audience Award, and his performance in *Eden* was nominated for an Oscar. But the frenzy didn't end with *Rebel*. Indeed, the anticipation of *Giant*, released a full year after his death, kept Dean alive in the public imagination in a way we can't quite understand. *Giant* grossed thirty-five million dollars, Dean won another Oscar nomination, and the mourning of a swath of America began to consolidate into the amorphous yet enduring shape of a cult.

Writing in 2002, film critic David Thomson declared, "Many stars, no matter how well they survive passing time, are only eminent because of the way they first mark consciousness. Once penetrated, we never forget the star." He was talking about Dean and his own experience, as a young man, with the star—an experience that made him understand what it must have been like for the audience of the twenties to lose Rudolph Valentino.

Today, our closest analog is Heath Ledger, but his pain seemed too distant; his performances, however incendiary, were too far away, too far gone. His death was tragic, but it didn't move people the way Dean's did—perhaps because Ledger first touched teen

Acknowledgments

This book was a complete surprise to me. I mean that in so many ways: when I first started writing the columns that eventually inspired it, back in May 2011, I had no inkling that they would ever turn into anything as substantive as a book. I also thought that my years studying Hollywood stars and scandal meant that I understood each of chapters before I even started writing them, but the time I spent immersed in the piles of discourse that surrounded each proved otherwise. There's the story as we understand it now, and then there's the story as it was understood then—rarely did those two narratives match up. The writing of this book has thus been a study in patience, diligence, and a willingness to let go of what I wanted to believe.

It was also a work of untraditional collaboration. I may not have had cowriters, but I've had dozens of people assist in ways they might not even have realized. First and foremost, this project never would have been possible if Edith Zimmermann, editor emeritus at *The Hairpin*, hadn't taken a chance on me. I sent her a fragmented 1,500 words on Ingrid Bergman and she saw nothing but possibility and has been my champion ever since. I can't overstate this: without her, my writing career would not be what it is.

I simply can't thank her enough. At the Hairpin/Awl Network, Jane Marie, Nicole Cliffe, Choire Sicha, Carrie Frye, Emma Carmichael, and Jia Tolentino have not only supported the Scandals series but encouraged my weird forays into all corners of the pop culture universe. Writing for these sites introduced me to Mallory Ortberg and Simone Eastman, who are as close to Internet feminist partners in crime as a girl can get.

But let's be truthful: I only know this stuff the way that I know it because of what I learned in school. At Whitman College, Robert Sickels has been my mentor and friend for more than fourteen years, and his slides (actual slides) of Hollywood Stars, ca. 1999, were my first introduction to the cult of classic stardom. He's also responsible for the line "Cary Grant knew how to wear clothes," and for that insight I am forever grateful. Whitman also provided generous support for research materials, including piles of beautiful old fan magazines, over the course of the writing of this book. Kathleen Rowe Karlyn introduced me to the work of my academic theorist boyfriend, Richard Dyer, who really provides the foundation on which all of my work rests. My dissertation adviser, Janet Staiger, has such a knack for seeing nuance where others see a straight narrative, and conversations with her have significantly informed my understandings of so many of the stars included in this book. In addition to teaching me almost all I know about the industrial workings of Classic Hollywood, Tom Schatz also cured me of writing like an academic. It's his book, *Genius of the System*, that served as a model for the sort of academic/ popular hybrid text that I hoped to write.

Because this book isn't a traditional academic publication, I haven't been able to underline the work of various scholars who have so deeply informed my understanding of these stars and their respective scandals. A brief list: Gaylyn Studlar on Mary Pickford, Mark Lynn Anderson on Wallace Reid, Sam Stoloff on Fatty

Arbuckle, Ramona Curry on Mae West, Mia Mask on Dorothy Dandridge, Richard Dyer on Judy Garland, Amy Lawrence on Montgomery Clift, Mary Desjardins on *Confidential* magazine, and Adrienne McLean's work on Hollywood scandal have provided the theoretical foundation on which each scandal narrative was built. If you'd like to read more about any of the stars featured in this book, these scholars' works are the place to start.

I've been lucky to have found an inspiring and supportive academic and writing community via social media, including Rebecca Onion, Angela Serratore, Jason Mittell, Allison Wright, Karen Petruska, Amanda Ann Klein, Alisa Perren, Kristen Warner, and Courtney Brannon Donoghue. Phil Maciak, Janu Hu, and Lili Loofbourow—my Dear Television cohort—make me a better writer and thinker every day. Emily Carman, Ross Melnick, and Eric Hoyt have all challenged me to think expansively about film history, and without Eric's initiative digitizing old fan magazines via the Media History Digital Library, this book, as is, would have frankly been impossible.

I'm so incredibly grateful to the faithful readers of both the original *Hairpin* column and my blog, many of whom have been reading and sharing my work long before this project. Without their support, I never would've kept with the blog, and probably never would've gained the gumption to start writing for a larger audience. They are the engine that keeps me writing—the thing that makes all of this worth it.

My agent, Allison Hunter, took a chance on me when I was just a girl with a bloggy column that used a lot of swear words. From the beginning, she saw the vision I had for the project and worked diligently until we found an editor who saw it as well. That editor, Kate Napolitano, has been so generous, insightful, and deft with her shaping of my thoughts. The difference between good writing and great writing is excellent editing, and if this book approximates anything close to "great," it's all thanks to Kate.

In order to write a book, you have to have a whole host of people who will be willing to help you get away from that book. Alaina Smith, Beth Randall, and Anna Pepper served that incredibly crucial function in Seattle while Matt Detar, Adam Gordon, Jen Cohen, Lucy Schwallie, Lisa Uddin, Josh Slepin, Jamie Warren, and Melissa Salrin distracted me in Walla Walla. My mom paid for a subscription to *Entertainment Weekly* when I was ten and watched Mae West movies with me when I was thirty-two: she's the consummate supporter of my work and the strongest, most resilient woman I know. My brother, Charles Petersen, provided me with the access to the African American newspaper archive that gave the chapter on Dorothy Dandridge life; he also was the first person to encourage me to publish my work in a public forum, and for that I owe him a huge thank-you and a massive noogie. Finally, my partner, Krzys, makes the ordinary seem extraordinary, the quotidian seem like an adventure. I so love living this screwball life with you.

Notes

Chapter One

5 **In 1909 alone:** Christine Gledhill, "Mary Pickford: Icon of Stardom," in *Flickers of Desire: Movie Stars of the 1910s*, ed. Jennifer M. Bean (New Brunswick, NJ: Rutgers University Press, 2011), 47.

5 **A review in *The Bioscope*:** Cited in Gaylyn Studlar, "Oh, 'Doll Divine': Mary Pickford, Masquerade, and the Pedophilic Gaze," *Camera Obscura* 16, no. 3 (2001): 196–227.

6 **IMP, their studio at the time, exploited the pairing:** Gledhill, "Mary Pickford," 60.

7 **as historian Scott Curtis describes:** Scott Curtis, "Douglas Fairbanks: Icon of Americanism," in *Flickers of Desire: Movie Stars of the 1910s*, ed. Jennifer M. Bean (New Brunswick, NJ: Rutgers University Press, 2011), 219.

8 **Fairbanks replied:** "A Close-Up of Douglas Fairbanks," *Everybody's Magazine,* December 1916.

9 **Even the April 1918 announcement:** "Owen Moore Says He'll Act in Own Protection," *Los Angeles Times*, April 14, 1918.

9 **Moore emphasized that it was Fairbanks:** Ibid.

10 **In April 1918, she announced her plans:** "Mary Pickford Will Go into Total Retirement," *Los Angeles Times*, April 30, 1918.

10 **By the time Pickford filed for divorce in March 1920:** "Mary Pickford Denies She'll Wed Fairbanks," *Los Angeles Times*, March 6, 1920.

11 **It was a gossip dream come true:** "Mary Pickford and Douglas Fairbanks Are Secretly Married Here," *Los Angeles Times*, March 31, 1920.

11 **The pair were criticized for their choice of minister:** "Resident Divorce Crux," *Los Angeles Times*, April 1, 1920; "Brougher Gives Wedding Views," *Los Angeles Times*, April 3, 1920.

11 **The *Washington Post* framed the culmination as a "real life drama":** "Mary Pickford Stars in Real Life Drama," *Washington Post*, April 4, 1920.

12 **In an issue released two months after the marriage:** Billy Bates, "The Pickford-Fairbanks Wooing," *Photoplay*, June 1920, 70–73.

12 **Upon their much-vaunted return to Hollywood:** "Doug and Mary Home Again," *Los Angeles Times*, August 11, 1920.

13 **"I've never been to any of the places in Hollywood":** "Horrible Hollywood, Home of Hokum," *Literary Digest*, June 10, 1922, 42–46.

Chapter Two

15 **He attended Santa Clara College:** Alfred A. Cohn, "He Never Laughs on Sunday," *Photoplay*, June 1919, 58.

16 **He was championed as a master director:** "Arbuckle Worth Nearly a Million," *Los Angeles Times*, September 12, 1921; "Estimate Cash for Arbuckle," *Los Angeles Times*, September 13, 1921.

16 **Even his history was reshaped:** "Weighed 16 Pounds at Birth," *New York Times*, September 14, 1921.

16 **A 1915 *Photoplay* article offered tongue-in-cheek advice:** K. Owen, "Heavyweight Athletics," *Photoplay*, August 1915, 35.

17 **He was the punch line for one-liners:** "The Answer Man," *Photoplay*, August 1921, 82.

17 **When a fan queried *Photoplay* as to the identity of Arbuckle's wife:** Ibid.

18 **When Rappe and her friends arrived:** "Mystery Death Takes Actress," *Los Angeles Times*, September 10, 1921.

18 **Lowell Sherman reported that her behavior:** "Did Not Think Girl Was Hurt," *Los Angeles Times*, September 23, 1921.

18 **Delmont told Arbuckle to get out of the room:** "Arbuckle Charge to Be Fixed Today," *Washington Post*, September 28, 1921.

19 **They took off her clothes:** Ibid.

19 **Semnacher alleged:** "Testifies Arbuckle Admitted Attack," *New York Times*, September 22, 1921.

20 **What's more, he was negligent:** "Grave of Arbuckle's Mother Neglected," *Los Angeles Times*, September 13 1921; "Bulldog Mourns for Arbuckle," *Los Angeles Times*, September 14, 1921.

20 **The papers framed the party:** "Discover Long Liquor Trail," *Los Angeles Times*, September 19, 1921; "Booze Parties Reported," *Los Angeles Times*, September 13, 1921; "Many Theatres Ban Arbuckle Pictures," *New York Times*, September 13, 1921.

20 **He proclaimed his innocence:** "Comedy and Tragedy," *Los Angeles Times*, September 13, 1921.

20 **Even men unconnected to the film industry:** "Booze Parties Reported," *Los Angeles Times,* September 13, 1921.

21 **For Myra Nye . . . the entire industry was at fault:** Myra Nye, "The Tin Gods," *Los Angeles Times*, September 16, 1921.

21 **dozens of religious leaders:** "To Preach on Arbuckle," *Los Angeles Times,* September 17, 1921.

21 **Producers must thus:** "Unjust to Blame All Filmdom," *Los Angeles Times*, September 19, 1921.

21 **Senator Henry Myers claimed:** "Movie Arraigned by Senator Myers," *New York Times,* July 30, 1922.

22 **No matter that his actual films:** "Clean Pictures That Will Please Children, Arbuckle's Aim," *Motion Picture News*, May 12, 1917.

23 **They appointed devout Presbyterian:** "Moving-Picture Morals Attacked and Defended," *Current Opinion*, April 1922, 505.

23 **Hays's first act as head of the MPPDA:** "Arbuckle Films Banished from Film by Hays," *New York Times*, April 19, 1922.

23 **The ban resulted in the loss of ten thousand booking contracts:** Ibid.

24 **Arbuckle stood trial three times:** "Appeal Made by Arbuckle," *Los Angeles Times*, December 25, 1922.

24 **Hays even lifted the ban on his films:** "Hays Insists Stand Right," *Los Angeles Times*, December 24, 1922.

24–25 **The National Education Association publicly insisted:** "National Educational Body Protests Arbuckle Return," *Washington Post*, December 22, 1922; "Directors Not for Arbuckle," *Los Angeles Times*, December 23, 1922.

Chapter Three

27 **he starred in five race car films:** Wallace Reid, "What I Think of Myself," *Washington Post*, May 29, 1921.

28 **Yet Reid was keen to disassociate himself:** "We Interview Wally," *Motion Picture*, September 1921.

29 **But his "dabblings" marked him:** Mark Lynn Anderson, *Twilight of the Idols: Hollywood and the Human Sciences in 1920s America* (Berkeley: University of California Press, 2011), 16.

29 **that's what the fan magazines worked very hard to suggest:** Mrs. Wallace Reid, "Getting Back at Friend Husband," *Photoplay*, November 1921, 20–21.

29 **the star theorized that the best way:** Cited in ibid.

29 **Reid was hospitalized:** "Report Wally Reid," *Los Angeles Times*, October 21, 1922.

29 **The press explained:** Ibid.

30 **His recovery was framed:** "Narcotics Given Up," *Los Angeles Times*, December 16, 1922.

30   **These ruffians . . . were the source**: Ibid.

30   **"My husband is a sick, sick boy"**: Ibid.

31   **the man in question**: "Wally Reid Ruined by Drugs, Is Charged," *Washington Post*, December 17, 1922.

32   **One thing led to another**: "Evelyn Nesbit Thaw Tells of Hollywood Dope Parties," *Washington Post*, December 18, 1922.

32   **Hays, working with Davenport**: "Wally Reid Better; Wife Talks of Case," *New York Times*, December 19, 1922.

32   **Various bits of information**: "Had Dope for Star," *Variety*, November 19, 1920.

32–33   **When *Motion Picture* interviewed him**: Adele Whitely Fletcher and Gladys Hall, "We Interview Wally," *Motion Picture*, September 1921.

33   **Davenport also claimed**: Dorothy Davenport Reid, "Wally Reid's Confirmed Use of Drugs Revealed," *San Francisco Examiner*, January 3, 1923.

33   **she somewhat unconvincingly averred**: "Drug Quiz Is Asked," *Los Angeles Times*, December 19, 1922.

33   **His mother-in-law claimed**: "Wally Reid Better; Wife Talks of Case," *New York Times*, December 19, 1922.

33   **Because Reid was such a hardworking, selfless guy**: William Parker, "Reid Got 'Dope' Habit in N.Y., Says Wife," *Los Angeles Evening Herald*, December 22, 1922.

34   **The train wreck didn't happen**: Dorothy Davenport Reid, "Wife Pens Dramatic Story of Wallace Reid's Drug Ruin: Dope Curse Traced to Car Injury in 1919," *San Francisco Examiner*, December 31, 1922.

34   **Reid attended to fellow passengers**: Ibid.

34   **These melodramatic explanations**: "Wallace Reid Improved," *Los Angeles Times*, December 23, 1922.

34   **His purported last words**: "Wally Reid Dies After Long Fight," *Los Angeles Times*, January 19, 1923.

35 **His equally heroic wife:** "Thousands to Honor Reid," *Los Angeles Times*, January 20, 1923.

35 **Hays announced that the Prohibition commissioner:** "Haynes Finds Orgies in Films Exaggerated," *New York Times*, January 25, 1923.

35 **Just weeks after Reid's death:** "Mrs. Wallace Reid, Author; Widow Will Carry On," *Los Angeles Times*, January 29, 1923.

35 **Because Reid was pure "life":** Ibid.

36 **Trumpeted as "a great success":** "Mrs. Reid's 'Human Wreckage' a Great Success," *Photoplay*, September 1923.

Chapter Four

43 **He would dance with them:** Alexander Walker, *Stardom: The Hollywood Phenomenon* (New York: Stein and Day, 1970), 158.

44 **But as critic Alexander Walker points out:** Ibid.

44 **the press worked to construct Valentino:** Quoted in Amy Lawrence, "Rudolph Valentino: Italian American," *Idols of Modernity: Movie Stars of the 1920s*, ed. Patrice Petro (Rutgers University Press, 2010).

45 **Dick Dorgan exclaims:** Dick Dorgan, "A Song of Hate," *Photoplay*, July 1922, 26.

46 **Following the release of *Beyond the Rocks*:** Rudolph Valentino, "Woman and Love," *Photoplay* March 1922, 40–43.

46 **He was also a sexual conservative:** Ibid.

47 **Valentino countered that all her correspondence:** "Wedded, Found Spouse Broke," *Los Angeles Times*, November 24, 1921; "Stars to Battle in Court," *Los Angeles Times*, November 14, 1921.

47 **Valentino busied himself with buying:** Harry Carr, "The Hollywood Boulevardier Chats," *Motion Picture Classic*, April 1922, 64–65.

47 **Lest he be embarrassingly charged:** Harry Carr, "On the Camera Coast," *Motion Picture*, August 1922, 74.

48 **Rambova established herself as the better of every reader:** Ruth Waterbury, "Wedded and Parted, or, in Other Words, the Story of Natacha Rambova Valentino," *Photoplay*, December 1922, 58.

48 **He had been unhappy for months:** Walker, *Stardom*, 164.

49 **He published a very plaintive:** Rudolph Valentino, "Open Letter to American Public," *Photoplay*, January 1923.

49 **He wrote for *The Bookman*:** Gladys Hall, "Are the Movie Folk Morons?" *Motion Picture*, April 1923, 53.

49 **If all the Renaissance man activity:** Walker, *Stardom*, 166.

49 **When Valentino finally reached a deal:** "Valentino Coming Back," *Los Angeles Times*, December 26, 1923.

49 **His return to the screen was eagerly anticipated:** Tamar Lane, "That's Out," *Motion Picture*, September 1924, 61.

50 **Valentino's performance and wardrobe:** "News and Views of Eastern Stars," *Motion Picture*, December 1924, 64–65.

50 **He was roundly ridiculed:** Allan R. Ellenberger, *The Valentino Mystique: The Death and Afterlife of the Silent Film Idol* (Jefferson, NC: McFarland & Co, 2005), 14.

50 **As a writer for the *Chicago Tribune* exclaimed:** Quoted in "Sufferin' Powder Puffs! Why Rudolph Wants a Duel," *Los Angeles Times*, July 21, 1926.

50 **independent producer Joseph Schenck:** Walker, *Stardom*, 167.

50 **In late August 1925:** "Screen Sheik Admits Break," *Los Angeles Times*, August 21, 1925.

51 **Amid rumors of new dalliances:** Agnes Smith and Milton Howe, "Gossip of the Camera Coasts," *Motion Picture*, May 1926, 46.

51 ***Motion Picture* declared that Valentino was old news:** Don Ryan, "Has the Great Lover Become Just a Celebrity?" *Motion Picture Classic*, May 1926; Tamar Lane, "That's Out," *Motion Picture*, April 1925, 58.

51 **Judging from the writer's reaction:** "Sufferin' Powder Puffs," *Chicago Tribune*, July 18, 1926.

51 *Los Angeles Times* **columnist Harry Carr:** Harry Carr, "The Lancer," *Los Angeles Times*, July 21, 1926.

52 **By August 20, 1926:** "Valentino Gaining; Asks to Leave Bed," *New York Times*, August 21, 1926.

52 **In the aftermath of Valentino's death:** Edwin Schallert, "Colony Mourns Rudy's Passing," *Los Angeles Times*, August 24, 1926.

52 **Even Carr . . . admitted that the star had broken:** Carr, "The Lancer."

53 **At the suicide inquest:** "Denies Girl Suicide Had Known Valentino," *New York Times*, October 6, 1926.

53 **In September, a nineteen-year-old girl:** "Girl Dies Grasping Valentino Picture: Body Found in Room in Newark . . ." *New York Times*, September 22, 1927; "Tries to Join Valentino: Woman Declaring Love for Dead Actor Fails in Suicide Attempt," *New York Times*, October 31, 1926.

53 **months before Valentino's death:** "Cites Three Causes for Suicide Wave," *New York Times*, March 9, 1927.

Chapter Five

56 **Growing up in Brooklyn:** Adela Rogers St. Johns, "My Life," *Photoplay*, February 1928, 30.

56 **But the cameraman was a local guy:** "Clara Bow Puts Over a Rapid One," *Washington Post*, April 21, 1928.

57 **On loan to First National:** "New Pictures," *Photoplay*, July 1924.

57 **She moved on to Victor Fleming:** Adela Rogers St. Johns, "The Hollywood Story," *American Weekly*, December 24, 1950.

58 *Photoplay* **heralded:** Portrait of Clara Bow, *Photoplay*, December 1924.

58 **columnist Alma Whitaker warned:** Alma Whitaker, "A Dangerous Little Devil Is Clara, Impish, Appealing, but Oh, How She Can Act!" *Los Angeles Times*, September 7, 1924.

58 **This noncompliance was part of what the columnists meant:** Marquis Busby, "All Flappers Don't Flap," *Los Angeles Times*, May 29, 1927.

58 **She loved going to football games:** Janet French, "Do You Believe This?" *Photoplay*, May 1930, 78.

59 **She was, in her words, "a big freak":** Lois Shirley, "Empty Hearted," *Photoplay*, October 1929, 29.

59 **By the mid-twenties, the Hays office:** Sara Ross, " 'Good Little Bad Girls': Controversy and the Flapper Comedienne," *Film History* 13, no. 4 (2001): 410.

59 **as she told the *Los Angeles Times*:** Busby, "All Flappers Don't Flap."

59 **If even the so-called super-flapper:** "New Pictures," *Photoplay*, August 1927, 19.

59 **The concept of the "It" girl:** Quoted in Lori Landay, *Madcaps, Screwballs, and Con Women: The Female Trickster in American Culture* (Philadelphia, University of Philadelphia Press, 1998), 80.

61 **One play-by-play of a rendezvous:** Cal York, "News! Views! Gossip! of Stars and Studios," *Photoplay*, April 1930, 48.

61 **Pearson's wife . . . was six months pregnant:** David Stenn, *Clara Bow: Runnin' Wild* (New York: Cooper Square Press, 2000), 195.

61 **The head of Paramount ordered her home:** "Clara Bow Ordered Home," *Los Angeles Times*, June 20, 1930.

62 **Bow emerged from the ordeal without punishment:** Ibid.

62 **the gossip press began to note an expansion of her figure:** Leonard Hall, "Star Names That Mean Fight!" *Photoplay*, June 1930, 38–39.

62 **When fans wrote in protest:** Ibid.

62 **She had ignored . . . DeVoe's insistence:** "Ex-Aide of Clara Bow Hints at Contract Suit," *Los Angeles Times*, November 13, 1930.

62 **her flippant reply:** "Clara Bow Challenges Gaming Debt Seekers," *Los Angeles Times*, September 24, 1930.

62 **Henry Herzbrun, attorney for Paramount:** "Clara Warned to Watch Step," *Los Angeles Times*, September 26, 1930.

62–63 **From that point forward:** Stenn, *Runnin' Wild*, 164–65.

63 **The friendship soured:** "Miss Bow Case in Grand Jury," *Los Angeles Times*, November 15, 1930.

63 **DeVoe was indicted on thirty-seven counts of grand theft:** "Daisy De Voe Indicted," *Los Angeles Times*, November 26, 1930.

63 **But as Bow testified:** "Clara Bow Counters Aide's Henna Charge," *New York Times*, January 18, 1931.

63 **These telegraphs were introduced:** "Love Missives in De Voe Case," *Los Angeles Times*, January 14, 1931.

64 **She lashed out at DeVoe:** Ibid.

64 **In a description dominating the front page:** "Temper Loosed by Clara Bow," *Los Angeles Times*, January 15, 1931.

64 **She was especially enraged:** "Clara Bow Counters Aide's Henna Charge."

64 **DeVoe fired back:** "Clara Bow's Secrets Told," *Los Angeles Times*, January 17, 1931.

64 **The judge realized:** " 'Mud Slinging' Banned," *Los Angeles Times*, January 20, 1931.

65 **Riverside, California, censors:** "Riverside Censors Bar Clara Bow Film," *Los Angeles Times*, January 22, 1931.

65 **Paramount withdrew Bow:** "Clara Bow Taken from Film Cast," *Los Angeles Times*, January 17, 1931.

65 **Starting in late March, a pulpy tabloid:** Stenn, *Runnin' Wild*, 227–28; see *Coast Reporter* from March 28, April 4, April 11, and April 18, 1931.

65 **DeVoe would deny this claim:** "Temper Loosed by Clara Bow."

66 **Girnau was subsequently arrested:** Stenn, *Runnin' Wild*, 228.

66 **she had a nervous breakdown:** "Clara Bow Plays Role of Invalid," *Los Angeles Times*, May 7, 1931.

66 **Paramount and Bow came to a mutual agreement:** "Clara Bow Out at Paramount," *Los Angeles Times*, June 9, 1931.

66 **The exhausted Bow was pleased:** "Cal York on Hollywood," *Photoplay*, March 1931, 48–51.

67 **And so the new, "rough," Clara emerged:** Harry Lang, "Roughing It with Clara," *Photoplay*, September 1931, 30.

67 **But the simplicity of Bow's new life:** Ibid.

67 **But as *Photoplay* columnist Leonard Hall pointed out:** Leonard Hall, "Where Now, Clara?" *Photoplay*, August 1931, 55.

68 **The studio was careful:** Henry Crosby, "The Return of Clara Bow," *Photoplay*, November 1932, 27.

68 ***Photoplay*, ever eager to trumpet a comeback:** Portrait, *Photoplay*, October 1932, 20.

68 **Bow retreated again to ranch life:** "Clara Hates to Take Time Out to Be a Vamp," *Daily Boston Globe*, December 10, 1933.

Chapter Six

73 **Harlow was the original "blonde bombshell":** Mary Anderson, "The Sex-Jinx on Stardom," *Photoplay*, August 1935, 28.

74 **On-screen, her characters took what they wanted:** Ibid.

77 **she was a Kansas City society girl:** "In Case You Were Interested in that Kansas City Blondie," *Washington Post*, November 30, 1930.

77 **The exact shade evaded description:** Leonard Hall, "Hell's Angel," *Photoplay*, January 1931, 69.

77 **only one woman in a thousand had hair and coloring:** May Allerton, "Don't Go Platinum Yet! Read Before You Dye!" *Photoplay*, October 1931, 30.

77 **It's no wonder she became known:** Marion Martone, "Your Gossip Test," *Motion Picture*, September 1931, 96.

77 **Print ads for the film promised:** Cited in Hell's Angels ad, *New York Times*, August 18, 1930.

79 **In April, a catty *Motion Picture* columnist:** Robert Fender, "The Hollywood Circus," *Motion Picture*, April 1931, 16.

79 **In September, *The Saturday Evening Post* emphasized:** Frank Condon, "Kansas City Platinum," *Saturday Evening Post*, September 19, 1931.

79 **She appeared on Hollywood Boulevard:** Gladys Hall, "The Hollywood Frivolities of 1931," *Motion Picture*, February 1932, 35.

80 **And so the women gathered:** Condon, "Kansas City Platinum."

80 **After describing a night out on the town:** Ruth Leiber, "But I Can Unmask Jean Harlow!" *Photoplay*, October 1931, 71.

80 **a feature on her autumn style:** "Jean Harlow Sets the Styles for Autumn," *Motion Picture*, October 1931, 65.

81 **Whether or not Crawford ever actually feuded:** "Jimmy Fidler in Hollywood," *Washington Post*, October 12, 1936. See also: Dorothy Manners, "Has Jean Become Joan's Rival?" *Movie Classic*, July 1933, 23.

81 ***Red-Headed Woman* was thus sold:** Susan Ohmer, "Jean Harlow: Tragic Blonde," in *Glamour in a Golden Age: Movie Stars of the 1930s*, ed. Adrienne L. McLean (Piscataway, NJ: Rutgers University Press, 2011), 174–95.

82 **The film was a triumph:** Ibid, 181.

82 **But during the filming of *Red-Headed Woman*:** "What Red Hair Did to a Platinum Blonde," *Photoplay*, August 1932, 69.

82 **It was the red hair that brought her love:** Ibid.

83 ***Motion Picture* reported that Bern was well known:** Dorothy Donnell, "Jean Harlow Marries Paul Bern," *Motion Picture*, September 1932, 64.

83 **He was so beloved:** Faith Service, "The Man Jean Harlow Has Married—Paul Bern," *Photoplay*, October 1932, 51.

83 **Nearby, a cryptic suicide note:** Muriel Babcock, "The Headline Career of Jean Harlow," *Motion Picture*, December 1932, 30.

84 **Harlow had been staying with her parents:** Ibid.

84 **At some point in the mid-1920s:** "Tells of Other Woman," *New York Times*, September 8, 1932.

84 **Bern's brother, Henry:** "Girl Here Entered Paul Bern's Life," *New York Times*, September 8, 1932.

84 **When he emerged from the MGM offices:** "New Complications Add Mystery," *Los Angeles Times*, September 9, 1932.

85 **The next day, Bern's doctor:** "Bern Last Will Gone from Box," *Los Angeles Times*, September 14, 1932.

85 **acting on pressure from MGM:** From the Coroner's Inquest transcript; see David Stenn, *Bombshell: The Life and Death of Jean Harlow* (Lightning Bug Press, 2000), 112.

85 *Time* **extrapolated on the findings:** "Death in Hollywood," *Time*, September 20, 1932, 20.

85 **Even when the coroner clarified:** Adela Rogers St. Johns, "The Jean Harlow Story Hollywood Suppressed," *Photoplay*, August 1937, 19.

86 **The inquest endured for months:** Elza Schallert, "Jean Harlow Gives First Statement on Tragedy," *Los Angeles Times*, October 2, 1932.

86 **In the weeks after the suicide:** Ibid.

86 **Harlow's future was nevertheless framed:** Edwin Schallert, "Will Bern Tragedy Kill Jean Harlow's Career," *Los Angeles Times*, September 18, 1932.

86 **The film grossed $1.2 million:** Edwin Schallert, "Crisis in Film Career Passed," *Los Angeles Times*, October 22, 1932.

87 **To further distract from the scandal:** Louella Parsons, *Los Angeles Examiner*, June 13, 1937; Louella Parsons, *Los Angeles Examiner*, August 24, 1933.

87 **When gossip columnist Louella Parsons interviewed:** Ibid.

87 **MGM planted a few gossip bits:** "News and Gossip of the Studios," *Motion Picture*, October 1933.

88 **Rosson maintained that he had loved Harlow:** "Jean Harlow Explains Elopement," *Los Angeles Times*, September 19, 1933.

88 **Louella Parsons called the press reception:** Louella Parsons, *Jean Harlow's Life Story* (New York: Dell Publishing, 1937).

88 **A lengthy feature:** Dorothy Manners, "Explaining Jean's 'Surprise' Marriage," *Motion Picture*, October 1933, 51.

88 **Rosson was also presented as the reason:** John C. Moffitt, "Inside Story of Star's Three Weddings Told," *Los Angeles Times*, September 24, 1933.

88 **As for elopement:** "Why Do Movie Couples Elope," *Motion Picture*, December 1933, 64.

88 **She was, in her words:** Manners, "Explaining Jean's 'Surprise' Marriage."

88 **A week after the wedding:** Grace Kingsley, "Hobnobbing in Hollywood," *Los Angeles Times*, September 20, 1933.

88 **Their planned honeymoon to Hawaii:** "Actress in Emergency Operation," *Los Angeles Times*, October 16, 1933; Ruth Rankin, "Jean Battles a Sea of Rumors," *Photoplay*, April 1934, 32.

89 **While many female stars had played:** "Hollywood Cleans House," *New York Times*, June 15, 1934.

89 **And so the Legion issued:** Ibid.

90 ***Never Been Kissed* thus transformed**: Philip K. Scheuer, "Harlow Seeks Pal, Husband," *Los Angeles Times*, August 3, 1934.

90 **Howard Strickling, head of MGM publicity:** Howard Strickling, "A Hollywood Observer Appraises Star of Whose Nature Public Knows Little," *Washington Post*, October 20, 1935.

90 **She was hanging out with William Powell:** Sidney Skolsky, "Hollywood," *Washington Post*, November 26, 1935.

90 **The doyennes of the studio:** Catherine Jurca, *Hollywood 1938: Motion Pictures' Greatest Year* (Berkeley: University of California Press, 2012), 102.

91 **She was drinking heavily:** See Stenn, *Bombshell*, 207.

91 **when Gable came to visit her:** Taylor Orci, "The Original 'Blonde Bombshell' Used Actual Bleach on Her Head," *The Atlantic*, Feb-

ruary 22, 2013, http://www.theatlantic.com/health/archive/2013/02/
the-original-blonde-bombshell-used-actual-bleach-on-her-
head/273333.

91 **Obituaries and remembrances emphasized:** "Burial Dress Will Be
White," *Los Angeles Times*, June 8, 1937.

91 **A *Washington Post* headline promised:** "Jean Harlow's Charm Will
Be Missed," *Washington Post*, June 8, 1937.

Chapter Seven

96 **According to oft-repeated lore:** Mae West, "I'm No Angel! Why
Should I Be?" *Los Angeles Times*, October 29, 1933.

96 **She claimed that to achieve the "fine figure":** Cecilia Ager, "Mae
West Reveals the Foundation of the 1900 Mode," *Vogue*, September 1, 1933, 67.

96 **she insisted that during her teens:** West, "I'm No Angel!"

97 **Testimony from others on Broadway:** Harry Richman, "West of
Broadway," *Hollywood*, October 1934, 17.

97 **West may have *seemed* very à la mode:** Dana Rush, "Back of the
West Front," *Photoplay*, February 1932, 60.

97 **The newspapers refused to run the print ads:** Ruth Biery, "The Private Life of Mae West," *Movie Classic*, February 1934, 32.

97 **When West was arrested and jailed:** Ibid.

98 **Future projects . . . benefited from the same type of publicity:**
"Mae West Trial Feb. 3.: Date Tentatively Set at Crain's Request
in 'Pleasure Man' Case," *New York Times*, January 14, 1930.

99 **The somewhat devious solution:** Ramona Curry, *Too Much of a
Good Thing: Mae West as Cultural Icon* (University of Minnesota
Press, 1996), 30–31.

99 ***Photoplay* ran an anticipatory piece:** Leonard Hall, "Look Out!
Here's Mae West!" *Photoplay*, January 1933, 46.

100 **Across the country, there were reports:** Jay Brien Chapman, "Is

Mae West Garbo's Greatest Rival?" *Motion Picture*, July 1933, 28.

100 **The film was not immune to censorship:** Ibid.

100 **As one fan exclaimed in the "letter of the month":** "Letters from Our Readers," *Motion Picture*, August 1933, 8.

101 **But in print and in interviews:** Maude Lathem, "'Will I Last' Asks Mae West," *Motion Picture*, June 1934, 28.

101 **Sex, to West:** "The Crime of the Day in Hollywood," *Motion Picture*, January 1934, 70.

101 **Critics affirmed her rhetoric:** Andre Sennwald, "Lines for a Mae West Scrap-Book," *New York Times*, September 30, 1934.

101 ***Motion Picture* asserted that even with its sexual explicitness:** "The Picture Parade," *Motion Picture*, April 1933, 68.

101 **But West's frankness:** Elza Schallert, "Go West—If You're an Adult!" *Motion Picture*, May 1933, 32.

101 **She wasn't ashamed of her body:** "'Remain Young,' Is Mae West's Tip to Women: 'Don't Diet,' She Advises; Play Dumb Enough, and Be a Pal," *Washington Post*, June 6, 1936.

102 **in the era of Roosevelt:** Chapman, "Is Mae West Garbo's Greatest Rival?"

102 **The earliest Hollywood publicity:** Hall, "Look Out!"

102 **a sentiment echoed by countless:** Dorothy Donnell, "Mae West Is Robbed of Famous Diamonds in Daring Hold-Up," *Movie Classic*, January 1933, 25; "Three Men—And All Kissed by Mae West," *Motion Picture*, November 1933, 34; Alma Whitaker, "Mae West Loves to Shock 'Em, for Business Reasons: And Anyway, Out-and-Out Vulgarity More Moral Than Refined Sin, She Asserts," *Los Angeles Times*, April 16, 1933.

102 **She never drank or smoked:** Schallert, "Go West."

102 **she went to church every Sunday:** Cornelius Vanderbilt Jr., "Who's Really Who in Hollywood Society," *Photoplay*, April 1938, 21–22.

102 **As she told one fan magazine:** Aileen St. John Brenon, "The Real Mae West," *New Movie Magazine*, August 1934, 32.

102 **when a fan asked her whether she lived:** Eric L. Ergenbright, "Mae West Answers Your Questions," *Motion Picture*, August 1933, 55.

102 **While some doubted the earnestness of West's claims:** Dorothy Calhoun, "Hollywood Starts a Big Clean-up," *Movie Classic*, February 1934, 68.

103 **It's like West was the new girl:** Biery, "The Private Life of Mae West."

103 **West was such a threat:** Chapman, "Is Mae West Garbo's Greatest Rival?"

103–4 **The feud was exacerbated when Dietrich:** "War Clouds in the Sky?" *Photoplay*, December 1933, 47.

104 **Paramount and the fan magazines:** Sonia Lee, "Dietrich Isn't Afraid of Mae West," *Motion Picture*, January 1934, 49.

104 **Paramount had to beg its *own* stars to attend:** C. B. Gray, "Green-Eyed Jealousy," *Photoplay*, February 1934, 50–51.

104 **it was the stars, who were jealous:** Ibid.

104 ***I'm No Angel*, sold under the luscious tagline:** "So Mae West's Slipping? Not So She Can Notice It!: 'I Was a Finished Product When I Started and I'm Getting Better,' She Says," *Los Angeles Times*, May 20, 1934.

104 **her apparent refusal to grant interviews:** Kirtley Baskette, "Has Mae West Gone High Hat?," *Photoplay*, June 1934, 39.

106 **The original plan:** Edwin Schallert, "'Indo-China,' Film With Foreign Background, Will Prove Change for Joan Crawford," *Los Angeles Times*, July 5, 1934.

106 **West then purportedly acquired:** Will F. French, "What Price Glamour?," *Motion Picture*, November 1934, 29.

106 **it wasn't entirely her fault:** "What's New on the Screen," *Hollywood*, October 1934, 6.

106 **Paramount and the press reinvigorated efforts to disassociate West:** William F. French, "It's All In Fun," *Movie Classic*, December 1934, 27; Mark Dowling, "Don't Get Me Wrong," *Motion Picture*, December 1934, 33.

106 **she was also framed as classy:** Ibid.

107 *Photoplay* **paired the feature with drawings of West:** "Mae West Can Play Anything," *Photoplay*, June 1935, 90.

107 **in anticipation of her next film,** *Goin' to Town*: Ad for the "New Stream-Lined Mae West" in *Photoplay*, May 1935.

107 **West even admitted that** *Belle* **had been a disaster:** "Miss West Talks Shop: In Which the Buxom Mae Discusses the Theories That Motivate Her Art," *New York Times*, February 3, 1935.

107 **It was just dull:** Andre Senwald, "The Paramount Presents Mae West in 'Goin' to Town'—'Bride of Frankenstein,' at the Roxy," *New York Times*, May 11, 1935.

108 **She claimed it must've been some other Mae West:** "Marriage in Milwaukee in 1911 Denied by Mae West," *Los Angeles Times*, April 22, 1935.

108 **Then there was the matter of the annoying ex-husband:** "Mae West Faces Tilt: Wallace Asks That Court Declare Him Husband of Film Star," *Los Angeles Times*, May 11, 1935.

109 **In June 1934, a fan magazine had questioned West:** Lathem, " 'Will I Last.' "

Chapter Eight

113 **After several months of speculation:** "Gable Will Become Army Private Today," *New York Times*, August 12, 1942.

114 **In high school, Gable was good at sports:** "The Cinema's Ranking 'Matinee Idol' Had Hard Row to Hoe to Reach Heights," *Washington Post*, September 29, 1935.

115 **Dillon polished his acting skills:** "Open Letters to Clark Gable from His Former Wife," *Motion Picture*, July 1933, 27.

115 **He was . . . a bit of a kept man:** Sheilah Graham, "Gable Discusses Ladies but Keeps It Professional," *Los Angeles Times*, June 8, 1936.

115 **He found various roles:** "Clark Gable, the Lonely Man," *Look*, September 14, 1954, 60–65.

116 **He did a screen test for Warner Bros.:** Turner Classic Movies, *Leading Men: The 50 Most Unforgettable Actors of the Studio Era* (San Francisco: Chronicle Books, 2006).

116 **MGM cast him in increasingly prominent roles:** "News from the Hollywood Studios," *New York Times*, August 2, 1931.

116 **Like Valentino, Gable sent an "electric shock":** Harry Carr, "Can He Be Another Valentino?" *Los Angeles Times*, August 2, 1931.

116 **But it was a specific type of physical presence:** James R. Quirk, "Why Women Go Crazy About Clark Gable," *Photoplay*, October 1931, 67.

117 **He was quoted:** J. Eugene Chrisman, " 'I'm No Saint,' Says Clark Gable," *Motion Picture*, February 1932, 28.

117 **authors emphasized his mighty build:** Harry Long, "What a Man—Clark Gable," *Photoplay*, October 1931, 34.

117 **His shoulders were so broad:** "The Cinema's Ranking 'Matinee Idol.' "

117 **He hated wearing neckties and other fancy clothes:** "Clark Gable Pictorial," *Motion Picture*, June 1932, 20; Cal York, "Newest Hollywood Fad," *Photoplay*, June 1932, 36.

117 **He gives the same impression of "physical power":** Chrisman, " 'I'm No Saint.' "

117 **Hollywood was far too civilized:** Jerry Lane, "Why I Like to Be Alone," *Motion Picture*, October 1932, 51.

117–18 **His house proved he was a "he-man":** Dorothy Calhoun, "Any

Man Would Like Clark Gable's House!" *Motion Picture*, August 1934, 52.

118   **This was certainly no Valentino:** Lane, "Why I Like to Be Alone"; Chrisman, " 'I'm No Saint.' "

118   **Gable himself underlined the association:** William F. French, "Clark Gable Cuts the Apron Strings," *Photoplay*, April 1934, 28.

119   **This "New Gable":** Ibid.

119   **When Gable didn't wear one:** Jack Kofoed, "Life Imitates the Movies, Not Art: Gable Even Influences the Undershirt Business," *New York Times*, July 17, 1938.

119   **He and his second wife, Ria:** Evaline Lieber, "The High Price of Screen Love-Making," *Photoplay*, December 1932, 32–33.

119   **To assuage rumors of adultery:** Kay Proctor, "Why Male Stars Marry Plain Girls," *Photoplay*, October 1935, 38–39.

120   **when Gable returned from filming *The Call of the Wild*:** Sara Hamilton, "At Last! Mrs. Clark Gable Talks," *Photoplay*, December 1938, 18.

120   **Yet with whispers of his potential dalliance:** Dennison Hastings, "Clark Gable's Romantic Plight," *Photoplay*, September 1936, 12.

121   **Gable never spent a waking moment:** "Gable Great Outdoor Fan," *Los Angeles Times*, January 26, 1935.

121   **But Lombard was also madcap:** David Thomson, *Biographical Dictionary of Film*, 3rd ed. (New York: Knopf, 1994), 529.

122   **In a 1932 tell-all:** Elisabeth Goldbeck, "Bill Powell Talks About His Wife," *Movie Classic*, November 1932, 15.

123   **But for those reading closely:** Gladys Hall, "There Are 7 Kinds of Love," *Photoplay*, October 1933, 50.

124   **At one such fete:** Tip Poff, "That Certain Party," *Los Angeles Times*, June 23, 1935.

124   **She publicly advised her fans:** William F. French, "Be Modern or Be a Wallflower . . . Says Carole Lombard," *Motion Picture*, August 1935, 28.

125 **While she had developed a reputation:** Portrait, *Photoplay*, November 1934.

125 **with her new, so-called lunatic persona:** "Carole Lombard Likes Lunatic Roles," *Los Angeles Times*, November 28, 1937.

125 **Throw a party during the day:** Dennison Hastings, "Clark Gable's Romantic Plight," *Photoplay*, September 1936, 12.

126 **it was simply a wear-formalwear-in-the-afternoon affair:** Edward Doherty, "Can the Gable-Lombard Love Story Have a Happy Ending?" *Photoplay*, May 1938, 18; "Boy Gets Girl," *Time*, April 1939, 66.

126 **she impressed him with her utter lack of self-consciousness:** Hastings, "Clark Gable's Romantic Plight."

126 **Lombard arranged for an ancient, rusted-out Ford Model T:** Doherty, "Can the Gable-Lombard Love Story Have a Happy Ending?"

126 **They were public enough:** Harry Lang, "The Talkie Town Tattler," *Motion Picture*, August 1936, 8.

126 **But there were still attempts to squelch:** Sheilah Graham, "Two Stars Discover Their Temperaments Differ," *Los Angeles Times*, September 12, 1936.

127 **Gable was still married:** Hastings, "Clark Gable's Romantic Plight."

127 **fan mag pictorials framed Lombard:** "Infant Plays Show Lead," *Los Angeles Times*, January 9, 1937; "Gable's Girl," *Photoplay*, February 1937, 17; "Skipper Gable," *Photoplay*, January 1937, 41.

127 **Lombard's resistance and self-advocacy:** Emily Susan Carman, *Independent Stardom: Female Stars and Freelance Labor in 1930s Hollywood* (Los Angeles: ProQuest, UMI Dissertation Publishing, 2011), 599.

128 **But lest Lombard appear too spoiled:** Janet Bentley, "She Gets Away with Murder," *Photoplay*, March 1938, 89.

128 **Her rules:** Hart Seymore, "Carole Lombard Tells: 'How I Live by a Man's Code,'" *Photoplay*, June 1937, 12–13.

129 **Gable had purchased:** Kirtley Baskette, "Hollywood's Unmarried Husbands and Wives," *Photoplay*, January 1939, 22–23.

130 **But it was suggestive enough:** Anthony Slide, *Inside the Hollywood Fan Magazine* (Jackson, MS: University Press of Mississippi, 2010), 89.

130 **While details of the divorce decree:** E. J. Fleming, *The Fixers: Eddie Mannix, Howard Strickling, and the MGM Publicity Machine* (Jefferson, NC: McFarland & Company, 2005), 185.

130 **an MGM publicity exec arranged for the pair:** "Clark Gable and Carole Lombard Wed by Minister in Arizona Ceremony," *New York Times*, March 30, 1939.

130 **Their wedding, and its importance to Hollywood:** Edwin Schallert, "Clark and Carole Now Face Super Test," *Los Angeles Times*, April 2, 1939.

130 **Instead of a pool:** "Swimmin' Hole for Gable Ranch," *Washington Post*, January 25, 1940.

131 **Gable arranged for a cake:** Gladys Hall, "The Gags of the Gables," *Motion Picture*, May 1941, 22.

132 **Back in Hollywood:** Ruth Waterbury, "What the Loss of Carole Lombard Means to Clark Gable," *Photoplay*, April 1942, 28.

132 **Still in mourning:** "$112,000 Film Pay to Go to Charities," *New York Times*, January 29, 1942.

132 **The fan magazines attempted to process the nation's grief:** Ruth Waterbury, "How Clark Gable is Conquering Loneliness," *Photoplay*, August 1942, 34; Waterbury, "What the Loss of Carole Lombard Means to Clark Gable."

132 **What made sense, and what made Gable a hero:** "Gable Will Become Army Private Today."

Chapter Nine

135 **He was the consummate tough guy:** Michael Minen, "The New Bogart," *Hollywood*, November 1940, 21.

136 **he was a bona fide blue blood:** Katharine Albert, "Meet Humphrey Bogart," *Photoplay*, July 1937, 44.

136 **With schooling out of the question:** "Bogey Man Goes Beatific," *Chicago Daily Tribune*, December 6, 1942.

137 **The navy did more than make Bogart a man:** Mayme Peak, "Bad Man Goes Romantic," *Daily Boston Globe*, April 28, 1940.

137 **After an honorable discharge:** Grace Mack, "Meeting Up with a New Menacing Man," *Motion Picture*, January 1937, 34.

137 **It was in his role as stage manager:** Ibid.

137 **But they quarreled incessantly:** Ibid.

138 **His first real stage role was as a Valentino-like sheik:** Peak, "Bad Man Goes Romantic."

138 **He also paid his dues:** Ed Sullivan, "Looking at Hollywood," *Chicago Daily Tribune*, April 8, 1939.

138 **These romantic parts:** Carlisle Jones, "Fugitive from a Racquet," *Atlanta Constitution*, May 31, 1936.

138 **Bogart was too skinny:** "Bouquet for Bogart," *Chicago Daily Tribune*, July 11, 1948.

140 **His name also became synonymous with villainy:** Minen, "The New Bogart"; Louella Parsons, "Close-ups and Long Shots of the Motion Picture Scene," *Washington Post*, February 28, 1939; Mack, "Meeting Up with a New Menacing Man."

140 **Gossip columnist Grace Wilcox reported:** Grace Wilcox, "The Hollywood Reporter," *Atlanta Constitution*, March 15, 1936.

140 **Fans even began to claim:** Mack, "Meeting Up with a New Menacing Man."

140 **Bogart claimed to have taken a cue:** John Durant, "Tough On and Off," *Collier's*, August 31, 1940, 24.

141 **But in case you thought he was just a jerk**: Mack, "Meeting Up with a New Menacing Man."

141 **He called his house**: Kirtley Baskette, "Hollywood's Trigger Man," *American Magazine*, June 1943, 43; "Swings Ax on Formal Dinners," *Washington Post*, March 5, 1942.

141 **He hated formal clothes**: Minen, "The New Bogart"; Sara Hamilton, "Things We Like About Bogie," *Photoplay*, October 1942.

141 **Even his food had to be straightforward**: Peak, "Bad Man Goes Romantic"; Hamilton, "Things We Like About Bogie."

142 **He hated working with "dames"**: Harold Heffernan, "Bogart's Love Making Is Strictly Business," *Daily Boston Globe*, October 24, 1943.

142 **"If I have to make love to dames"**: Ibid.

142 **To his mind, the perfect world**: Ibid.

142 **Words, especially romantic ones**: Peak, "Bad Man Goes Romantic."

142 **How, then, did such a terse, self-proclaimed "ugly" man**: Baskette, "Hollywood's Trigger Man."

143 **He had been ascribed with sex appeal before**: Mack, "Meeting Up with a New Menacing Man."

144 **Bogart, however, quickly discovered**: Albert, "Meet Humphrey Bogart."

144 **No matter that Philips**: "Humphrey Bogart's Wife Files Plea for Divorce," *Los Angeles Times*, June 22, 1937.

144 **He claimed that she was "perfectly content"**: Peak, "Bad Man Goes Romantic"; Cameron Shipp, "The Adventures of Humphrey Bogart," *Saturday Evening Post*, August 2, 1952.

144 **She was obsessively jealous**: Heffernan, "Bogart's Love Making Is Strictly Business"; "Bouquet for Bogart."

144 **They fought *constantly***: George Frazier, "Humphrey Bogart," *Life*, June 12, 1944, 55.

145 **The brawls between the "Battling Bogarts"**: Shipp, "The Adventures of Humphrey Bogart."

146 **With the film still in the early stages of production**: Kyle Crichton, "Watch for Bacall," *Collier's*, October 1944, 64.

146 **When the exasperated Hawks:** Ibid.

146 **He wanted to make her voice huskier:** Ibid.

146 **When Hawks first introduced Bogart and Bacall:** Thomas Meehan, "She Travels by Roller Coaster," *Saturday Evening Post*, May 21, 1966.

147 **when Warner Bros. president Jack Warner saw:** Ibid.

148 **Given the extensively chronicled disputes:** "Bogarts Stop 6 Year Battle and Separate," *Chicago Daily Tribune*, October 20, 1944.

148 **some must have speculated about the timing:** Meehan, "She Travels by Roller Coaster."

148 **But there was no mention of a relationship:** Crichton, "Watch for Bacall"; Inga Arvad, "Glimpses of Hollywood," *Atlanta Constitution*, October 20, 1944.

148 **Bogart allowed several months to pass:** Sheilah Graham, "Bogart Leaves for Rest in Ohio," *Atlanta Constitution*, January 15, 1945.

148 **Hedda Hopper playfully reported:** Hedda Hopper, "All Is Not Sunshine!" *Washington Post*, January 18, 1945.

149 **Bogart made sure that the couple:** Francis Sill Wickware, "Lauren Bacall," *Life*, May 7, 1945, 101.

149 **The two absconded to Bromfield's farm:** Carolyn Bell, "Town Talk," *Washington Post*, March 11, 1945.

149 **with the divorce from Methot finalized:** "Bogey, Like Soft Egg, 'Cooked in 3 Minutes,'" *Atlanta Constitution*, May 22, 1945; "O Goody! Gasps 'The Look' as She Weds 'The Leer,'" *Chicago Tribune*, May 22, 1945.

149 **They seemed the picture of wedded bliss:** "Bogart Returns with Bride Bacall," *Los Angeles Times*, May 26, 1945.

149 **And the fans *loved* it:** "Fans Sanction Union of 'Look' and Bad Boy," *Atlanta Constitution*, July 8, 1945.

149 **Apart from a bit of squawking:** "Backstage by Paul Jones," *Atlantic Constitution*, March 19, 1945.

150 **As for concern over the gap in their ages:** Hedda Hopper, "This King Business!" *Washington Post*, February 6, 1945.

151 **People were seldom nice:** Wickware, "Lauren Bacall."

151 **She was the female counterpart:** Arvad, "Glimpses of Hollywood"; *Variety* review of *To Have and Have Not*, January 1, 1944, 82; Bob White, "Bogart Pair Setting Pace for Hollywoodians," *Los Angeles Times*, September 15, 1946; "New Horizons," *Time*, February 12, 1945, 42; Hedda Hopper, "The Stars of 1945," December 31, 1944; "Lauren Bacall," *Life*, October 16, 1944, 17.

151 **At least four articles penned:** Bosley Crowther, "A Big Hello," *New York Times*, October 22, 1944; Crichton, "Watch for Bacall"; Harold Heffernan, "Lauren Bacall, Hollywood's Latest Vamp, Is Sleek, Sophisticated Type," *Daily Boston Globe*, December 10, 1944; Wickware, "Lauren Bacall."

151 **Bogart was an unspoken opponent:** "Bogart Admits Red Defense Was 'Mistake,'" *Los Angeles Times*, December 3, 1947. See also: Humphrey Bogart, "I'm No Communist," *Photoplay*, May 1948, 53.

152 **Bogart praised Bacall's independence:** Lydia Lane, "Simplicity, Individuality Traits of Lauren Bacall," *Los Angeles Times*, December 13, 1953.

152 **Bacall, fashion model:** Ibid.

152 **In 1951, Bogart wrote an editorial:** Humphrey Bogart, "Love Begins at Forty," *Los Angeles Times*, October 7, 1951; "Lauren Bacall Tells 'Why I Hate Young Men,'" *Look*, November 3, 1953.

152 **Bogart had always hated the social scene:** Arlene Dahl, "Lauren Bacall Advises Tall Girls on Dress," *Chicago Tribune*, February 12, 1951.

152 **the Bogarts and their tight group of neighbors:** "Hollywood Report," *Boston Globe*, October 2, 1955.

152 **They were "fun-loving bohemians":** Ibid.

153 **his last words to Bacall:** Meehan, "She Travels by Roller Coaster."

153 **It was a narrative of death**: Alistair Cooke, "Bogey's Tough Shell Masked a Fine Core," *Washington Post*, January 27, 1957.

Chapter Ten

158 **In actuality, Garland, given name Frances Gumm**: "Judy Garland's Life Story," *Atlanta Constitution*, October 6, 1940.

158 **According to well-worn legend**: "Judy Garland's Life Story"; Jingle Bells story repeated: John Chapman, "Looking at Hollywood," *Chicago Tribune*, October 6, 1940; Hedda Hopper, "A Garland for Judy," *Chicago Tribune*, January 19, 1947.

159 **The rest of her early childhood**: Hopper, "A Garland for Judy."

159 **They were continually rejected**: Ibid.

159 **The family . . . settled in California**: Judy Garland, Guest Editor, *Movie Mirror*, December 1937.

159 **According to one version**: Dixie Wilson, "A Garland for Judy," *Photoplay*, September 1940.

159 **Mayer signed her on the spot**: Wilson, "A Garland for Judy"; "Judy Garland's Life Story."

160 **Garland's status as undesirable ugly ducking**: Mary Jane Manners, "The Ugly Duckling Who Became a Swan," *Silver Screen*, June 1940.

160 **She was called ungraceful**: Sheilah Graham, "Young Stars Have Big Problem," *Atlanta Constitution*, August 1, 1940, 16; Cameron Shipp, "The Star Who Thinks Nobody Loves Her," *Saturday Evening Post*, April 1955.

161 **As press for *Oz* built**: "Mickey and Judy Mobbed by Fans," *Daily Boston Globe*, August 11, 1939; "5,000 Greet Screen Stars," *New York Times*, August 15, 1939.

161 **The movie made $3.3 million**: Thomas Schatz, *Boom and Bust: American Cinema in the 1940s* (Berkeley: University of California Press, 1999), 105.

161 **When the nation's exhibitors voted**: Nelson B. Bell, "Box Officers Elect Ten Money-Making Stars," *Washington Post*, December 29, 1940.

162 **she was a stereotypical female teen**: Sheilah Graham, "Cupid Waits Patiently on Judy Garland," *Atlanta Constitution*, May 4, 1941; Kay Proctor, "Judy Garland's Guide Book to Dating," *Movie Mirror*, August 1940, http://www.jgdb.com/articl57.htm.

162 **When Sheilah Graham brought up the topic**: Graham, "Cupid Waits Patiently."

162 **In some interviews**: Sheilah Graham, "Judy Garland Will Remain a 'Spinster,'" *Atlanta Constitution*, November 10, 1939; Lucie Neville, "Judy Garland Recalls Her 'Corny' Days and Is Amazed by Her Success," *Washington Post*, January 21, 1940; Proctor, "Judy Garland's Guide Book."

162 **She didn't go to nightclubs**: James Carson, "I'm Not Boy Crazy!" *Modern Screen*, January 1940.

162 **In November 1939**: Graham, "Judy Garland Will Remain a 'Spinster.'"

163 **Garland was never fat**: Ibid.

163 **When she attempted to order a normal lunch**: Chapman, "Looking at Hollywood."

163 **The gossip columnists only fueled the process**: Sheilah Graham, "Everything Happens to Judy Garland," *Atlanta Constitution*, August 22, 1940.

163 **Graham noted that she hoped**: Graham, "Cupid Waits Patiently."

163 **A piece in the *Washington Post***: "Judy Reduces, Then Celebrates," *Washington Post*, July 4, 1941; Lydia Lane, "Diet and Exercise Keep Body Youthfully Slender," *Los Angeles Times*, March 19, 1942.

163 **Rose was bad news**: "Martha Raye Wins Divorce Decree, Accusing Second Husband of Cruelty," *Los Angeles Times*, May 18, 1940.

163 **The divorce was too fresh**: Sheilah Graham, "Real Romances in Hollywood," *Atlanta Constitution*, November 8, 1940.

164 **But Garland couldn't stay single forever:** Gordon Swarthout, "Should Judy Act Her Age?" *Movie-Radio Guide*, November 16–22, 1940, http://www.jgdb.com/articl16.htm.

164 **Garland's first on-screen kiss:** Graham, "Everything Happens to Judy Garland."

164 **But Garland was publicly established:** Graham, "Judy Garland Will Remain a 'Spinster.'"

165 **Presumably prompted by the studio:** Sheilah Graham, "Judy Garland Steals Show from Hedy!," *Atlanta Constitution*, April 22, 1941.

165 **MGM enlisted the most moralizing of the gossip columnists:** Louella Parsons, "Louella Parsons" column, *Washington Post*, June 8, 1941.

165 **The studio passive-aggressively responded:** Hedda Hopper, "When Love Is Young," *Washington Post*, August 5, 1941.

166 **The MGM publicity office:** "She's a Big Girl Now!" *Modern Screen*, October 1941, 106.

166 **Rose . . . was kind of a weird guy:** "Will Judy Be Happy Married?" *Screen Guide*, 1941, http://www.jgdb.com/articl67.htm.

166 **The dissonance was so acute:** Vern Haughland, "Judy Garland Is Two Persons, More or Less, Since Marrying," *Washington Post*, November 30, 1941.

166 **MGM was forced to give up the dream:** Chapman, "Looking at Hollywood."

167 **Amid all this confusing image manipulation:** *Los Angeles Examiner*, November 27, 1942; cited in Gerald Clarke, *Get Happy: The Life of Judy Garland* (New York: Random House, 2000), 163.

167 **The MGM fixers:** Clarke, *Get Happy*, 162–63; E. J. Fleming, *The Fixers*, 198.

167 **Rumors of marital unrest:** Louella Parsons, "Judy Garland Plays Sweetheart of the Navy," *Atlanta Constitution*, October 24, 1942.

167 **The separation would last more than a year:** Sheilah Graham, "Judy Garland & Dave Rose Show Promise of Reconciliation," *Atlanta*

Constitution, February 25, 1944; Hedda Hopper, "Garlands for Judy," *Chicago Tribune*, June 26, 1949.

168 **St. Louis went on to gross:** "All Time Domestic Champs," *Variety*, January 6, 1960, 34.

168 **At some point during the filming:** Imogene Collins, "All for Love," *Modern Screen*, May 1951, http://www.jgdb.com/articl40.htm.

169 **As the film's release approached:** Elinor Ames, "A Garland for Judy," *Chicago Tribune*, January 19, 1947; Edwin Schallert, "Judy Garland Achieves New Level of Poignancy," *Los Angeles Times*, June 2, 1946.

169 **In the months after Liza's birth:** Schallert, "Judy Garland Achieves New Level of Poignancy."

169 **In July 1947, she suffered:** Hedda Hopper, "Looking at Hollywood," *Los Angeles Times*, July 16, 1947.

169 **A month later, she reported:** Ibid.

170 **MGM replaced her:** Hedda Hopper, "Doctor Rules Long Rest for Judy Garland," *Los Angeles Times*, July 18, 1948.

170 **MGM suspended her yet again:** "Judy Garland Plays Hooky, Is Suspended," *Daily Boston Globe*, May 11, 1949.

170 **This time, however, Hopper was on her side:** Hedda Hopper, "Judy Garland Film Role Goes to Betty Hutton," *Los Angeles Times*, May 20, 1949.

171 **The suggestion that Betty Hutton replace Garland:** Edwin Schallert, "Metro Postponements Cause Many Headaches," *Los Angeles Times*, May 23, 1949.

171 **It's unclear whether Alsop or MGM was supervising:** Marjory Adams, "People Here Don't Bother Judy," *Daily Boston Globe*, May 31, 1949.

171 **In truth, when she presented herself:** Ibid.

171 **Garland had been causing problems for weeks:** Marjory Adams, "Judy Isn't Temperamental," *Daily Boston Globe*, June 7, 1949; Hopper, "Garlands for Judy."

171 **And Garland's exhaustion:** Carleton Alsop, "Judy's Singing Again," *Photoplay*, November 1949, http://www.jgdb.com/articl41.htm.

172 **Alsop's piece, along with similar ones:** "Poundage Nearly Costs Judy Garland a Role," *Los Angeles Times*, November 1, 1949.

172 **In January 1950, Hopper countered rumors:** Hedda Hopper, "John Wayne to Make Another Cavalry Film," *Chicago Tribune*, January 12, 1950.

172 **Headlines did not proclaim:** "Judy Garland, Suspended Again, Slashes Throat," *Daily Boston Globe*, June 21, 1950; "Judy Garland Found with Throat Wound," *New York Times*, June 21, 1950; "Judy Garland's Career Appears in the Balance," *Chicago Daily Tribune*, June 22, 1950.

173 **The doctor who had treated Garland:** "Judy Garland, Suspended Again."

173 **Two days later, Garland was heavily sedated:** "Judy Garland Not Told of Suicide Try Publicity," *Los Angeles Times*, June 23, 1950.

174 **Garland had been working:** Joe Hyams, "Judy Garland Real Trouper," *Daily Boston Globe*, September 19, 1956; Shipp, "The Star Who Thinks Nobody Loves Her."

174 **Louis B. Mayer called her:** Hyams, "Judy Garland Real Trouper."

175 **Ethel Gumm was quick to shoot down:** "Judy Garland Had Fine Care," *Los Angeles Times*, July 22, 1950.

175 **Later in life, Ethel became petty:** Shipp, "The Star Who Thinks Nobody Loves Her."

175 **And so Garland remained a girl:** Lee Rogers, "Judy Garland Plays Wife of George Murphy," *Atlanta Constitution*, December 1, 1940; Inga Arvad, "Judy Garland Celebrates 22nd Birthday," *Atlanta Constitution*, June 22, 1944; Ames, "A Garland for Judy"; Alsop, "Judy's Singing Again"; Collins, " All for Love"; Hedda Hopper, "Great Garland Talent in Critical Jeopardy," *Los Angeles Times*, June 2, 1950; Richard L. Coe, "Judy's No Problem in Trim Musical," *Washington Post*, September 9, 1950; Hedda Hopper, "MGM's

Golden Girl," *Los Angeles Times*, September 30, 1950; "Judy Garland Plans Long Screen Absence," *New York Times*, October 2, 1950.

175   **Even after her comeback**: Albert Goldberg, "Judy Garland Scintillates in Philharmonic Comeback," *Los Angeles Times*, April 22, 1952; Mae Tinee, "Judy Garland is Wonderful in New Movie," *Chicago Tribune*, October 18, 1954; Joe Hyams, "A Future Full of Doubt," *Boston Globe*, September 20, 1956; Shipp, "The Star Who Thinks Nobody Loves Her."

176   **psychologically stuck in adolescence**: "An Open Letter from Judy Garland," *Modern Screen*, November 1950, http://www.jgdb.com/article6.htm.

176   **But that very emotionality**: Maxine Arnold, "The Punch in Judy," *Photoplay*, August 1948, 41; Schallert, "Judy Garland Achieves New Level."

176   *A Star Is Born* **director**: Dorothy Kilgallen, "Judy Garland Can Take It—For Art," *Washington Post*, June 8, 1954.

177   **And the resilience**: See Richard Dyer, "Judy Garland and Gay Men," in *Heavenly Bodies: Film Stars and Society* (New York: Routledge, 2004).

Chapter Eleven

180   **But it was a surprise blessing**: Dorothy Dandridge, "How I Crashed the Movies," *Afro-American*, April 26, 1941.

180   **She wrote a feature**: Dandridge, "How I Crashed the Movies"; Ted Yates, "Around Harlem Town," *Atlanta Daily World*, April 21, 1941.

180–81 **In later years, Dandridge would speak openly**: "Dandridge Says Stardom a Must and Tells Why," *Chicago Defender*, June 11, 1955.

181   **Eventually, she won a chance gig**: "Dot Dandridge to Star in CBS-TV Life Program," *Chicago Defender*, September 29, 1956.

181   **She split from Nicholas:** "Dorothy Dandridge: Boasts New Glamour," *Chicago Defender*, January 27, 1951.

181   **In 1951, this "new" Dorothy Dandridge:** "Skylarking with James Copp," *Los Angeles Times*, May 9, 1951.

181   **The piece was accompanied:** "Shy No More," *Life*, November 5, 1951, 65.

182   **But you weren't someone in café society:** Walter Winchell, "Walter Winchell: Man About Town," *Washington Post*, December 3, 1951.

183   **As one black columnist explained:** Stanley G. Robertson, "LA Confidential," *Los Angeles Sentinel*, September 16, 1965.

183   **A female columnist:** Gertrude Gipson, "Dorothy Dandridge: She's Pretty, Shapely, Talented Now a Star," *Los Angeles Sentinel*, November 8, 1951; George E. Pitts, "10 Sexiest Women in Show Business," *Pittsburgh Courier*, May 12, 1956.

183   **She was "shapely":** Gerry Fitz-Gerald, "Low Notes Not Sexy," *New Journal and Guide*, August 30, 1952.

183   **In interviews, Dandridge declared herself:** "La Dandridge, Alhambra Star is 'Pretty Enough,'" *Cleveland Call and Post*, June 7, 1952; Alvis Moses, "Nitelife in New York," *Philadelphia Tribune*, February 5, 1952; Fitz-Gerald, "Low Notes Not Sexy."

183   **And it worked:** "Star Dot Dandridge in Chez Paree Show," *Pittsburgh Courier*, October 3, 1953.

183   **By the summer of 1952:** "Dorothy Dandridge to Make Two New Pictures," *New Journal and Guide*, November 22, 1952.

184   **Hedda Hopper stated it plainly:** Hedda Hopper, "Looking at Hollywood," *Chicago Daily Tribune*, September 7, 1953.

184   **Preminger told Dandridge:** Louie Robinson, "The Private World of Dorothy Dandridge," *Ebony*, June 1962, 116–21.

185   **Forget all that:** Lucy Key Miller, "Front Views and Profiles," *Chicago Daily Times*, October 5, 1953.

185   **She wasn't a nerd:** Marjory Adams, "Dorothy Dandridge Given

Voice of Another in Carmen Jones," *Boston Globe*, November 17, 1954.

185 **Hopper got so excited:** Hedda Hopper, "Liberace and Movie Firm Are Discussing Picture Deal," *Chicago Daily Times*, October 15, 1954.

185–86 **Gossip columnist Dorothy Kilgallen:** Dorothy Kilgallen, "Pier Gets Cold Stare," *Washington Post*, October 15, 1954; Louella Parsons, "Oh No, Says Mr. Hughes, I'm Holding," *Washington Post*, October 3, 1954; Walter Winchell "The Broadway Lights," *Washington Post*, November 1, 1954.

186 **London's *Daily Express* even placed her:** Quoted in Rudolph Dunbar, "Writer Says Carmen Jones Brings Heat Wave to London," *Atlanta Daily World*, January 20, 1955.

186 ***Carmen Jones* was roundly praised:** Marion Jackson, "Carmen Jones is Saga of Coquetry," *Atlanta Daily World*, November 4, 1954.

186 **The only solution was independent producers:** "On the Right Road of Carmen and Joe," *New York Times*, October 24, 1954.

187 **the Academy didn't go in for "sexy" roles:** Lin Holloway, "Dorothy and Harry Named Tops in Field," *New Journal and Guide*, March 19, 1955.

187 **She also refused to use:** Hedda Hopper, "Napoleon's Invasion of Spain Will Be Presented on Screen," *Chicago Daily Times*, February 16, 1955.

187 **It was the first time a black actor:** Harry Levette, "D misses Oscar but Scores Elsewhere," *Philadelphia Tribune*, April 9, 1955.

187 **Opportunities for Dandridge:** "Carmen Success Leads to 12 All-Tan Features," *Afro-American*, January 29, 1955.

187 **Dandridge also became the first black person to appear:** Izzy Rowe, "Dandridge Makes 'Em Love Her at Waldorf," *Pittsburgh Courier*, April 23, 1955.

187 **There were reports that Dandridge had negotiated:** Lulu Garrett, "Gadabouting in the USA," *Afro-American*, May 7, 1955.

187 **Rumors floated of all sorts of roles:** "Reports Dorothy Dandridge May Get Commandments," *Afro-American*, February 5, 1955; Louella Parsons, "Van Johnson Signs for Rosalinda," *Washington Post*, March 3, 1955.

187 **But the choice offer:** Hedda Hopper, "Dorothy Dandridge in 'The King and I,'" *Los Angeles Times*, February 19, 1955.

188 **In April 1956:** Louella Parsons, "'Carmen' Star Heads Back to Filmland," *Washington Post*, April 5, 1956.

189 **And general gossip around the film:** "Dorothy Dandridge Learns Her Lesson," *Daily Defender*, November 5, 1956.

189 **Dorothy Kilgallen was reporting:** Dorothy Kilgallen, "Callas Puts on a Real Good Show," *Washington Post*, November 30, 1956.

189 **Before the *Confidential* issue hit stands:** "La Dandridge Sues Hep for $2 Million," *New York Amsterdam News*, February 16, 1957.

190 **To avoid losing:** "Confidential Backs Off Dotty Dandridge Yarn," *Los Angeles Sentinel*, May 23, 1957.

191 **racial prejudice was so rampant:** "Dot Describes Race Prejudice," *New York Amsterdam News*, September 14, 1957; Gladwin Hill, "2 Film Actresses Testify on Coast," *New York Times*, September 4, 1957; Lee Belser, "Dandridge, Maureen Proud of Each Other," *Daily Defender*, September 5, 1957.

191 **But the jury couldn't reach a verdict:** Mary Desjardins, "Systematizing Scandal: *Confidential* Magazine, Stardom, and the State of California," in *Headline Hollywood: A Century of Film Scandal*, eds. Adrienne L. McLean and David A. Cook (New Brunswick, NJ: Rutgers University Press, 2001), 206–31.

191 **In February 1955:** Louella Parsons, "Gentlemen Now Chase Redheads," *Washington Post*, February 25, 1955.

192 **Dandridge managed to extricate herself:** Masco Young, "The Grapevine," *Pittsburgh Courier*, October 19, 1957.

192 **Dandridge's role, if not her performance:** Rob Roy, "Dandridge Superb in 'The Decks Ran Red,'" *Chicago Defender*, October 25, 1958.

193 **The reason for the fire:** Hazel A. Washington, "This Is Hollywood," *Chicago Defender*, July 9, 1958.

193 **Following Mamoulian's dismissal:** Hedda Hopper, "Stars Comment on Porgy Row," *Los Angeles Times*, August 5, 1959.

194 **Even the head of the NAACP:** "Leigh Whipper Resigns Porgy Role in Protest," *Los Angeles Times*, August 7, 1958.

194 **He had pursued her:** Rick Brow, "Dot Seeks Day When Race Won't Matter," *New Journal and Guide*, November 21, 1959.

194 **As Dandridge explained to the press:** Brow, "Dot Seeks Day."

195 **At the post-screening celebration:** Doc Young, "Dorothy Dandridge Told All," *Los Angeles Sentinel*, March 9, 1967.

195 **Hollywood had finally gotten past stereotypes:** Hal Humphrey, "Wanted: A Brave Sponsor for Cole and Dandridge," *Los Angeles Times*, February 14, 1962.

195 **Some of the work she refused:** "Dot Dandridge Turns Back on Pigskin Bias," *Pittsburgh Courier*, August 19, 1961.

195 **One day, her marriage was reported:** "Dot Dandridge Wedding on the Rocks?," *New Journal and Guide*, October 1, 1960; Doc Young, "One Greek, One Negro," *Los Angeles Sentinel,* December 15, 1960; "The Big Beat," *Los Angeles Sentinel*, December 15, 1960.

195 **A writer for the *Chicago Defender*:** Bob Hunter, "Is Dandridge New Mistress of Mystery?," *Chicago Defender*, August 23, 1962.

195 **Dandridge filed for divorce:** "Dot Dandridge Wants Out," *New Journal and Guide*, November 17, 1962.

195 **The black press had never:** "Dorothy Dandridge Ousts Blond Hubby," *Philadelphia Tribune*, November 6, 1962.

196 **Dandridge saw this clearly:** Dorothy Dandridge and Earl Conrad, *Everything and Nothing: The Dorothy Dandridge Tragedy* (New York: HarperCollins, 2000), 183.

197 **"If I were Betty Grable":** Janet Maslin, "Hollywood's Tryst with Dorothy Dandridge Inspires Real Love at Last," *New York Times*,

June 19, 1997, http://www.nytimes.com/1997/06/19/movies/
hollywood-s-tryst-with-dorothy-dandridge-inspires-real-love-at-
last.html.

Chapter Twelve

201 **It was an odd childhood:** Stanley Frank, "Hollywood's New Dreamboat," *Saturday Evening Post*, August 27, 1949.

201 **But it was in Florida:** Howard Thompson, "The Barefoot Boys," *Motion Picture*, October 1951, 43.

202 **But Clift was no blazing talent:** Frank, "Hollywood's New Dreamboat."

202 **He was in a string of Pulitzer Prize–winning plays:** Thompson, "The Barefoot Boys."

202 **Somewhat hilariously:** "Montgomery Clift," *Life*, August 16, 1948, 73.

203 *Red River* **finally hit theaters:** Frank, "Hollywood's New Dreamboat."

203 **his skill was . . . an amalgamation of acting styles:** Amy Lawrence, *The Passion of Montgomery Clift* (Berkeley: University of California Press, 2010), 14.

203 **Clift used this synthetic approach:** Louis Berg, "Rumpled Movie Idol," *Los Angeles Times*, May 15, 1949.

203 **Zinnemann told Hedda Hopper:** Hedda Hopper, "Elusive Monty Clift Is Purist About Work: Actor Would Like to Have . . . ," *Los Angeles Times*, August 9, 1953.

203–4 **Elizabeth Taylor said that the first time she saw him:** Elizabeth Taylor narrating a Turner Classic Movies tribute to Montgomery Clift; cited in Lawrence, *The Passion of Montgomery Clift*, 1.

204 **When photographer Richard Avedon saw him:** Lawrence, *The Passion of Montgomery Clift*, 12; see Patricia Bosworth, *Montgomery Clift: A Biography* (New York: Limelight Editions, 2004), 138.

204 **Why all the excitement, then:** Frank, "Hollywood's New Dreamboat."

204 **When the press talked about Clift:** Hedda Hopper, "Legend of
Montgomery Clift's Character Oddities Punctured," *Los Angeles
Times*, March 26, 1950; Aline Mosby, "Montgomery Clift Breaks
Down, Buys Suit No. 2," *Daily Boston Globe*, October 30, 1949.

205 **He survived on two meals a day:** " 'I Like It Lonely!' says Monty
Clift to Ernst Jacobi," *Motion Picture*, November 1954, 33; Frank,
"Hollywood's New Dreamboat"; Elsa Maxwell, "The New Clift
Cut," *Photoplay*, December 1951, 56.

205 **When he wasn't reading:** Maxwell, "The New Clift Cut."

205 **When he came to visit:** Ibid.

205 **His beat-up car:** Frank, "Hollywood's New Dreamboat."

205 **He was, in his words:** Ibid.

205 **Yet Clift would come to hate:** " 'I Like it Lonely!' " *Motion Picture*.

206 **He had a close friendship:** Sheilah Graham, "It Looks Like Cupid
Has Caught Hollywood's No. 1 Bachelor," *Daily Boston Globe*, October 30, 1949.

206 **But Clift's rebuttal was firm:** Hopper, "Legend of Montgomery
Clift's Character Oddities."

206 **Clift was so protective of Holman:** Lawrence, *The Passion of Montgomery Clift*, 145.

206 **Clift was unperturbed:** Frank Neill, "In Hollywood," *New Journal
and Guide*, December 31, 1949.

207 **When another columnist asked:** Hopper, "Legend of Montgomery
Clift's Character Oddities."

207 **the title of a *Motion Picture* article:** " 'I Like it Lonely!' " *Motion
Picture*.

207 **Other testimonies to Clift's gayness:** Margot Peters, *Design for Living: Alfred Lunt and Lynn Fontanne* (New York: Knopf, 2003), 187;
Lawrence, *The Passion of Montgomery Clift*, 239.

208 **After the success of *Place*:** "Montgomery Clift Meets Elizabeth

Taylor at Plane: Romance Denied," *Los Angeles Times*, June 18, 1951.

209 **His emotional connection:** Lawrence, *The Passion of Montgomery Clift*, 168.

209 **Charlie Chaplin, he of faint and sporadic praise:** Bosworth, *Montgomery Clift*, 212.

210 **And as Clift himself explained:** Lawrence, *The Passion of Montgomery Clift*, 167.

210 **Where his letters to Zinnemann:** Ibid., 149.

210 **When asked what he had been doing:** Edwin Schallert, "Self-Imposed Hollywood Exile Ends for Montgomery Clift," *Los Angeles Times*, May 6, 1956.

211 **Moments after the accident:** Bosworth, *Montgomery Clift*, 298.

212 **According to Clift's doctors:** "Actor Clift, 35, Hurt Seriously in Auto Crash," *Chicago Daily Tribune*, May 14, 1956.

212 **And thus began what Robert Lewis . . . called:** Gerald Clarke, "Sunny Boy," *Time*, February 20, 1978, 98.

212 **Even before *Raintree*:** Christopher Isherwood, *Diaries*, quoted in Lawrence, *The Passion of Montgomery Clift*, 236–37.

212 **And it wasn't just in private record:** Louella Parsons, "Libby's Nursing Montgomery Clift Along," *Washington Post and Times Herald*, October 7, 1956.

212 **While filming his next picture:** Philip K. Scheuer, "Montgomery Clift States His Credo: Actor, Not Angry or Beat, He Says," *Los Angeles Times*, October 13, 1958.

213 **But even Monroe reported:** Bosworth, *Montgomery Clift*, 330.

214 **It was also a dark, melancholy film:** Film review of *The Misfits*, *Variety*, February 1, 1961.

214 **Or, as Bosley Crowther . . . explained:** Bosley Crowther, "Gable and Monroe Star in Script by Miller," *New York Times*, February 2, 1961.

215 **But something of the old talent remained:** David Thomson, *The*

New Biographical Dictionary of Film (New York: Random House, 2010), 164.

215 **Plans for Clift to play the lead:** Dorothy Kilgallen, "Troubles Beset Monty Clift Film," *Washington Post*, September 15, 1963; Hedda Hopper, "Looking at Hollywood: Actor Michael Caine Introduced at Party," *Chicago Tribune*, December 22, 1965.

215 **His perpetual question:** Bosworth, *Montgomery Clift*, 162.

215 **For Clift, the task proved impossible:** Ibid., 376.

Chapter Thirteen

217 **The story of Brando's upbringing:** "A Tiger in the Reeds," *Time*, October 11, 1954, 8.

217 **Brando's father provided for the family:** Richard Gehman, "The Marlon Brando Story," *Cosmopolitan*, May 1955, 42; James Bacon, "Wacky—Or Great Artist?" *Washington Post*, May 9, 1954.

217 **His mother was an actress:** Grady Johnson, "Marlon Brando: Actor on Impulse," *Coronet*, July 1952, 75.

218 **He hated authority:** Pete Martin, "The Star Who Sneers at Hollywood," *Saturday Evening Post*, June 6, 1953.

218 **His family was solidly middle class:** Theodore Strauss, "Brilliant Brat," *Life*, July 31, 1950.

218 **He loathed the school clock tower:** Martin, "The Star Who Sneers at Hollywood."

218 **He found the work:** Johnson, "Marlon Brando: Actor on Impulse."

218 **While waiting for classes to start:** Marjory Adams, "Marlon Brando, New Movie Idol, Quitting Films to Resume School," *Daily Boston Globe*, July 13, 1950.

219 **In *Truckline Cafe*, he caught the eye:** Louis Calta, "Brando May Play 'Streetcar' Role: Young Actor Is Mentioned for Lead," *New York Times*, September 1, 1947.

219 **Williams later recounted:** Gehman, "The Marlon Brando Story"; Bacon, "Wacky—Or Great Artist?"

219 **As famed *New Yorker* film critic Pauline Kael would recall:** Pauline Kael, *Reeling* (New York: Warner Books, 1977), 57.

219 **Brando regularly incited:** Hedda Hopper, "Brando—Showman and Show-Off!," *Chicago Daily Tribune*, March 30, 1952.

221 **To prep for his role in *The Men*:** "Preparing for Paraplegia," *Life*, June 12, 1950, 129.

221 **As one producer explained:** Martin, "The Star Who Sneers at Hollywood."

222 **Hedda Hopper called him:** Hedda Hopper, "Hollywood's New Sex Boat," *Photoplay*, July 1952.

222 **he commonly referred to her:** "A Tiger in the Reeds."

223 **In 1951, he ran an advertisement:** Elsa Maxwell, "That Mad Man Marlon," *Photoplay*, December 1950.

223 **He didn't like "glamour girls":** Hopper, "Hollywood's New Sex Boat."

223 **And his hobbies skewed to the eccentric:** "The Brandos," *Life*, March 22, 1948.

223 **he was known to make an entire meal:** "A Tiger in the Reeds."

223 **When asked why he didn't fall:** Strauss, "Brilliant Brat."

223 **Brando . . . wasn't mean-spirited:** Louis Berg, "Streetcar to Hollywood: Only One Thing Troubles Marlon Brando," *Los Angeles Times*, July 16, 1950; "The Unbelievable Brando," *Motion Picture*, November 1954, 20.

223 **As a "close friend" explained:** "The Unbelievable Brando."

223 **The real Brando:** Martin, "The Star Who Sneers at Hollywood"; "A Tiger in the Reeds."

225 **He turned up in New York City:** Bacon, "Wacky—Or Great Artist?"

225 **Fox sued for breach of contract:** "Fox Scores Brando in $2,000,000 Claim," *New York Times*, February 17, 1954.

225 **his real problem with *The Egyptian*:** Gehman, "The Marlon Brando Story."

225 **Here was a new, "domesticated" Brando:** Cecelia Ager, "Brando in Search of Himself: A Complicated Joe Is Marlon," *New York Times*, July 25, 1954.

225 **A scandal rag even declared him:** "Marlon Brando: World's Worst Lover," *Rave*, December 1953.

226 **But the details of Brando and Mariana-Berenger's whirlwind courtship:** Steve Cronin, "How Marlon Brando Proposed," *Modern Screen*, February 1955, 52.

226 **The fan magazines also constructed:** Ibid.

226 **And as she told the press:** Ibid.

226 **she was a "sloppy dresser":** "Marlon's Pals Cool on His Gal," *Washington Post*, December 26, 1954.

226 **As Castaneda commented:** Cronin, "How Marlon Brando Proposed."

226 **She was right:** Sheilah Graham, "Marlon Brando and Josanne," *Daily Boston Globe*, July 25, 1955.

227 **But after the press descended:** Josanne Mariani, "Marlon Brando: A French Girl Relives the Wonder and Happiness," *Chicago Daily Tribune*, September 18, 1960.

227 **while filming *Guys and Dolls* in 1955:** Marjory Adams, "'Rude' Marlon Brando Proves Well-Mannered and Outspoken," *Daily Boston Globe*, July 19, 1953; "The Visible Invisible," *Photoplay*, September 1955, 54.

227 **The magazines were predictably indignant:** "The Visible Invisible."

227 **A year after their marriage:** "Down Beatnik," *Time*, October 13, 1958, 55.

228 **Yet she found herself pregnant:** Dorothy Kilgallen, "Marlon Brando's Bride Loses Expected Baby," *Washington Post*, January 27, 1958.

228 **In a custody trial:** "Brando Says He Tied and Spanked Ex-Wife: Actor, in Custody Hearing," *Los Angeles Times*, November 19, 1959.

228 **He became a political firebrand:** See, for example, Drew Pearson, "Marlon Brando: On 'Ugly-Senators,'" *Washington Post*, April 25, 1963.

228 **And so Brando turned rancid:** Joe Hymans, "Marlon Brando: Acting Is a Bum's Life!" (1960), reprinted in *Motion Picture*, December 1976, 8.

228 **once the film became a global blockbuster:** "Brando Sues on 'Superman' Film," *New York Times*, December 16, 1978.

Chapter Fourteen

231 **Before Dean became an icon:** "A Star Is Born," *Movie Stars Parade*, May 1956, 28.

231 **But his mother died:** Hedda Hopper, "Keep Your Eye on James Dean," *Chicago Daily Tribune*, March 27, 1955.

231 **For the state competition:** David Dalton, *James Dean: The Mutant King: A Biography* (Chicago: Chicago Review Press, 2001), 175.

232 **He enrolled in a prelaw class:** Herbert Mitgang, "Strange James Dean Death Cult," *Coronet*, November 1956, 110.

232 **The bit parts were unsatisfying:** "What Made Jimmy Run?," *Movie Stars Parade*, May 1956, 28.

232 **Once Dean was in New York:** Ibid.

232 **But it was that role that attracted the attention:** Ibid.

233 **In a letter sent to his on-again, off-again girlfriend:** James Dean, "Wow! Am I Fucked Up," Letters of Note, http://www.lettersofnote.com/2010/08/wow-am-i-fucked-up.html.

233 **In Brando's memoir:** Marlon Brando and Robert Lindsey, *Songs My Mother Taught Me* (New York: Random House, 1994), 20.

233–34 **the *New York Times* highlighted:** Howard Thompson, "Another Dean Hits the Big League," *New York Times*, March 13, 1955.

234 **Hopper declared him:** Hedda Hopper, "Helen Traubel Will Play Dressler Role," *Los Angeles Times*, December 13, 1954.

234 *Life* **commissioned Dean's friend:** "Moody New Star," *Life*, March 7, 1955, 125.

234 **That moodiness:** Thompson, "Another Dean Hits the Big League."

234 *Life* **reported his "militantly independent" behavior:** "Moody New Star."

234 **When Hopper first saw him:** Hedda Hopper, "Looking at Hollywood: New Film Type, the Slouch, Gives Writer the Creeps," *Chicago Daily Tribune*, July 7, 1954.

234 **Dean was "beautifully nuts":** Ezra Goodman, "Delirium Over Dead Star," *Life*, September 24, 1956, 75.

234 **He also didn't tolerate:** Hedda Hopper, "Keep Your Eye on James Dean," *Chicago Daily Tribune*, March 27, 1955.

235 **While filming *East of Eden*:** "His Searching Heart," *Movie Stars Parade*, May 1956, 34.

235 **But Angeli's mother never approved:** Seymour Korman, "James Dean: Brilliant Young Star Met Tragic End on Eve of His Greatest Success; but Even in Death His Fame Continues to Grow," *Chicago Daily Tribune*, February 5, 1956.

235 **Angeli announced her engagement:** Hedda Hopper, "Actress Pier Angeli Engaged to Vic Damone," *Los Angeles Times*, October 5, 1954.

235 **as the sixteen-year-old president:** Mitgang, "Strange James Dean Death Cult."

236 **Bosley Crowther . . . was scathing:** Bosley Crowther, "The Screen: 'East of Eden' Has Debut: Astor Shows Film of Steinbeck," *New York Times*, March 10, 1955.

236 **Brando himself recoiled:** Joe Morella and Edward Z. Epstein, *Brando: The Unauthorized Biography* (New York: Nelson, 1973), 58.

236 **Hopper declared that she couldn't remember a time:** Hopper, "Keep Your Eye on James Dean."

237 **Even the crotchety Crowther:** Bosley Crowther, "Screen: Large Subject: The Cast," *New York Times*, October 11, 1956.

237 *Giant* **wrapped filming in late August:** Korman, "James Dean: Brilliant Young Star."

237 **he had shown the car to actor Alec Guinness:** Harry Harper, "Alec Guinness Warned James Dean About Car Crash," Ozzie News, http://www.ozzienews.com/chin-wag/alec-guinness-warned-james-dean-about-car-crash.

237 **He had been pulled over below Bakersfield:** Korman, "James Dean: Brilliant Young Star."

238 **Dozens of "one-shot" magazines:** "Dean of the One-Shotters," *Time*, September 3, 1956, 54.

239 **In a one-shot titled** *The Real James Dean*: "The Star They'll Never Forget," *The Real James Dean Story*, undated.

239 **Others reported seeing:** "The Star They'll Never Forget"; "Dean of the One-Shotter"; Mitgang, "Strange James Dean Death Cult."

239 **Writing in 2002:** David Thomson, *The New Biographical Dictionary of Film* (New York: Knopf, 2002), 212–13.

240 **As Humphrey Bogart explained:** Cited in Murray Pomerance, "James Stewart and James Dean: The Darkness Within," in *Larger than Life: Movie Stars of the 1950s*, ed. R. Barton Palmer (New Brunswick, NJ: Rutgers University Press, 2010), 85.

Printed in the United States
by Baker & Taylor Publisher Services